40 Days of Discipleship
A Self-Paced Doctrinal Education Plan
Volume 2: The Second 40 Days

By Joseph Tkach, Michael D. Morrison, Gary W. Deddo, and others

Published by Grace Communion International

3120 Whitehall Park Dr.

Charlotte, NC 28273

www.gci.org

All Scripture quotations, unless otherwise indicated, are taken from the Holy Bible, New International Version®, NIV®. Copyright ©1973, 1978, 1984, 2011 by Biblica, Inc.™ Used by permission of Zondervan. All rights reserved worldwide. www.zondervan.com. The "NIV" and "New International Version" are trademarks registered in the United States Patent and Trademark Office by Biblica, Inc.™

First edition

Copyright © 2016 Grace Communion International

Minor edits 2018

All rights reserved.

ISBN 13: 978-1535172448

ISBN 10: 1535172444

Contents

Day

Introduction iii

Theology in general
1. An Introduction to Trinitarian Theology, by Michael Morrison 1
2. An Introduction to Trinitarian Theology, part 2 4
3. An Introduction to Trinitarian Theology, part 3 8
4. An Introduction to Trinitarian Theology, part 4 13

The Triune God
5. Responding to God With Faith, by Joseph Tkach 17
6. Who Is God? by Joseph Tkach 21
   Humanity's Relationship With God 22
7. Knowing God, by Joseph Tkach 25
   Who's Afraid of God's Judgment? by Neil Earle 26
8. One in Three and Three in One 28

Jesus Christ
9. Jesus — Alive Forevermore! by Michael Morrison 33
   Jesus Was Not Alone, by Joseph W. Tkach 35
10. Evidence of the Resurrection, by Michael Morrison 37
    The Power of the Resurrection 39
11. Why Jesus Gives Us Hope, by Joseph Tkach 41
    Did You Kill Jesus Christ? By Don Mears 44
12. Two Truths We Learn From Jesus' Death, by Joseph Tkach 45
    Commemorating the Crucifixion, by Joseph Tkach 46

The Holy Spirit
13. Can You Hear the Holy Spirit? by Joseph Tkach 49
    Do You Have the Holy Spirit? by Paul Kroll 51
14. The Deity of the Holy Spirit, by Michael Morrison 53
15. A Theology of the Holy Spirit, by Gary Deddo, part 1 57
16. A Theology of the Holy Spirit, by Gary Deddo, part 2 61

The Scriptures
17. God Speaks to Us! by Paul Kroll 66
    Five Simple Rules for Bible Study, by Michael Morrison 68
18. Scripture: God's Gift, by Gary Deddo, parts 1 and 2A 71
19. Scripture, God's Gift, by Gary Deddo, parts 2B and 3 75
20. Scripture, God's Gift, by Gary Deddo, part 4 79

The gospel
21. Preaching in the Book of Acts: Paul, by Michael Morrison 82
22. The Gospel Really Is Good News, by J. Michael Feazell 86
23. Sharing Your Faith With the Unchurched, by Neil Earle 91
    Heart Trouble, by Joseph Tkach 93
24. How Baptism Pictures the Gospel, by Joseph Tkach 95

Grace and salvation
25. Too Much Grace? By Gary Deddo, part 1 98
26. Too Much Grace? By Gary Deddo, part 2 102
27. Is Jesus the Only Way of Salvation? by Joseph Tkach 106
28. Parable of the Lost Son, by Michael Morrison 109

The church
29. Responding to God With Worship, by Joseph Tkach 114
30. Church: Some Assembly Required, by John Halford 118
31. Leadership in the Church: An Examination of Eight Words, by Michael Morrison, part 1 122
32. Leadership in the Church: An Examination of Eight Words, by Michael Morrison, part 2 127

Christian life
33. New Life in Christ, by Paul Kroll 131
34. The Goal of the Christian Life, by Joseph Tkach 135
    The Purpose of Blessings, by Joseph Tkach 137
35. Trials and Faith, by Joseph Tkach 140
    Life in Christ: Living Like a Christian, by Michael Morrison 142
36. Jesus Helps Us in Everyday Trials, by Joseph Tkach 145

The future
37. A Balanced Approach to Bible Prophecy, by Michael Morrison 148
38. How to Interpret Prophecy, by Michael Morrison 153
39. God's Wrath 157
40. The Coming of the Lord, by Norman Shoaf 161
    Here He Comes, Ready or Not, by James Henderson 163

About the Authors 165
About the Publisher 166
Grace Communion Seminary 167
Ambassador College of Christian Ministry 168

Introduction

A self-paced doctrinal education plan

This is the second volume in our series for people who want to begin or continue their theological education with free resources from the GCI website. For each day, we present (on average) 2500 words, which can be read in 15-20 minutes. We again aim for variety, and go deeper into some doctrines than we were able to go in the first volume.

All the articles are on our website; an index with links is at https://www.gci.org/articles/40-days-of-discipleship-the-second-40-days/.

Church leaders should already be familiar with most of the doctrines presented in these articles, but a review can be helpful in firming up a foundation for new pastors, bivocational pastors, and others who are unable to pursue formal seminary education.

Although this series is designed for pastoral education, completion of the series does not mean that a person is thereby qualified to be a pastor. Doctrinal knowledge is only one of the many skills that congregational leaders need. This series focuses on theology; it does not include the many GCI articles on biblical studies,[1] which pastors also need. Further, we do not have many articles available on ministry practices, such as preaching and counseling, which would normally form an important component of pastoral education.

Most importantly, no amount of reading can give people the spiritual gifts needed in the pastoral role. No amount of reading can give people experience with leading congregations and encouraging spiritual growth. Field experience is needed for that, perhaps as an intern, under the guidance of a mentor. Those who desire to lead in the church desire a good thing, but desire itself is not enough. Social skills and spiritual gifts are also needed, and the congregation itself must provide some confirmation that the leader has been gifted and called for this role.

Michael Morrison
Dean of Faculty
Grace Communion Seminary

---

[1] For an index of our biblical studies articles, go to https://www.gci.org/article-categories/the-bible/

An Introduction to Trinitarian Theology

I. Introduction: why we need this

A. Stating the topic

We say that we have a "Trinitarian theology." However, most churches accept the doctrine of the Trinity, and their theology is at least somewhat Trinitarian, but we emphasize the Trinity more than most churches do. Sometimes we say that we have an Incarnational Trinitarian theology, or a Trinitarian Christ-centered theology. None of these are completely distinctive terms, but they do mention some of the emphases that we have.

We call our theology Trinitarian because the doctrine of the Trinity is not a side point, or just one of many other doctrines. We are trying to be more consistent with it, to let it be the organizing principle for other doctrines. Whether we are talking about sin or salvation or the church, we want to ask, how does the doctrine of the Trinity help us understand this particular doctrine? How is it connected with the nature of God, and of who God is in his innermost being?

We are trying to understand a little better some points about God's relationship with humanity: his purpose in creating humanity, the way in which he saves us, and how we should respond to him. We believe that our theology is true to the Bible, and that it helps make sense of what we are doing on the earth and in the church. It helps tie different doctrines together.

B. Not trying to criticize others

In the process of explaining our theology, we find that our beliefs are sometimes a little different from other theological traditions, and in some points of doctrine, we conclude that those other Christians are mistaken. This does not mean that we think they are non-Christian, or that those people won't be saved. We all make mistakes, and we have no doubt made a few of our own.

We all believe that we are saved through the life, death and resurrection of Jesus – and it is good for us to have that in common with many other Christians around the world.

Thankfully, we are saved not by having absolutely perfect theology, but we are saved by Christ, by grace, by trusting in Jesus to do for us what we cannot do for ourselves. Other Christians are doing the best they can, and we are doing the best that we can, to understand the Bible, and to understand the meaning of life and how it all fits together. Our purpose here is not to criticize other people and other theologies, but simply to do the best that we can in explaining what we believe, and how we think it is true to the Bible, and how we think it helps us understand what our life is all about.

C. A desire to understand as much as we can

This is what the early church called "faith seeking understanding." We already understand some things about God, and we believe them, but we are convinced that this is something we'd like to know more about, and so we try to understand as much as we can. We have fallen in love with Jesus, and we'd like to learn more about who he is, and the relationship he has with us, and what he has in mind for our future.

We could also describe our goal as an act of worship: we want to praise God for who he is and what he has done and what he has promised to do in the future – and in order to praise God for these things, we need to understand what they are. The goal is to explain things as best as we can, based on the Bible and the way that God has revealed himself to us ultimately and personally in Jesus Christ.

D. Practical significance

We will not try to cover all the biblical or historical evidence for the doctrine of the Trinity. We have published other articles about that. What we would like to focus on here is the practical significance of the doctrine.

At first, it seems like the doctrine of the Trinity is just information about God: God is three Persons in one Being. It's about him. But what does that have to do with us? Does it make any difference to us here on earth?

Yes. That is because persons have relationships with one another, and relationships are important for all of us. God created us to have relationships similar to the relationships that exist for all eternity within the Triune God. The divine Persons in the Godhead have relationships, and persons here on earth have relationships, too, and there is supposed to be some similarity in the kind of relationships we have.

The Bible tells us that "God is love" (1 John 4:8). Not that he has love, but that he IS love. That is descriptive of who he is and how he lives in eternity, how he interacts with other persons. Even before God created the universe, even before God created angelic beings, he was love. When God was the only thing there is, God was love — love among the triune Persons.

Before God created anything, what would God be like? If there is only one person in God, there would be no one to love, because love means caring for and caring about someone else. But if God were somehow loving but alone, that would mean that God would be unable to fully be or express some of his internal nature. God would be deficient. The statement that "God is love" would be meaningless before creation, if God were only one Person, because the love could not be expressed.

The doctrine of the Trinity tells us that even before God created anything, he could be love, because the Father loved the Son, and the Son loved the Holy Spirit, and the Spirit loves the Father, and so forth. There was love within the Triune God, even before anything had been created (John 17:24). The three Persons were distinguishable from one another, but united to one another in love. This is important for who God is, and it's important for who we are, as well.

II. Centered on Jesus Christ

As mentioned above, we sometimes say that we have a Trinitarian, *Christ*-centered theology. Some people wonder, if all three Persons in the Godhead are fully divine, and *equal* in being divine, why should we center our theology on *one* of them in particular?

A. Jesus is fully divine

God is revealed to us *most clearly* in the Person of Jesus Christ. Jesus is where God has chosen to make himself *visible* to us (Colossians 1:15). Jesus is the Word made flesh — God the Son become human. He has revealed himself in a way that we could see him, touch him, hear him and see how he lives. Jesus is the way that God has chosen to reveal himself to us.

In John 14:8, Philip asked Jesus: "Lord, show us the Father and that will be enough for us." Jesus responded in verse 9: "Don't you know me, Philip, even after I have been among you such a long time? Anyone who has seen me has seen the Father."

Jesus is not saying that God the Father is 5 foot 8 inches tall, with brown hair and Middle Eastern features. Rather, he is saying that in his most important respects (his character, purposes, heart, and mind), *God the Father is like Jesus Christ* in terms of the way he interacts with others. The compassion that Jesus had shows us what God is like. The zeal for righteousness, that's what God is like. The willingness to sacrifice for others, God is like that, too. Jesus helps us see what God the Father is like – and the Holy Spirit is like that, too.

When Jesus became a flesh-and-blood human being, he was showing us in a tangible and visible way what the Triune God is like. The apostle Paul says, "The Son is the image of the invisible God" (Colossians 1:15). Even though we cannot see God directly, Jesus shows us what he's like, in a way that we *can* see and hear.

Colossians 2:9 says, "In Christ all the fullness of the Deity lives in bodily form." Jesus is the summary that we are given of what we need to know about God. We can never know God completely – he is much bigger than our minds are capable of comprehending – but we are able to have an accurate understanding of at least *some* things about God, because Jesus embodies all that any human being can know of God, and he came to reveal God to us. He does not reveal everything, but what he does reveal is accurate. John 1:18 says, "No one has ever seen God, but the one and only Son, who is himself God and is in closest relationship with the Father, *has made him known*."

B. Jesus is fully human

All orthodox Christian theology includes the teaching that Jesus is fully human. That might seem obvious to many people – he was born as a baby, grew as a boy, and he died. As the Bible says, in John 1:14, "The Word *became flesh* and made his dwelling among us." He didn't just put on a costume that made him *look* human – no, he was a real human being. He ate ordinary food, breathed air like an ordinary person, his fingernails grew and he got thirsty and tired. When he scraped his knee, he bled, and when they crucified him, he died just like other people would have.

He was fully God and fully human – both at the same time. We have never seen that combination before, but with God, all things are possible, and so if that's what he did, then we have to make room in our theology for it. God can do one-of-a-kind things that aren't comparable to anything else. He is able to be in his own creation. The Incarnation of the Son of God is that unique kind of thing.

There are a number of reasons as to why a divine Person might want to become a human being. He came to communicate to us on a level we could understand; he came to die for us; he came to experience life as a human so that we could know for sure that he understood what it's like for us to be human. But just as Jesus shows us what God is like, he also shows us what *humanity* is really like. He is the perfect human.

C. Connecting human beings to God

Jesus has a unique role. He has been part of the circle of God's triune life, and he's been part of the human circle of life, and because of that, he provides a unique connection between humanity and God. In a sense, he is a bridge between the two, a bridge God uses to bring us into the divine fellowship. Not that we are part of the Trinity, but in and through his humanity, we do share in God's life.

2 Peter 1:4 says, "He has given us his very great and precious promises, so that through them you may *participate* in the divine nature." So in some way we participate in what God is. We are in the family of God, or the kingdom of God. We are in fellowship with God, in a *relationship* with God – and this is all made possible by Jesus.

1 Timothy 2:5 says, "There is one God and one mediator between God and mankind, the man Christ Jesus." A mediator is a person in the middle – in this case, a person serving to connect humanity with God. God initiated this; he is the one who sent Jesus to earth to become a human being, and to be resurrected back into heaven to make this connection work. Jesus is the key link or connector between humanity and God.

The doctrine of the Trinity is important for this understanding. For our connection with God, for our future with God, it is essential that our mediator be fully God in his own right. No human being is good enough to *earn* a connection with God, who is infinitely far above us in power, glory, wisdom and righteousness. No created human being could rise up to God's level as Creator, but God is able to put himself at *our* level.

Jesus is perfect in righteousness and holiness, and yet one of us. He is the pathway by which other human beings are brought *into* the presence of the holy and perfect God. The doctrine of the Trinity says that Jesus is fully God, and the doctrine of the Incarnation says that Jesus became fully human, and he continues to be both divine and human, and with that combination, now we are ready to talk about a relationship between God and humanity.

An Introduction to Trinitarian Theology
continued

III. Humanity in the image of God

A. Created in his image

Jesus shows us what God is like, and he also shows us what humanity is supposed to be like, and this implies that there is some important *similarity* between God and humans. This is not because humans are good enough to rise up to the level of God. No, it all comes from God as a gift given to us. He is the one who created us this way in the first place. We find it stated in the first chapter of the Bible:

> God said, "Let us make mankind in our image, in our likeness, so that they may rule over the fish in the sea and the birds in the sky, over the livestock and all the wild animals, and over all the creatures that move along the ground." 27 So God created mankind in his own image, in the image of God he created them; male and female he created them. (Genesis 1:26-27)

God did it, and he said it was good. Humanity was created "in the image of God," to somehow look like God and to represent God here on earth. Again, we are not supposed to think of skin color, hair color or the number of fingers on our hands. Those things are incidentals that only apply to creatures. What is important is that humanity should be like God in a *spiritual* sense, and we see that emphasis in Galatians 5:22, where the apostle Paul describes the results of the working of the Holy Spirit in us: "love, joy, peace, forbearance, kindness, goodness, faithfulness, gentleness and self-control." Humans are supposed to be like God in *these* ways.

Now we can ask the Trinitarian question: In what way does the doctrine of the Trinity help us understand what humanity is? The answer is, that just as the Persons in the Trinity interact with one another in love, so also we as persons ought to interact with all other human persons *in love*. That's the first item Paul lists in the fruit of the Spirit (Galatians 5:22), and the primary way that we were made to be like God. Love should be the basis for our lives and our societies.

Just as the Triune God is essentially relational, with the Persons defined in reference to one another, so humans are also essentially *relational*, and our identity as persons depends on our relationships with other people. "Who we are" depends on the relationships we have with others. No one is a solitary individual; the meaning of life is not in *self*-existence, but it is to be found in our relationships with each other, in the way we live and think about other people. We were created to be in right relationship with the Triune God and also to be in right relationship with each other in a way that mirrors Jesus' relationship with the Father and the Spirit.

B. Sin defaces the image

Genesis tells us that humans didn't want life on the terms that God had given them. They wanted to define their own life, doing their own thing, instead of having to do God's things. So instead of love, joy and peace, they choose selfishness, and they got strife and unhappiness.

What does the doctrine of the Trinity reveal about the nature of *sin*? How does it help us better understand what sin is? If good is defined as humanity being in the image of God, then sin is doing things that are unlike God. If God is a relational being, and humans were created to be in relationships of love, then sin is a disruption in our relationships – problems in our relationships with God, and problems in our relationships with one another.

As a practical matter, we have rules that describe what a good relationship is. In a good relationship, we don't lie to each other, we don't steal from one another, we don't dishonor or disrespect the other, and so forth. Avoiding these problems doesn't necessarily *create* a good relationship, but breaking these rules *hurts* our relationships. Rules do not exist for their own sake, but in order to serve something more important, and that is relationships based on love.

When humanity rejected God, we also rejected him as the source of the *love* that we need. We were created to be like God in that respect, but we went in a wrong direction.

C. God restores the image – in himself

The Old Testament doesn't say much more about the image of God, but the New Testament picks up the phrase "image of God" and applies it to Jesus Christ. We have already looked at Colossians 1:15: "He is *the image of the invisible God.*" He is the image that Adam failed to be. He shows us in a *visible* way what God is like in the invisible, spiritual world.

Hebrews 1:3 tells us something similar: "The Son is the radiance of God's glory and *the exact representation of his being.*" When we see Jesus, we see what the Father is like in relationship to Jesus. So we expect God to be like Jesus, in his compassion and mercy and love.

D. We are in the image of Christ

This concept becomes directly relevant to us when we see that the Bible talks about <u>us</u> being formed in the image *of Christ*. We can see this in 2 Corinthians 3:18: "We, who with unveiled faces all reflect the Lord's glory, are being transformed *into his likeness* with ever-increasing glory, which comes from the Lord, who is the Spirit." That is, we look more and more like him – and again, that's not talking about his physical shape, size and color – it's talking about the way he is spiritually, in relationship to the Father and the Spirit from all eternity.

- Galatians 4:19 talks about how "Christ is formed in you."
- Ephesians 4:13 talks about how "we all reach unity in the faith and in the knowledge of the Son of God and become mature, attaining to the whole *measure of the fullness of Christ.*"
- Colossians 3:10 says we "have put on the new self, which is being renewed in knowledge *in the image of its Creator*" – and that is Jesus Christ.

Since Christ is the image of God, when we become more like Christ, we are being brought back toward the image of God that we are supposed to be. Right now, it is a spiritual transformation, a *mental* and ethical or relational transformation, and eventually, it will be a physical transformation as well, all based on God's original plan.

This concept is seen in a different way in Romans 5. In that chapter, Paul is comparing Adam with Jesus Christ. Verse 14 says that Adam was a type, or a model, "a pattern of the one to come." Just as the first Adam brought in sin and death, the second Adam brought in righteousness and life. Just as we shared in the results of the first Adam, so also we share in the benefits of the second Adam. Paul summarizes it in verses 18-19:

> Just as one trespass [Adam's sin] resulted in condemnation for all people, so also one righteous act [that of Jesus] resulted in justification and life *for all people.* For just as through the disobedience of the one man [Adam] the many were made sinners, so also through the obedience of the one man [Jesus] the many will be made righteous.

All humanity was included in the results of the first Adam, and all humanity is included in the results of the second Adam, Jesus. It's not just a few people that God chose ahead of time, and it's not just one particular nation, or one particular social class – God's plan is for everyone he has created. Jesus is Lord of all.

Adam messed it up, but Jesus did it right—and in Christ, all humanity has a fresh start on being "the image of God." Jesus is the key to our transformation – not only is he the model that we copy, but he is also the engine that drives the whole process. He supplies the power and the direction.

IV. The covenant relationship

A. The covenant formula

Even though the Old Testament does not use the phrase "image of God" very often, it does talk about the relationship we have with God, and the term it uses for that most of the time is *covenant*. We can see the basic idea in Exodus 6:7: "I will take you as my own people, and I will be your God." And we see it in

- Leviticus 26:12: "I will walk among you and be your God, and you will be my people."
- Jeremiah 7:23: "I will be your God and you will be my people."
- Ezekiel 36:28: "You will be my people, and I will be your God."

Old Testament scholars call this the "covenant formula." It's found more than 20 times in the Bible. It is an adaptation of words that people in the ancient Middle East used for marriages, adoptions, and political treaties. In a marriage, it would go something like this: "I will be your husband, and you will be my wife." In an adoption, it would be "I will be your father, and you will be my son." In a political treaty, it would be adapted: "I will be your king and you will be my people." It is declaring a relationship that the people intend to be permanent, a relationship that now defines who they are in relation to the other.

In the Law and in the Prophets, God repeatedly talks about covenants between God and humanity. He made covenants with Abraham, Isaac, Jacob, Aaron and David. In each covenant, he says, in effect, I have made with you a covenant relationship, and as you live according to it, then our relationship will be a good one. *The goal* is to have an ongoing relationship.

B. A new covenant promised

The people of Israel broke the covenant time and time again. Eventually through the prophets God promised that there would be a *new* covenant, made in the hearts of the people, and God's Spirit would be in them. This is not something that the people could achieve for themselves – it would be something that God would have to do *for* them. He would *give* them a new heart, a new Spirit.

- Jeremiah 31:33: "This is the covenant I will make with the people of Israel after that time," declares the Lord. "I will put my law in their minds and write it on their hearts. I will be their God, and they will be my people."
- Ezekiel 36:26-27: "I will give you a new heart and put a new spirit in you; I will remove from you your heart of stone and give you a heart of flesh. I will put my Spirit in you and move you to follow my decrees and be careful to keep my laws."

In Isaiah 42:6, God promises to make his servant "to be a covenant for the people and a light for the Gentiles." The covenant relationship between God and humanity would be focused and embodied in one person – who we now know as Jesus Christ. The covenant that we have with God is found in him; <u>he</u> is the covenant for all the people; our connection to God depends 100 percent on him.

C. Relationship terms in the New Testament

The New Testament says that we have this new covenant in Christ. The Lord's Supper reminds us that we have a new covenant in the blood of Christ. But this is not the only relationship term in the New Testament. For example, it calls us children of God; we are *adopted* into the family of God.

- Romans 8:15 says, "The Spirit you received does not make you slaves, so that you live in fear again; rather, the Spirit you received brought about your adoption to sonship."
- Ephesians 1:5 says, "He predestined us for adoption to sonship through Jesus Christ."

This means we become part of God's family, with rights and privileges that are part of being in the royal family. We are in a new social class.

Paul uses a different relationship term in 2 Corinthians 11:2: "I promised you to one husband, to Christ, so that I might present you as a pure virgin to him." This marriage concept is used in the book of Revelation, too: "Let us rejoice and be glad and give him glory! For the wedding of the Lamb has come, and his bride has made herself ready" (Revelation 19:7).

I saw the Holy City, the new Jerusalem, coming down out of heaven from God, prepared *as a bride* beautifully dressed for her husband. And I heard a loud voice from the throne saying, "Look! God's dwelling place is now among the people, and he will dwell with them. *They will be his people,* and God himself will be with them *and be their God.*" (Revelation 21:2-3)

Here the covenant formula is used again, this time in the context of a wedding. God will live with us, and we will live with him. We will be his children, adopted as siblings of Jesus Christ, part of the royal family forever. Through Jesus, we are brought into fellowship with the Triune God, sharing in his status as Son.

Another way to describe this is "the kingdom of God." That biblical phrase means being part of the universe in which life is lived in the way that God lives. We become part of the ruling family, with the privileges and responsibilities of that.

It means that eternal life is *not just living for a really long time* – it means that we live *with each other, and with God,* forever and ever. It is social, not solitary, because that is *the way that God made us to be.* We were made in his image, and he is social, and not solitary. The doctrine of the Trinity helps us understand who we are, what life is all about, and how God is bringing it about for us. The Triune God who began a good work in us is sure to finish the job, creating humanity to be a reflection of what God is: Persons in perfect community and harmony.

V. Salvation is more than a verdict

Understanding where we started, and where we will end up, can help us understand a little more about what *salvation* is. Some people think that salvation is just a matter of going to heaven when you die. But when it comes to salvation, there's a lot more to it than just a change in location.

Some people think that salvation is just a matter of getting a favorable verdict on the day of judgment. There's going to be a day of judgment, they warn, and everybody is guilty and deserves to be thrown into hell. But if you believe in Jesus, that guilty verdict will be changed to "innocent." It is *true* that there will be a day of judgment, and that everyone is guilty of sin, and that Jesus allows us to escape the verdict we deserve, and he allows us to enter a heavenly paradise.

But doesn't salvation have anything to do with life right now? Yes, it does. There's more to salvation than just a change in our future verdict.

A. Restoring us to God's image

Salvation means that we are rescued from *sin*, not just guilt, and we are rescued from the results of sin. It means that God's original plan gets back on track – and the original plan is that we were made in the image of God and we were to live in that covenant relationship. It is a *spiritual* likeness that God wants us to have, and that can be summed up in the word *love*. We are to love God with everything we have, and we are to love other people in the way that we love ourselves.

Just changing our location isn't going to restore us to being like God. Just changing the final verdict isn't going to make us the people we were meant to be. The goal in salvation is to change *us* – so that we are spiritually like God, so that we are his children in a way that mirrors Jesus' own sonship. That's the original plan, and God hasn't given up on it. He sent Jesus to show us the way and to be the way, for all humanity to be brought back into fellowship with the Triune God. The Father initiated the plan, the Son of God carried out key steps in the plan, and the Holy Spirit also has *an ongoing role* in the transformation, the change that we all need. We will briefly look at each of those.

An Introduction to Trinitarian Theology
continued

B. The role of the Father

Some people describe the gospel as the Father setting the rules, and getting angry at us because we have broken the rules. He says that we deserve to die, but then the Son has compassion on us and volunteers to pay the penalty for us. So the Father pours out his anger on his Son, and then he says, "Justice has been done. Those sinners can come into my kingdom, because the penalty has been paid." We have an angry Father and a compassionate Son who is able to get his Father to change his mind.

Maybe that's the way it works in some human families, but that's not the way it works in the Triune God. It's not true to the Bible, and not true in any system of theology, whether it's Trinitarian or Calvinist or Catholic or Eastern Orthodox.

Trinitarian theology reminds us that Jesus is fully God. He is just like God the Father. He is just as angry as the Father is, and just as *loving* as the Father is. He didn't change the Father's mind about anything. Rather, he *reveals* the Father's mind – the Father wants us to be saved just as much as Jesus does. Let's look at a couple of scriptures that show that.

- John 3:16 says it well: "*God* so loved the world that he gave his one and only Son, that whoever believes in him shall not perish but have eternal life." God the Father loves humanity and he wants us to be saved, not to be condemned or punished.
- Romans 5:8: "God demonstrates *his own love* for us in this: While we were still sinners, Christ died for us." God did not demonstrate his love for us by sending *somebody else* to die. It is only because Christ is God, that *his* death could demonstrate the love of God. They have equal love for us, equal compassion for us. The Triune God is in *full agreement* on our salvation. Father, Son and Spirit created us for a purpose, and they are working together to bring us to completion.

C. The role of the Son

Even though the Father initiated the plan, we often forget that, and usually think of Jesus as the Savior, the one who carried it out. He has the more visible role. How did Christ save us? Christians usually think that we were saved by Jesus' death on the cross. That is an important part of the picture, but it is only *part* of the picture.

1. The first step in our salvation was the Incarnation, when Jesus was made a flesh-and-blood human being. He took our nature as his own. That is when he became the second Adam, the new *leader* of all humanity. Just as we were all guilty because of the sin of Adam, so also we are made righteous in the righteousness of Jesus, because Jesus came to give all humanity a new beginning (Romans 5). This is not a matter of genetics – it is a *spiritual* reality, that the Incarnation includes all of us in the salvation that Jesus brings. In himself, Jesus reconnects all humanity to God.

2. The next step in our salvation is that Jesus had to live a righteous life, without any sin – because if he sinned, then he would simply be like one of us, needing to be saved. He would not even be able to save himself, and not anyone else. He lived without sin – he had a perfect relationship with the Father and the Spirit and, as much as could be done from his side, with all humans. Since he is our Creator, he represented us, and we are allowed to share in his righteousness.

3. Third, Jesus had to *die* for us. The wages of sin is death, the Bible says, and death is the result we would *expect*, if we try to live independent from the creator and sustainer of the universe. Jesus, as a mortal human being, experienced death, the result of our sins. He took our sins upon himself, so that we might share in his righteousness. Since the Creator of all humanity became a human, he had an essential unity with all of us. As our Creator, he was able to accept responsibility and the consequences for all of our sins, and to die for the sins of all humanity.

4. Fourth, Jesus had to be resurrected. Romans 5:10 says that we are "saved by his life." Jesus is able to save us from death because he has overcome death. He has been there, done that, and now he can do it for us, too.

5. Last, Jesus had to ascend into heaven as one of us, fully human, and be restored to complete fellowship with the Father and Spirit. The Bible says he ascended bodily into heaven, as a glorified human being, and he is now at the Father's right hand, which is a figure of speech meaning the most honored position. His is eternally, even now, our mediator, our intercessor, praying for us, and *transforming* us to become more like he is. By the Spirit he is sharing with us his regenerated and perfected humanity.

Our salvation is not complete with just the forgiveness of sins. We *need* that, but if that's all we got, we'd still have a big problem, because we all have a tendency to sin again, and we want to be *freed* from that tendency. Paul calls it a slavery to sin, and we want to be liberated from that slavery. So, by sending us his Spirit, all that Jesus had done for us on earth and completed for us in heaven is now being worked out in us. Jesus by his Spirit is continuing to work for our transformation.

We can rightly say that we are saved by the death of Jesus, but that is only part of the picture. A more complete statement is that we are saved by the incarnation, life, death, resurrection and ascension of Jesus. If that's too much to say at one time, then just say that we are saved *by Jesus*. We are saved by who he is, and what he has done.

How did Jesus save us?

Let's focus on the death of Jesus for a few minutes, because it is an important part of the picture, and perhaps the most distinctive part of Christian theology. How can the death of Jesus do anything for our salvation?

One common explanation is that our sin requires a penalty, and Jesus serves as a substitute to pay the penalty on our behalf. This is called the penal substitutionary theory of the atonement, and it is so common that some people think that it's the only explanation. But there is a danger in this theory, and the Bible gives us other ways to explain it, as well.

1) Danger: a focus on punishment

First, the danger. A problem can arise if we focus on the "penalty" part of the theory, by suggesting that God had to *punish* Jesus for all the sins that we committed. This suggests that one Person in the Godhead is inflicting pain on another Person in the Godhead; this suggests separation rather than unity in the Triune God. This does not seem like a very righteous thing for God to do; we do not allow substitutions in our penal codes and systems of justice.

This theory acts as if the primary problem with sin is the punishment, as if the primary problem with crime is that our prisons are full. But this is focusing on the results, not the real problem. It focuses on the verdict, and it still leaves people with a problem: we all have a tendency to sin, and the death of Jesus does not address that problem. The problem is not just in the things that we do, but in the kind of people that we are.

What has happened here is that people have let a legal metaphor, a figure of speech, become the controlling description of what God is doing. All our words are based on human experiences, and the meaning of our words depends on how they are used in human affairs. But our experiences are not the measure of what such words mean in the divine realm. When God uses courtroom terminology to describe sin and salvation, we should not let *our* concepts of legal procedure to be the final description of what God is doing. When we say that the penalty of sin is death, we should not think that "penalty" is an exact description of what is going on, as if God is obligated to inflict punishment for every transgression of his law.

"Consequence" would probably be a more appropriate term. The result of sin is death, even without God having to step in to inflict it. When Jesus died for us, he experienced the consequence of our sin, the result of the way of life human beings chose, but God did not have to perform additional pain and suffering so that Jesus could pay the penalty we deserved. No, he suffered and died without any need for extra punishments coming from God.

God does pronounce a judgment on sin. He says, "If you sin, you're going to die." He does not say, "If you sin, I'm going to kill you." Death is a *natural* result of us turning our backs on the One who gave us life. God doesn't have to do anything extra to us in order for us to suffer from the results of sin and to die from the results of sin. We experience the judgment, the result he warned us about, without him having to do anything extra to punish us. Similarly, he didn't have to do anything extra to Jesus for Jesus to die for our sins. When God *did* intervene, he gave Jesus life instead of death.

That's what he does for us, too. God is angry about sin, but as Ezekiel says, he takes no pleasure in the death of the wicked (18:23, 32). Death does not serve his purpose. His goal is salvation, not punishment. The reason that he sent Jesus to us is so that we could *escape* the consequences of sin. He wants to *rescue* us, not punish us. We should not force God into our legal metaphor.

Trinitarian theologians accept the idea that Jesus' death was substitutionary, that Jesus died as a substitute for us. But we generally avoid the word "penal," because that word suggests that God the Father punished his one and only Son, and did something to increase his pain. It puts legal requirements and demands as putting requirements on what God has to do, as if law and punishment is the most important description of what good relationships ought to be. When we bring the doctrine of the Trinity into the picture, it helps us see that *punishment* is not the best way to think about it.

2) Biblical descriptions of salvation

If the Bible does not describe the death of Jesus as a punishment required by some law that God had to obey, how does it describe it? In several ways. Articles could be written about each one, but here we will give only a summary:

1. Jesus said that he would die as a ransom: "The Son of Man did not come to be served, but to serve, and to give his life as a ransom for many" (Mark 10:45). The word "ransom" suggests a payment that we might give to a kidnapper. Some people in the early church made elaborate theories of how Jesus paid a price to Satan, as if Satan had some legitimate claims over us. But they were making the mistake of letting a figure of speech turn into an exact description of what was going on.

2. We see a similar figure of speech in the word "redemption." That word describes people getting friends and relatives out of

slavery. They bought them back; that is the original meaning of "redeem." Jesus bought us with a price, Paul says, but we should not think that anyone actually *received* that payment. It is a figure of speech. The Old Testament says that God redeemed the Israelites out of slavery in Egypt, but he did not pay anyone in order to do it. We should not let the figure of speech dictate to us what happened in spiritual reality.

3. The Bible describes Jesus as a sacrificial lamb. John the Baptist called him the "the Lamb of God, who takes away the sin of the world!" (John 1:29). The apostle Paul says that "Christ our Passover has been sacrificed" (1 Corinthians 5:7). But again, the picture is not exact. Passover lambs were not designed as payments for sin, but they were associated with escaping slavery and death.

4. Jesus is called "an offering and a sacrifice to God" (Ephesians 5:2). In the Old Testament, there were a wide variety of sacrifices – some of animals, some of flour and oil, some for sin, some for purity rituals, some for thanksgiving, and so forth, and Jesus fulfilled the symbolism of all of them.

5. Jesus is our place of atonement. Romans 3:25 says, "God presented Christ as a sacrifice of atonement." Some translations say *propitiation,* and some say *expiation,* and scholars have argued about that for a long time. The Greek word meant one thing in a pagan context, and another thing in a Jewish context, but the Greek word is also the word used for the mercy seat on top of the ark of the covenant, the place where the high priest sprinkled blood on the day of atonement. So the NIV quoted above calls it the "sacrifice of atonement." But the sacrifice was never done at the mercy seat; a better translation might be "the place of atonement," without trying to be more precise than the word actually is. Jesus is the place, or the way that our sins are atoned, so there is nothing between us and God, so that we are restored to fellowship with God.

6. Reconciliation is a similar term; it refers to people who were once enemies or alienated, but are now on good terms with each other. Romans 5:10 says, "While we were enemies we were reconciled to God by the death of his Son." Colossians 1:20 says that "God was pleased…to reconcile to himself all things, whether things on earth or things in heaven, by making peace through [the Son's] blood, shed on the cross."

7. Justification is another important term. Some say it is the most important term of all, the one that makes sense out of all the others. Romans 5:9 says that we are "justified by his blood," or by his death on the cross. Justification means to make something right. The word could be used for making a relationship right, or it could be used for making something legally right. In a trial, a person could either be found guilty – condemned – or found righteous (cf. 2 Corinthians 3:9). When the judge declared a person to be in the right, this was justification. This can be a helpful way of looking at salvation, but it misses out on the fact that God wants more from us than to be declared legally innocent – he also wants us to be in fellowship with him forever. Yes, we are guilty of a crime, but the solution is not just to let us out of jail, but it is to transform who we are, so that we are more like Christ.

8. In Colossians, Paul gives us another interesting way to look at the death of Jesus: "Having disarmed the powers and

authorities, he made a public spectacle of them, triumphing over them by the cross" (2:15). By his death on the cross, Jesus won a victory! He defeated spiritual powers that were fighting against us. Paul does not explain the logic in how that works, but he says that it does.

The Bible uses a few additional figures of speech, but the point is clear, that there are several ways to look at it, and we should use all of these ways.

Trinitarian theology says that the meaning of human life is to be found in relationships, and relationships cannot be put into precise formulas. But we can state some basic facts about it. First, Jesus became a real human, and he was mortal. Even if the Jews and the Romans didn't kill him, he had a mortal body that would eventually get old and he would die. He was part of the Godhead, but he became part of humanity, and he accepted all the negative consequences of that. Why did he do it? Out of love. God loved us so much that he sent his only Son to die for us, and the Son loved us so much that he did it.

So Jesus has connected the world of heaven and earth, divine and human. In his death, Jesus demonstrated that he was a real human, completely in union with humanity. He completed his identification with us, sharing in everything that it means to be human. By doing that, he reversed the curse that was against us (Genesis 3:19; Galatians 3:13). He was able, on behalf of all humanity, to suffer the consequences of sin, and yet since he was personally without any sin, death did not have a legitimate claim on him. He had to be resurrected, and as the new Adam, the new head of humanity, he sets the pattern for what will happen to all of us, and that's resurrection – not just a life that lasts forever, but a life that is in fellowship with the Triune God.

An Introduction to Trinitarian Theology
conclusion

D. Role of the Spirit in our salvation

The Father sent the Son to save us, and the Son did his work. Does that mean that there's nothing left to do until the Last Judgment? Certainly not! Trinitarian theology reminds us that we should expect the Spirit to have an important role in our salvation.

Shortly before Jesus died, he told his disciples:

> It is for your good that I am going away. Unless I go away, the Advocate will not come to you; but if I go, I will send him to you…. When he, the Spirit of truth, comes, he will guide you into all the truth…. He will tell you what is yet to come. (John 16:7, 13-14)

So, even though Jesus completed *his* earthly job, part of the work must be completed after Jesus goes away – and that work is done by the Holy Spirit, the Advocate, the Comforter, who is sent by Jesus. What does the Holy Spirit do in our salvation? We don't need to present a complete theology of the Spirit here, but let's mention a few points:

1. The Spirit gives us new birth. In John 3, Jesus told Nicodemus, "No one can enter the kingdom of God unless they are born of water *and the Spirit*…. You must be born again" (verses 5, 7). We need a *new start in life*, and in one sense, Jesus gave all humanity that when he became "the second Adam." But for individuals, this is done by the Holy Spirit.
2. The Spirit helps us realize that we *are* born again, that we are children of God. Romans 8:15 says, "The Spirit you received brought about your adoption to sonship. And by him we cry, 'Abba, Father.'"
3. The Spirit also enables us to understand the gospel. In 1 Corinthians 2:14, Paul writes, "The person without the Spirit does not accept the things that come from the Spirit of God but considers them foolishness, and cannot understand them because they are discerned only through the Spirit." Unbelievers might understand what the words of Scripture mean, but people don't accept those words as *true* without the Spirit leading them. The Spirit helps us see truth about God and truth about ourselves, and helps us continue growing in the truth. As John 16 says, the Spirit teaches us and guides into the truth. No one has all the truth *yet*, so this is still a work in progress.
4. The Holy Spirit *sanctifies* us, or sets us apart for God's use. 2 Thessalonians 2:13 supports this: "God chose you as firstfruits to be *saved* through the sanctifying work of the Spirit and through belief in the truth."
5. The Spirit gives us power over sin. "If you live according to the flesh, you will die; but *if by the Spirit* you put to death the misdeeds of the body, you will live" (Romans 8:13). As the Spirit leads us, helps us understand, and gives us strength, we are to stop doing bad things and start doing more godly things. This does not mean that we stop all sin (even though we wish we could), but that our basic orientation in life is now

toward the good. Christian life and good behavior are part of the process of sanctification. The Spirit sets us apart for God's use, and God wants to use us for good.

6. The Spirit produces results in our lives: love, joy, peace, and other good qualities. These are the results God wants to see in us. This is a transformation in our attitudes as well as our actions – we are being changed from the inside out.

More could be said on each of these points – and more points could be added. Our main purpose here is just to make the larger point that the Spirit has a vital role in our salvation – we cannot be saved without the work of the Spirit in our lives. Salvation is a Trinitarian work, involving the Father, Son, and Spirit working in harmony to bring us to the kind of persons we are supposed to be.

VI. How do we respond?

We have seen some of the ways that God is working in our lives: He is restoring in us the divine image, so that we are living representatives of who he is and what he is like. It is a *spiritual* image, started when God said, "Let *us* make mankind in our image, in our likeness." We were made to be like God, and since Jesus is the perfect image of God, we are being conformed into *his* image, changed so that we are more like he is. The Spirit is doing that work in us, producing in us the fruit of the Spirit: love, joy, peace, and other attitudes and actions that help us have better relationships. This is part of the ongoing work of salvation that God is doing within us.

But a time is coming when we will be transformed into God's image in additional ways, too. Romans 6:5 says, "If we have been united with him in a death like his, we will certainly also be united with him in a *resurrection* like his." Our physical nature will be changed, and we will share in the glory of Jesus Christ. In 1 Corinthians 15, Paul describes the resurrection, and he says in verse 49, "just as we have borne the likeness of the earthly man [Adam], so shall we bear the *likeness* of the man from heaven [Jesus]." We will have the image of Christ in a more glorious way.

1 John 3:1-2 gives us a similar picture:

> How great is the love the Father has lavished on us, that we should be called children of God! And that is what we are! The reason the world does not know us is that it did not know him. Dear friends, now we *are* children of God, and what we *will be* has not yet been made known. But we know that when he appears, we shall be like him, for we shall see him as he is.

We will be like he is; we will be even more fully made in his image.

All humanity has been created in the image of God, made for this purpose. We are already his children, already "in his image" in one sense, but there is more to come. As we are transformed into his image in this life in the way we live and think, we will be transformed *more completely* into his image when we are resurrected into glory and given immortality and incorruptibility. This is the wonderful future God has prepared for us.

What conclusion does John draw from this wonderful promise? He says it in the very next verse: "Everyone who has this hope in him purifies himself, just as he is pure" (verse 3). When we want to be like God is, then we want to be *like him in our thoughts and actions.* The glory that God has designed for us is that we should be like he is.

There's a lot more to eternal life than just living forever. A never-ending life of suffering would *not* be good, and that is not what God wants us to have. Rather, he wants us to have a never-ending life of love and joy, of good relationships – relationships with millions and billions of other people who *help* one another and *love* one another. The good news of the gospel, the good news of the Bible, the good news of salvation, is that not only do we live forever, but that we will live *with God*. That's the best part: God wants us to live with him. We can see this in the last book of the Bible, Revelation 21:1-4:

Then I saw "a new heaven and a new earth," for the first heaven and the first earth had passed away…. I heard a loud voice from the throne saying, "Look! God's dwelling place is now among the people, and he will dwell with them. They will be his people, and God himself will be with them and be their God. He will wipe every tear from their eyes. There will be no more death or mourning or crying or pain, for the old order of things has passed away."

God will live with us, and we will live with him. We will be his children, adopted as brothers and sisters of Jesus Christ, part of the royal family forever. We are *already* his children. We already have a relationship with the Father, Son and Spirit.

How can our vision of *future* life affect the way we live now? Here's another thought that many Christians struggle with: If salvation is by grace, why does the New Testament have so many commands about what we are supposed to do? Is it grace for how we get in, but works *after* we get in? No.

It is because God is not just giving us existence that lasts forever – he is giving us life of a certain *quality*, life that is based on love rather than selfishness and competition. That's the kind of life we will enjoy in eternity, and that's the kind of life that is *good*, not just in the future but also right now. When the New Testament gives us commands, it is *describing* for us the kind of life that God is giving us, the life of the age to come. Grace says: I am giving you a never-ending life of joy. The commands say: This is what it looks like. This is the way that will help you have joy and express love.

In a parable, we might say that God is at the gateway to his kingdom, and he invites us in. You are welcome to come in, he says, where there is no more pain or sorrow, or lying or cheating or selfishness. Some people may say, "I would like to have 'no more pain,' but can't I keep my selfishness?" God replies, "No, they are two sides of the same coin. Selfishness causes pain. If you go through this gate, I will scrub all the selfishness out of you, so that you don't cause pain either for yourself or for anyone else." It's possible that some people will be so in love with their selfishness that they will refuse to go in.

We do not want to be in love with our selfishness. Rather, we need to see selfishness as one of our enemies, an attitude that can rob us of joy and peace. It is part of the sin that so easily besets us – it is an enemy that keeps us in slavery – it is an enemy we need to be liberated from. It is an enemy that Christ has already defeated on the cross, and he wants us to share in that victory, and it is done though the Holy Spirit living in us.

A Trinitarian understanding of our purpose in life helps us see the purpose of salvation, and the purpose of the commands we see in the Bible. Once we see where we are going, it is easier to see how God is bringing us there. Love is central to the whole picture, because love is the life of the Father, Son and Spirit, and we are participating in the divine nature, sharing in the life and love of the Triune God.

As images of God, we want our life to be characteristic of *the age to come*, patterned after the life that God himself has. We are images of God and representatives of God, and we should want to live in the way that he does, the way that we will all live in eternity. This life is representative of God himself, a fulfillment of the image that we are supposed to be. In the age to come, we will forever be images of God, children of God, completely and perfectly.

VII. Conclusion

The doctrine of the Trinity has enriched our understanding of many other doctrines, and we will continue to learn more about it as we grow in grace and knowledge. It makes sense that God's nature is reflected in everything that God does, and that means it affects all other doctrines, because our doctrines are based on what God is doing in the people he has created.

We see God's *love* throughout the story, from before creation and in the cross of Christ, and on into eternity in the future. We see the Father, Son and Spirit in creation, in salvation, and in eternity.

God wants to live with us, and us to live with him, in love, forever and ever. In his love and grace, he has *given* this to us – and in our love for him, we enjoy learning about it. But we know that this is only the beginning of our understanding.

In 1 Corinthians 13:12, the apostle Paul says that now, "we see only a reflection as in a mirror; then we shall see face to face. Now I know in part; then I shall know fully, even as I am fully known." We have knowledge, but our knowledge is *partial,* and we look forward to learning more. We rejoice that God knows us fully, and we can be confident that he will continue to draw us toward himself, so that on some future day, we will see him face to face and know him fully, sharing in his life and love forever and ever.

Michael Morrison

Responding to God With Faith

God is powerful, and he is good. He always uses his enormous power to further his promise of love and grace toward his people. He is gentle, loving, slow to anger and full of mercy.

That's good, but what difference does it make in our lives? How do we respond to a God who is simultaneously powerful and gentle? We respond in at least two ways.

Trust

When we realize that God has all power to do anything he wants, and that he always uses it for the good of humanity, then we can have absolute confidence that we are in good hands. He has both the ability and the purpose of working all things (including even our rebellion, hatred and betrayal against him and one another) toward our salvation. He is completely trustworthy—worthy of our trust.

When we are in the midst of trials, sickness, suffering and even dying, we can be confident that God is still with us, that he cares for us, that he has everything under control. It may not look like it, and *we* certainly do not feel in control, but we can be confident that God isn't caught off guard. He can and does redeem any situation, any misfortune, for our good.

We need never doubt God's love for us. "God demonstrates his own love for us in this: While we were still sinners, Christ died for us" (Romans 5:8). "This is how we know what love is: Jesus Christ laid down his life for us" (1 John 3:16). The God who did not spare his own Son can be counted on to give us everything we need for eternal happiness.

God did not send somebody else: The Son of God, essential to the Godhead, became human so that he could die for us and rise again for us (Hebrews 2:14). We were redeemed not by the blood of animals, not by the blood of a very good person, but by the blood of the Creator God who became human. Every time we take Communion, we are reminded of the extent of his love for us. We can be confident that he loves us. He has earned our trust.

"God is faithful," Paul tells us. "He will not let you be tempted beyond what you can bear" (1 Corinthians 10:13). "The Lord is faithful, and he will strengthen and protect you from the evil one" (2 Thessalonians 3:3). Even "if we are faithless, he will remain faithful" (2 Timothy 2:13). He is not going to change his mind about wanting us, calling us, and being merciful to us. "Let us hold unswervingly to the hope we profess, for he who promised is faithful" (Hebrews 10:23).

He has made a commitment to us, a covenant with us, to redeem us, to give us eternal life, to love us forever. He will not be without us. He is trustworthy, but how do we respond to him? Do we worry? Do we struggle to be worthy of his love? Or do we trust him?

We need never doubt God's power. This is shown in the resurrection of Jesus from death. This is the God who has power over death itself, power over all the beings he created, power over all other powers (Colossians 2:15). He triumphed over all things through the cross, and this is demonstrated through his resurrection. Death could not hold him, for he is the author of life (Acts 3:15) and he never did anything deserving of death.

The same power that raised Jesus from death will also give immortal life to us (Romans 8:11). We can trust that he has the power, and the desire, to fulfill all his promises toward us. We can trust him with everything—and that's a good thing, since it is foolish to trust in anything else.

Of ourselves, we will fail. Left to itself, even the sun will eventually fail. Our only hope is in a God who has power greater than the sun, greater than the universe, more faithful than time and space, full of love and faithfulness toward us. We have that sure hope in Jesus our Savior.

Belief and trust

All who believe in Jesus Christ will be saved (Acts 16:31). But what does it mean to believe in

Jesus Christ? Even the devil believes that Jesus is the Christ, the Son of God. He doesn't like it, but he knows it's true. Moreover, the devil knows that God exists and that he rewards those who seek him (Hebrews 11:6).

So what is the difference between our belief and the devil's belief? James gives us an answer: True faith is shown by action (James 2:18-19). What we do shows what we really believe and trust. Behavior can be evidence of faith, even though some people obey for wrong reasons.

So what is faith, and how does it differ from belief?

Saving faith is *trust*. We trust God to take care of us, to do good rather than evil, to give us eternal life. Trust means knowing that God exists, knowing that he is good, knowing that he has the power to do what he wants, and trusting that he will use it to do whatever is best for us. Trust means a willingness to put ourselves under him, to be willing to obey not out of fear but out of love. When we trust God, we love him.

Trust is shown by what we do. But the action is not the trust, and it does not create the trust—it is only the result of trust. Faith is, at its core, trust in Jesus Christ.

A gift of God

Where does this kind of trust come from? It is not something we can work up for ourselves. We cannot talk ourselves into it or use human logic to build an airtight case. We will never have the time to cover all the philosophical arguments about God. But we are forced to make a choice each day: Will we trust God, or not? Trying to delay the decision is a decision in itself: We do not yet trust him.

Each Christian has at some point or another made a decision to trust in Christ. For some, it was a well-thought-out decision. For others, it was an illogical decision, made for wrong reasons—but the right decision anyway. We could trust no one else, not even ourselves. On our own, we would mess our lives up. Nor could we trust other people. For some of us, faith was a choice of desperation—we had nowhere else to go but to Christ (John 6:68).

It is normal that our first faith is an immature faith—a good start, but not a good place to stay. We need to grow in our faith. As one man said to Jesus, "I do believe; help me overcome my unbelief!" (Mark 9:24). The disciples themselves, even after worshiping the resurrected Jesus, had some doubts (Matthew 28:17).

So where does faith come from? It is a gift of God. Ephesians 2:8 tells us that salvation is a gift of God, which means that the kind of faith that leads to salvation must also be his gift. In Acts 15:9 we are told that God purified the believers' hearts by faith. God was working in their hearts. He is the one who "opened the door of faith" (Acts 14:27). God did it, because he is the one who enables whatever faith we have.

We would not trust God unless God himself gave us the ability to trust him. Humans have been too corrupted by sin to believe or trust in God on our own strength or wisdom. That is why faith is not a "work" that qualifies us for salvation. We get no credit for meeting the qualification—faith is merely receiving the gift, being thankful for the gift. God gives us the ability to receive his gift, to enjoy his gift.

Trustworthy

God has good reason to give us faith, for there is someone completely trustworthy for us to believe in and be saved by. The faith he gives us is rooted in his Son, who became flesh for our salvation. We have good reason to have faith, for we have a Savior who has obtained salvation for us. He has done all that it takes, once for all, signed, sealed and being delivered.[1] Our faith has a firm foundation: Jesus Christ.

Jesus is the author and perfecter of our faith (Hebrews 12:2)—but he does not work alone. Jesus does only what the Father wants, and he works by the Holy Spirit in our hearts. The Holy Spirit

---

[1] Salvation is still "being delivered." It is not yet complete – there is work for the Holy Spirit to do in our salvation. We should also note that not everyone wants the salvation he gives.

teaches us, convicts us, and gives us faith (John 14:26; 15:26; 16:10).

Through the word

How does the Father, Son, and Holy Spirit give us faith? It is usually through the preached word. "Faith comes from hearing the message, and the message is heard through the word of Christ" (Romans 10:17). The message is in the written word, the Bible, and it is in the spoken word, whether a sermon at church or a simple testimony of one person to another.

The gospel tells us about Jesus, the Word of God. The Holy Spirit uses this message to enlighten us, and somehow allows us to trust in this word. This is sometimes called "the witness of the Holy Spirit," but it is not like a courtroom witness we can ask questions of. It is more like a switch inside us that is turned on, allowing us to accept the good news that is preached. It feels right. Though we may still have questions, we believe that we can live in this message. We can base our lives on it, we can make decisions based on it. It makes sense. It is the best possible choice.

God gives us the ability to trust him. He also gives us the ability to grow in faith. The down payment of faith is a seed that grows. It prepares and enables our minds and our emotions to understand more and more of the gospel. It helps us understand more about God as he reveals himself to us in Jesus Christ. To use a biblical metaphor, we begin to walk with God. We live in him, think in him, and believe in him.

Doubts

But most Christians struggle with faith at some time or another. Our growth is not always smooth and steady—it comes through trials and questions. For some, doubts come because of a tragedy or severe suffering. For others, it is prosperity or good times that subtly tempt us to rely on material things instead of God. Many of us will face both sorts of challenges to our faith.

Poor people often have stronger faith than rich people do. People beset by constant trials often know they have no hope except God, no choice but to trust him. Poor people tend to give a higher percentage of their income to the church than rich people do. It appears that their faith (even though not perfect) is more consistent. Often, the greatest enemy of faith is when all goes well. People are tempted to think that it was by their strength or their intelligence that they achieved as much as they have. They lose their sense of child-like dependence on God. They rely on what they have, rather than on God.

Poor people are in a better position to learn that life on this planet is full of questions, and God is the least questionable thing they have. They trust in him because all else has proven itself to be untrustworthy. Money, health, and friends are all fickle. We cannot depend on them. Only God is dependable, but even so, we don't always have the evidence we would like. So we have to trust him. As Job said, even though he kills me, I will trust him (Job 13:15). Only he offers the hope of eternal life. Only he offers hope that life makes sense or has any purpose.

Part of growth

Even so, we sometimes wrestle with doubts. That is part of the process of growing in faith, of learning to trust God with yet more of life. We face the choices set before us and once again choose God as the best choice. As Blaise Pascal said centuries ago, if we believe for no other reason, then at least we ought to believe because God is the best bet. If we follow him and he does not exist, then we have lost nothing. But if we do not follow him and he does exist, we have lost everything. We have nothing to lose and everything to gain by believing in God, by living and thinking that he is the surest reality in the universe.

This does not mean that we will understand everything. We will never understand everything. Faith means trusting in God even though we do not always understand. We can worship him even when we have doubts (Matthew 28:17). Salvation is not an intelligence contest. The faith that saves does not come from philosophical arguments that answer every doubt. Faith comes from God. If we rely on having answers to every question, we are not relying on God.

The only reason we can be in God's kingdom is by grace, through faith in our Savior, Jesus Christ. If we rely on our obedience, or anything else that we do, then we are relying on the wrong thing, an unreliable thing. We need to re-form our faith (allowing God to re-form our faith) into Christ, and him alone. Works, even good works, cannot be the basis of our salvation. Obedience, even to the commands of Jesus, cannot be our source of assurance. Only Christ is trustworthy.

As we grow in spiritual maturity, we often become more aware of our own sins, and our own sinfulness. We realize how far we are from Christ, and this can lead us to doubts, too, that God would really send his Son to die for people as unreliable as we are.

No matter how real our doubts, they should lead us back to greater faith in Christ, for only in him do we have any chance at all. There is no other place to go. In his words and his actions, we see that he knew how bad we were before he came to die for us. The better we see ourselves, the more we see the need to cast ourselves into the mercy of God. Only he is good enough to save us from ourselves, and only he will save us from our doubts.

Fellowship

It is by faith that we have a fruitful relationship with God. We pray by faith, worship by faith, and hear his words in sermons and fellowship by faith. Faith enables us to have fellowship with the Father, Son, and Holy Spirit. By faith we are enabled to give our allegiance to God, through our Savior Jesus Christ, by means of the Holy Spirit working in our hearts.

It is by faith that we can love other people. Faith frees us from the fear of ridicule and rejection. We can love others without worrying about what they will do to us, because we trust in Christ to reward us generously. Through faith in God, we can be generous with others.

Through faith in God, we can put him first in our lives. When we believe God is as good as he says he is, then we will treasure him above all else, and be willing to make the sacrifices that he asks of us. We will trust him, and it is by that trust that we will experience the joys of salvation. Christian life is, from first to last, a matter of trusting God.

Joseph Tkach

Five facts about faith

- God loved us even when we were his enemies; he will be faithful in all circumstances.
- The resurrection of Jesus shows that God has the power to save us even from death.
- When we trust God, we obey him, knowing that his commands are for our good.
- No one has perfect faith; we grow in faith through life experiences.
- Doubts and questions can lead us to trust Christ even with the unknown.

Who Is God?

Is God a nice old man in the sky? A cranky being who wants to dish out "justice" on you? Is he like a human father or mother?

Charles Haddon Spurgeon was England's best-known preacher for most of the second half of the 19th century. In a sermon he gave when he was only 20, Spurgeon declared that the proper study for a Christian is the Godhead. Here is a quote from that sermon—it's one of my favorites:

> The highest science, the loftiest speculation, the mightiest philosophy, which can ever engage the attention of a child of God, is the name, the nature, the person, the work, the doings, and the existence of the great God whom he calls his Father. There is something exceedingly improving to the mind in a contemplation of the Divinity. It is a subject so vast, that all our thoughts are lost in its immensity; so deep, that our pride is drowned in its infinity. Other subjects we can compass and grapple with; in them we feel a kind of self-content, and go our way with the thought, "Behold I am wise." But when we come to this master-science, finding that our plumb-line cannot sound its depth, and that our eagle eye cannot see its height, we turn away with the thought, that vain man would be wise, but he is like a wild ass's colt; and with the solemn exclamation, "I am but of yesterday, and know nothing." No subject of contemplation will tend more to humble the mind, than thoughts of God.

As have many other preachers and teachers, Spurgeon reminds us that the great and central question of Christianity is this: "Who is God?"

God's own answer is not a proposition, but a person: the incarnate Son of God, Jesus Christ. As the self-revelation of God, Jesus is the focal point of our knowledge of God's nature. Jesus, who takes us to the Father and sends us the Spirit, teaches us to ask, "Who is God?," then bids us look to him for the definitive answer.

Throughout history, many great thinkers pondered the question, "Who is God?" Unfortunately, they often did not make Jesus the center of their investigations. Working from the central revelation of God in Jesus Christ, the doctrine of the Trinity was developed to answer the false reasoning and heretical ideas about God that had infiltrated the church in its first three centuries. Though the Trinity doctrine doesn't answer all questions about God's nature, it helps us focus on who God is without wandering away from sound doctrine.

The early Christians were not unique in developing errors of reasoning as they pondered the nature of God. Theologians and philosophers of every age got it wrong, and our time is no exception. Old ideas have a way or repackaging themselves and worming their way into contemporary thinking. It is important that we are aware of two errors that are prevalent in our day. Both lead to wrong conclusions and a distorted picture of who God is.

The first error is a modern version of pantheism—the idea that God is part of his creation instead of being distinct from it and Lord over it. Though Scripture tells us that creation tells us about God (Romans 1:20), there is an important difference between believing that God is *present to everything* and believing that *everything is God.*

Unfortunately, a belief in the divine spirituality of everything (often referred to as "the Universe") is common today. Hungry for spirituality and put off by traditional religion, many people are seeking "enlightenment" in obscure and fringe ideas. Go into any large bookstore and you'll find sections devoted to fantasy fiction and the occult. Video gamers are obsessed with ever more bizarre themes and fantastic creatures wielding supernatural powers. Technology is blurring the line between fantasy and reality, and the spiritual landscape is becoming cluttered with offbeat ideas.

The same thing happened in the early years of the church. People had an appetite for magic and mystery. As a result, many non-apostolic epistles and gospels were in circulation—offering a mix of truth and bizarre ideas about God, reflecting the popular culture of that day. Paul reminds us what happens when people lose their spiritual moorings:

> For although they knew God, they neither glorified him as God nor gave thanks to him, but their thinking became futile and their foolish hearts were darkened. Although they claimed to be wise, they became fools and exchanged the glory of the immortal God for images made to look like a mortal human being and birds and animals and reptiles. (Romans 1:21-23)

A second prevalent error in our day concerning the nature of God is conceiving of God as a spirit force that dwells in everyone individually. From this perspective, God is viewed as a genie that we carry with us, making use of him as the need arises. It's as though God is a cosmic smartphone with all kinds of useful apps.

Following this line of faulty reasoning, we wrongly conclude that when we travel, we are taking God somewhere that he is not already present. God becomes dependent on us and limited by our limitations. As a result, God can't be more faithful than we are. Though this false idea may boost our sense of self-importance, it is a false idea that negates the grace of God.

The truth of God's nature, revealed in Jesus, is the opposite of this error. As the authors of the New Testament remind us, God remains faithful even when we are faithless. Our true importance is related to our identity as children of the God who not only dwells within us by his Spirit, but far beyond us. Our calling is to join God in what he is doing. We do so with great anticipation knowing that he has been at work long before we arrive on the scene. We are greatly privileged to share in what the Holy Spirit is doing to turn people around and to draw them into a reconciled relationship with the Father and the Son.

The more clearly we understand who God is, the better will be our understanding of who we are and of our calling to live in communion with Christ by the Holy Spirit.

Joseph Tkach

Humanity's Relationship With God

What do humans want to know about God? Perhaps the best initial question is, "Who are you?"

To such a question, God replied, "I AM WHO I AM" (Exodus 3:14). God declares himself to us in creation (Psalm 19:1). He has interacted with the human family ever since he made us. Sometimes he speaks through thunder, quaking or fire, and sometimes he speaks in a whisper (Exodus 20:18; 1 Kings 19:11-12).

In the biblical record, God reveals information about himself and inspired reports of how people responded to him. God also reveals himself through Jesus Christ and the Holy Spirit.

But we want to know more than who God is,

don't we? We want to know why he made us. We want to know what he wants us to do. We want to know how he affects us. We want to know what he has in store for us. We want to know not just *about* him — we want to know *him*. What is our relationship with God now? What should it be? And what will our relationship be in the future?

Where we find ourselves now

God made us in his image (Genesis 1:26-27). The Bible reveals a far more profound future than we can now imagine. Hebrews 2:6-11 tells us that we are made "a little lower than the angels." Yet God has crowned us with "glory and honor" and put everything under our rule. His future intent for humanity is to leave "nothing that is not subject to them. Yet at present we do not see everything subject to them."

God has prepared an infinitely glorious and joyous future for us. But something stands in the way. We find ourselves in a state of sin, feeling cut off from God. But the breach has been healed. Jesus tasted death for us so that he might bring "many children to glory" (Hebrews 2:9-10).

Revelation 21:7 says that God wants to unite us with him in a family relationship. Because of God's love for us and what he has done for us, and what he is doing for us now as the Author of our salvation, Jesus is "not ashamed to call [us] brothers and sisters" (Hebrews 2:10-11).

So what should we be doing now?

Acts 2:38 tells us to repent and to be baptized – to figuratively bury the old self. Those who believe that Jesus Christ is their Savior, Lord and King are led by the Spirit (Galatians 3:2-5). As he opens our minds to understand the gospel, we repent – turning to God from the selfish ways we followed in the past. In faith, we enter a new relationship with him. We are reborn (John 3:3), given a new life in Christ through the Holy Spirit, through God's grace and mercy and the work of Jesus Christ.

What happens then? We "grow in the grace and knowledge of our Lord and Savior Jesus Christ" (2 Peter 3:18) for the remainder of our lives, and then we will take part in the first resurrection, after which we will "be with the Lord forever" (1 Thessalonians 4:13-17).

Awesome inheritance

> [God] has given us new birth into a living hope through the resurrection of Jesus Christ from the dead, and into an inheritance that can never perish, spoil or fade – kept in heaven for you, who through faith are shielded by God's power until the coming of the salvation that is ready to be revealed in the last time. (1 Peter 1:3-5)

In the resurrection, we will be given immortality (1 Corinthians 15:54) and a "spiritual body" (verse 44). "As we have borne the likeness of the earthly man [Adam]," says verse 49, "so shall we bear the likeness of the man from heaven [Jesus]." As "children of the resurrection," we will no longer be subject to death (Luke 20:36).

Could anything be more wonderful than what the Bible says about God and our future relationship with him, a relationship that can begin right now? We will "be like him [Jesus], for we shall see him as he is" (1 John 3:2). Revelation 21:3 says that, in the time of the new heaven and new earth, "the dwelling of God is with humans, and he will live with them. They will be his people, and God himself will be with them and be their God."

We will be one with God in holiness, love, perfection, righteousness and spirit. As his immortal children, we will be the family of God in its fullest sense, sharing complete fellowship with him in perfect and everlasting joy. What a marvelous and inspiring message of hope and eternal salvation God has for us!

The Name of God — YHWH

When God called to Moses out of the burning bush, telling him to free the Israelites from bondage in Egypt, Moses asked: "Suppose I go to the Israelites and say to them, 'The God of your fathers has sent me to you,' and they ask me, 'What is his name?' Then what shall I tell them?" (Exodus 3:13).

God answered Moses, "I AM WHO I AM" (verse 14). The Hebrew word for "I AM" is *ehyeh*, which comes from the verb "to be." It can also be translated as "I SHALL BE."

God further told Moses: "Say to the Israelites, 'The Lord, the God of your fathers…has sent me to you'" (verse 15). Although the Hebrew word for "Lord" is *adon*, the word translated "Lord" in verse 15 is different. It is spelled with the four Hebrew consonants YHWH – "the tetragrammaton" (Greek for "four letters"). The word is related to *ehyeh* and also comes from the verb "to be." Both words have the sense of "being actively present."

Although most scholars pronounce the tetragrammaton as Yahweh, the correct pronunciation is not known for certain. The Hebrews avoided saying God's name because they believed that doing so might take God's name in vain. When reading a passage of the Hebrew Bible that contained it, they referred to God by one of his titles – *adonai* or "my Lord."

The oldest known manuscript fragments of the Septuagint leave the tetragrammaton untranslated. Later manuscripts, probably reflecting Christian editing, render the tetragrammaton as *kyrios*, Greek for "Lord." Later, English versions rendered the personal name YHWH as the impersonal "the Lord." They used all capital letters for "Lord" to indicate they were translating YHWH, rather than *adon* or *adonai*.

The text of the Hebrew Bible originally had only consonants. When vowels were added in the 10th century A.D., the vowels of *adonai* were also used for the tetragrammaton, reminding the readers to pronounce the word as *adonai*. In the 16th century, Latin translators combined the vowel points of *adonai* with the consonants of the tetragrammaton to produce the artificial form *Iehoua*. In 1530, Tyndale rendered the tetragrammaton as *Iehouah* in his translation of Exodus 6:3. Subsequently, the letter I became J, and the u became v, and Jehovah became the standard spelling. The King James Version uses this spelling (Psalm 83:18 is one example), but the KJV usually translates YHWH as "the Lord" and *adonai* as "the Lord."

Knowing God

In Psalm 113:5-6, the psalmist asks: "Who is like the Lord our God, the One who sits enthroned on high, who stoops down to look on the heavens and the earth?"

We still are asking that question. The self-help sections of bookstores and online catalogs offer seemingly countless books addressing ways to know God from Christian, quasi-Christian and other religious perspectives. Some of these books teach universalism; others teach pantheism or panentheism. Those with a New Age perspective often promise keys to finding secret knowledge concerning God.

Many people are seeking to know God or at least to connect with some sort of "higher power." That should not surprise us, since God created humans in his image, giving us a "spiritual appetite." Theologian and philosopher Blaise Pascal is credited with saying that within each person there is a "God-shaped hole looking to be filled."[1] We would hope that a person sincerely seeking to know God would receive clear direction from all Christian churches. Sadly, that is not always the case.

Given our limited minds, we humans are unable to fully comprehend all there is to know about God. Paul put it this way: "Oh, the depth of the riches of the wisdom and knowledge of God! How unsearchable his judgments, and his paths beyond tracing out!" (Romans 11:33). Though God lives in "unapproachable light" (1 Timothy 6:16), he has not left us completely in the dark. Note Jesus' remarkable statement in Matthew 11:27: "All things have been committed to me by my Father. No one knows the Son except the Father, and no one knows the Father except the Son and those to whom the Son chooses to reveal him." I love how the second-century Christian teacher Irenaeus explained this verse:

> No one can know the Father apart from God's Word, that is, unless the Son reveals him, and no one can know the Son unless the Father so wills. Now the Son fulfills the Father's good pleasure: the Father sends, the Son is sent, and he comes. The Father is beyond our sight and comprehension; but he is known by his Word, who tells us of him who surpasses all telling. In turn, the Father alone has knowledge of his Word. And the Lord has revealed both truths. Therefore, the Son reveals the knowledge of the Father by his revelation of himself. Knowledge of the Father consists in the self-revelation of the Son, for all is revealed through the Word. (in *Against Heresies*)

This means that no one can know God unless and until God reveals himself – and he has chosen to reveal himself through Jesus. The word *reveal* comes from the Greek word *apokalupto,* meaning to take off the cover—to disclose or reveal. It is the opposite of *kalupto,* which means to cover up; hide. The Old Testament speaks of the Shekinah glory of God, present within the innermost part of the Tabernacle behind the veil. No one was allowed behind that veil except the high priest, and then only once a year. For most of the time, God

---

[1] Pascal wrote: "What else does this craving, and this helplessness, proclaim but that there was once in man a true happiness, of which all that now remains is the empty print and trace? This he tries in vain to fill with everything around him, seeking in things that are not there the help he cannot find in those that are, though none can help, since this infinite abyss can be filled only with an infinite and immutable object; in other words by God himself."

remained hidden behind the veil. So when Jesus said he had come to reveal the Father, his followers were understandably intrigued.

When Philip asked Jesus to show the disciples the Father, Jesus replied: "Don't you know me, Philip, even after I have been among you such a long time? Anyone who has seen me has seen the Father" (John 14:9). God sent his Son to "pull back the covers" and reveal who he is through his Son. We must be careful not to let preconceptions of what God is like determine our thinking and behavior toward God. Only Jesus has perfect and complete knowledge of God, and he shares that knowledge with us.

Through the life and ministry of Jesus, we get the best look at what God is like this side of our resurrection. Jesus alone is one with the Father and the Holy Spirit. He alone brings "insider knowledge" of the whole of God as the eternal Son of God. He alone is God's self-revelation in time and space, flesh and blood. In Jesus, God has come to us in person, meeting us face-to-face so that we may know him truly and personally.

Jesus shared himself and what he knew with his disciples, whom he called his friends. He commissioned them, and those who follow them, to go into the world and make that knowledge known—not through books and programs offering esoteric, "hidden knowledge" or esoteric, private experiences—and certainly not through a complex web of philosophical arguments and counter-arguments. Jesus told his followers that they could come to know God through relationships, including relationships with each other and with those outside the Christian community. He said that the clearest sign that would point others to him would be the love that his followers have for each other—a love reflecting God's own love for all people.

Joseph Tkach

Who's Afraid of God's Judgment?

Imagine a courtroom scene. You are accused of a crime and now on trial. Problem is, you know you are guilty. But as you walk in, you notice the judge gives you a reassuring nod of recognition, as if he had known you all your life. He summons you to the bench. "Don't worry about a thing," he tells you with a warm fatherly smile. "I know all about this case. In fact, I'm going to be your defense attorney."

The late theologian Shirley C. Guthrie would explain that this is the way we should picture what the Bible calls the Judgment. "Must we talk about the wrath of God?" Guthrie asked. "Yes," he answers. "But God's wrath is not like that of the gods. It is the wrath of the God who was in Christ reconciling the world to God's self" (*Christian Doctrine*, pages 261-262).

Theological strait-jackets

Unfortunately, instead of allowing Jesus' love, compassion and kindness to shape their understanding of God, many Christians gravitate toward what we might call a "forensic" model of salvation. "Forensic" is a penal or legal term. This model sees God the Father as stern and vengeful, a frightening God from whom we need Jesus to save us. It assumes that the starting place for understanding God is not Jesus Christ, but "the law," or the commands of the Bible. This model sees the law as so important that even God is subject to it. Since God is concerned first about the demands of his law and only secondly about the well-being of humans, he will punish them for lawbreaking in the same way that the State and human courts and legal systems do — through a straightforward proving of guilt, a guilty verdict, followed by an appropriate punishment.

Front and center in the forensic model is God's anger against sinning humanity. God is offended, and someone must pay. Jesus steps forward and takes the full force of God's wrath against human sin. That means we have had our penalty paid for us, but this model does nothing for a restored relationship of love and trust. This "offended deity" picture forgets that first and foremost, God is love (1 John 4:16), that God is joyously working to bring "many children to glory," and that our salvation was in his mind "from the creation of the world" (Revelation 13:8).

This forensic model also forgets something even more basic — that Jesus Christ and the Father along with the Holy Spirit are the three Persons of the one God, and that the Son or Word made Incarnate in Jesus was the perfect revelation of the Father in human form. The Father is not some angry, vengeful deity that we need protection from; he is just like Jesus. Jesus, remember, is "the exact representation" of the being of God (Hebrews 1:3). The Father is full of compassion and mercy, a God who "desires mercy and not sacrifice," just like Jesus. Jesus is the starting place for understanding God; the law is not.

God is not schizophrenic. He does not have a split personality. There is not one "good God," Jesus, and one "bad God," the Father. There is one God — Father, Son and Spirit — who loves us unconditionally and has in Jesus made full provision not only for our sins to be forgiven and removed, but also for us to be fully included in the love relationship that the Son has shared with the Father from eternity.

Adoption

God is not in the business of training obedient servants, but in building a family. The apostle Paul used the word "adoption" in describing the kind of relationship that God has created for humanity in Jesus Christ (Ephesians 1:4-5). Through the Incarnation of the Son — by Jesus becoming one of us and taking up our cause as his own — God has drawn us into and made us part of the intimate relationship that Jesus has with the Father.

We see the power of this intimate love that God has for humanity in the parable of the Prodigal Son. The repentant son is welcomed home by the Father and restored to full rights of being part of the family (Luke 15:11-24). This depicts the God who was in Christ reconciling the world to himself (2 Corinthians 5:19). The death of Christ was not an act of divine child abuse, as some critics of Christianity have said. It was a divine rescue springing from God's love for us (John 3:16), an intervention designed to restore a purpose of which we were unaware in our ignorance and darkness (verses 19-20).

Set against this majestic purpose, God's wrath can be seen for what it is — anger not at the humanity he sent Jesus to save, but at sin, which destroys the relationship he has always intended for us in Christ. God is not some resentful, selfish parent in an emotional stew because we have not played by his rules. God is Father, Son and Spirit, loving, faithful and unconditionally committed to bringing humanity into the joy of knowing him for who he really is.

Mercy vs. judgment

God, however, will never be at peace with sin. The great human tragedy is that we have been unaware of the pardon and reconciliation the Father has brought about through Jesus Christ. We have loved darkness rather than light and have chosen to ignore what the Father offers us through the Son.

Through Christ, the disconnect between the world and God has been removed once and for all. The great majority of unbelievers are people who through weakness or ignorance are resisting the influence of the life-giving Holy Spirit of Christ, the Person of the Godhead who beckons to us to abandon our addiction to darkness and sin — who testifies in our hearts to God's saving, atoning and reconciling work in Jesus on our behalf (John 14:25-27; 15:26).

Jesus did not just *bring* good news, he *was* good news. The overwhelming emphasis of his teaching was mercy, not vengeance. His hallmark sayings reflect the God who is love, in whose mind mercy rejoices against judgment (James 2:13). Thus, what was hinted at in parts of the Old Testament becomes the major theme in the Gospels — "I will have mercy and not sacrifice." Jesus' word pictures show us a forgiving father, a Good Samaritan, seeking shepherds and splendidly generous employers, healings, exorcisms, a Great Physician who pleaded "Come to me, all you who are weary and burdened, and I will give you rest" (Matthew 11:28).

Neil Earle

One in Three and Three in One

The Bible never compromises the fact that God is one. Yet, Jesus' incarnation and work give us a greater depth of understanding of the way in which God is one. The New Testament testifies that Jesus Christ is God and that the Father is God. There is *more than one* Person in the *one* God.

The New Testament also presents the Holy Spirit as divine and eternal. Whenever we say that the Holy Spirit does something, we mean that God does it. The Holy Spirit is God. That means the Bible reveals one God who exists eternally as Father, Son, and Holy Spirit. It is for this reason that Christians are to be baptized "in the name of the Father and of the Son and of the Holy Spirit" (Matthew 28:19).

Throughout the centuries, many ideas have been developed that might seem, at first glance, to make these biblical facts easier to understand. But we must be careful not to accept any idea that contradicts what the Bible says. Some ideas might make things seem simple, in the sense of making God easier to comprehend and easier to picture in our minds. But what is important is whether an idea is consistent with the Bible, not whether it is simple or easy.

The Bible tells us there is one and only one God, and then presents us with more than one Person called God. The Father is called God, the Son is called God, and the Holy Spirit is called God. All three are eternal, and all three do things that only God can do. So there is one God, and three in the One.

"One in three" – or "three in one" – is a concept that, at first glance, appears illogical. But neither is it logical for us to assume that God could not be more than what we would expect if we simply sat down, with no revelation, to figure it out for ourselves.

God reveals many things about himself, and we believe them, even though we cannot explain them all. For example, we cannot completely explain how God can be without beginning. This is beyond our ability to understand. We cannot explain what eternal existence is like, yet we know that God is without beginning. Likewise, the Bible reveals that God is one and only one, yet is also Father, Son, and Holy Spirit. We believe it even though it is not simple or easy to explain. We believe it because the Bible reveals it.

The Holy Spirit is God

Acts 5:3-4 calls the Holy Spirit God:

> Peter said, "Ananias, how is it that Satan has so filled your heart that you have lied to the Holy Spirit and have kept for yourself some of the money you received for the land? Didn't it belong to you before it was sold? And after it was sold, wasn't the money at your disposal? What made you think of doing such a thing? You have not lied to men but to God."

When Ananias lied to the Holy Spirit, Peter says he was lying to God. He was not trying to deceive an impersonal force or an intermediate agency — he was trying to deceive God.

The Bible ascribes to the Holy Spirit attributes that belong only to God. For instance, the Holy Spirit is omniscient, or unlimited in knowledge. "God has revealed it to us by his Spirit. The Spirit searches all things, even the deep things of God…. No one knows the thoughts of God except the Spirit of God" (1 Corinthians 2:10-11).

The Holy Spirit is omnipresent, or unlimited in place. "Do you not know that your body is a temple of the Holy Spirit, who is in you, whom you have received from God?" (1 Corinthians 6:19). The Holy Spirit is in believers everywhere, not limited to any one place (see Psalm 139:7-8).

The Holy Spirit gives us new life. "No one can enter the kingdom of God unless they are born of water and the Spirit. Flesh gives birth to flesh, but the Spirit gives birth to spirit" (John 3:5-6).

The Holy Spirit speaks and knows the future. "The Spirit clearly says that in later times some will abandon the faith and follow deceiving spirits" (1 Timothy 4:1).

The Holy Spirit is equated with the Father and the Son in the baptismal ceremony. We are baptized "in the name of the Father and of the Son and of the Holy Spirit" (Matthew 28:19). There is one name, but three are included in the One.

The Spirit creates out of nothing (Psalm 104:30). Only God can create like that.

Hebrews 9:14 says the Holy Spirit is eternal. Only God is eternal.

Jesus told the apostles: "I will ask the Father, and he will give you another Counselor to be with you forever – the Spirit of truth. The world cannot accept him, because it neither sees him nor knows him. But you know him, for he lives with you and will be in you" (John 14:16-17).

Jesus identified the Counselor as the Holy Spirit: "The Counselor, the Holy Spirit, whom the Father will send in my name, will teach you all things and will remind you of everything I have said to you" (verse 26). The Counselor guides into all truth, something only God is capable of doing. As Paul affirmed, "We speak, not in words taught us by human wisdom but in words taught by the Spirit, expressing spiritual truths in spiritual words" (1 Corinthians 2:13).

Father, Son, and Holy Spirit: one God

When we understand that God is one, and that the Holy Spirit is God, just as the Father is God and the Son is God, we have no problem understanding a passage like Acts 13:2: "While they were worshiping the Lord and fasting, the Holy Spirit said, 'Set apart for me Barnabas and Saul for the work to which I have called them.'" Here Luke presents the Holy Spirit as speaking. The Holy Spirit is God at work in the church, speaking and calling people to do God's will.

The biblical revelation of the nature of God is beautiful. When the Holy Spirit speaks, or sends, or inspires, or leads, or sanctifies, or empowers, or gives gifts, it is God speaking, sending, inspiring, leading, sanctifying, empowering or giving gifts. But since God is one, and not three separate beings, the Holy Spirit is not a separate God.

God has one will, the will of the Father, which is also the will of the Son and of the Holy Spirit. It is not a matter of two or three separate God Beings deciding to be in perfect agreement with each other. This would contradict scriptures such as Isaiah 44:6-8. It is a matter of one God, one will. The Son is the very expression of the will of the Father. Similarly, the Holy Spirit constitutes the will of the Father at work in the world.

Paul says that "the Lord is the Spirit," and he speaks of "the Lord, who is the Spirit" (2 Corinthians 3:17-18). He says "the Spirit gives life" (verse 6), which is something only God can do. We know the Father, only because the Spirit enables us to believe that Jesus is the Son of God. Jesus dwells in us and the Father dwells in us, but that is only because the Spirit dwells in us (John 14:16-17, 23; Romans 8:9-11). Since God is one, if the Spirit is in us, then the Father and the Son are in us. The three can be distinguished, but not separated.

Paul equates the Spirit, the Lord, and God in 1 Corinthians 12:4-11. He says it is "the same God who inspires" in verse 6, and he says "these are the work of one and the same Spirit," and goes on to declare that the Spirit does all this as the Spirit wills (verse 11). How can the Spirit will? The Spirit wills because the Spirit is a person, and the Spirit is God, and God is one, and the will of the Father is the will of the Son and of the Holy Spirit.

To worship God is to worship the Father, the Son, and the Holy Spirit, the one and only one God. That does not mean we are to single out the Holy

Spirit and worship the Holy Spirit as though the Holy Spirit is a separate Being. We do not direct our worship to the Holy Spirit specifically, but to God, who is Father, Son, and Holy Spirit. It is God in us (the Holy Spirit) who causes us to worship God. The Comforter (like the Son) will not speak on his own (John 16:13), but what the Father gives him he will speak. He does not direct us to himself, but to the Father through the Son. Likewise, we don't normally pray specifically to the Spirit – it is the Spirit in us who helps us in our prayers, and intercedes for us (Romans 8:26).

Unless God himself is in us, we would not be turned toward God at all. Unless God himself is in us, we would not know God, and we would not know his Son. That is why all the credit for our salvation goes to God and not to us. The fruit we bear is the fruit of the Spirit – that is, God's fruit, not ours. But God gives us the privilege, if we will accept it, of participating with him in his work.

The Father is the Creator and Source of all things. The Son is the Redeemer and Savior, and the one by whom God created all things. The Holy Spirit is the Comforter and Advocate. The Holy Spirit is God in us, the one who leads us to the Father through the Son. Through the Son, we are cleansed and saved so that we can have fellowship with him and the Father. The Spirit stirs our hearts and minds and inclines us toward belief in Jesus Christ, who is the way and the gate. The Spirit gives us gifts, the gifts of God, including faith, hope and love.

All this is the work of the one God, who reveals himself to us as Father, Son, and Holy Spirit. He is not a different God from the God of the Old Testament, but in the New Testament something more is revealed about him: He sent his Son as a human being to die for our sins and to be raised to glory, and he sent us his Spirit – the Comforter – to dwell in us, to lead us into all truth, to give us gifts, and to conform us to the image of Christ.

When we pray, reaching God is the goal of the prayer, yet it is also God who leads us toward that goal, and it is also God who is the Way along which we are led toward the goal. In other words, it is to God (the Father) we pray; it is God in us (the Holy Spirit) motivating us to pray; and God is also the Way (the Son) along which we are being led toward that goal.

The Father initiates the plan of salvation. The Son embodies and executes the atoning, redemptive plan for the salvation of humanity. The Holy Spirit applies the benefits, or gifts, of redemption to empower the salvation of the believers. All this is the work of the one God, the God of the Bible.

Paul ended 2 Corinthians with the blessing: "May the grace of the Lord Jesus Christ, and the love of God, and the fellowship of the Holy Spirit be with you all" (2 Corinthians 13:14). In this verse, Paul highlights the love of God, which is shown to us through the grace he gives us in Jesus Christ and the unified fellowship with himself and one another he gives us through the Holy Spirit.

How many "Persons" is God?

Many people have only a hazy idea of what the Bible teaches about the oneness of God. Most do not think about it. Some imagine three separate Beings. Some picture one Being with three heads. Others think of one Being who changes from Father to Son to Holy Spirit whenever he wills. It is easy to make such mistakes.

Many people use the word Trinity as a definition of the biblical teaching about God. However, if asked, most would not be able to explain what the Bible actually teaches about how God is one. In other words, what many people envision when they speak of the Trinity is not biblical. Some of the confusion lies in the use of the word Persons.

The word Persons, which is normally included in English-language definitions of the Trinity, causes people to think of three Beings. "One God who is three Persons – Father, Son, and Holy Spirit," is a common way the Trinity is explained. But the ordinary meaning of the word "person" is misleading when it is applied to God. It gives the impression that God's threeness lies in being three separate individuals – which is not the case.

The English word "person" is derived from the Latin word *persona*. The word *persona* was used by theologians to describe the Father, the Son, and the Holy Spirit in the Latin language, but it did not convey the same meaning as the English word "person" conveys today. It was a word originally used for a role that an actor portrayed in a play. It was also the word for "mask," because actors wore different masks for each character they portrayed.

Even this concept, though it does not allow the error of three Beings, is still weak and misleading when referring to God. It is misleading because the Father, the Son, and the Holy Spirit are not mere roles being played by God. An actor can play only one role at a time, quite unlike God, who is Father, Son, and Holy Spirit all the time.

Even though a Latin theologian may have understood what was meant by the word *persona*, the average person today would not. The English word "person" is easily misunderstood by the average individual when referring to God, unless it is accompanied by an explanation that "Persons" in the Godhead should not be thought of in the same way as "persons" like humans.

When most English-speaking people think of one God who is three Persons, they cannot help but think in some way of three separate Beings. In other words, the terms *persons* and *beings* are usually thought of, in English, as meaning the same thing. But that is not how God is revealed in the Bible. There is only one God, not three. The Bible reveals that Father, Son, and Holy Spirit are the way the one true God of the Bible is, the way God exists always.

One God: three Hypostases

When we express the biblical truth that God is one and at the same time three, it is helpful to use words that do not imply three Gods. God's oneness cannot be compromised. The problem is, all words that refer to created things tend to mislead by their very context in ordinary language. Most words, including the word Persons, tend to confuse God's nature with the created order. On the other hand, all our words in one way or another refer to the created order. So it is important to know what we mean, and what we do not mean, when we use any word in reference to God.

A helpful word, one that was used by Greek-speaking Christians in expressing the oneness and threeness of God, is found in Hebrews 1:3. This passage is helpful in several ways. It states: "The Son is the radiance of God's glory and the exact representation of his being, sustaining all things by his powerful word."

From the description of the Son as "the radiance of God's glory," we learn a number of things. The Son is not a separate Being. The Son is not less divine than the Father. The Son is eternal, just as the Father is. In other words, the Son is to the Father as radiance or brightness is to glory. One cannot have radiance without the source of radiance, or a source of radiance without the radiance itself. Yet we distinguish between God's glory and the radiance of that glory. They are distinct, without being separate.

Likewise, there is much to learn from the words "the exact representation of his being." The Son is the full and complete expression of the Father. What God is in his being, the Son also is.

Now, let's look at the Greek word translated "being" in this passage. Some versions translate it "person." The word from which "being" and "person" in this passage are translated is *hypostasis*. It comes from Greek words meaning "standing under." It refers to that which "stands under," or that which makes something what it is. Hypostasis could be defined like this: "That without which something cannot be." It could be called "the ground of being."

God is personal

Hypostasis (in plural form, hypostases) is a good word to use of the Father, the Son, and the Holy Spirit. It is a biblical term, and it does not confuse God's nature with the created order.

The word Person may also be used, as long as one understands that Person must not be confused with the way humans are persons. One reason the word Person is helpful, if it is understood correctly, is that God interacts with us in a personal way. It is wrong to say that God is impersonal. We do not worship a rock or plant, or an impersonal "power that is behind the universe." Rather, we worship a "living Person."

God is personal, but he is not a person in the way humans are persons. He says, "I am God, and not man – the Holy One among you" (Hosea 11:9). God is Creator; he is not just another part of his creation. Humans have a beginning, grow up, have a body, are separate from one another, grow old, increase or decrease in size, strength, etc., and die. God has none of those characteristics, but is nonetheless personal in his relationship to humans. God is infinitely more than any human word can convey, yet he is personal and loves us dearly. God has revealed much about himself, but he has not revealed everything about himself – some things we are simply incapable of knowing. As finite beings, we cannot totally grasp the infinite. We can know God as he reveals himself to us, but we cannot know him exhaustively, because we are finite, and he is infinite. What God has revealed to us about himself is true. It is relevant. It is intimate. It is marvelous, and it is thorough. But we must never think we know everything about God. God has revealed all we *need* to know, and what he has revealed is wonderful!

God calls on us to continue to "grow in the grace and knowledge of our Lord and Savior Jesus Christ" (2 Peter 3:18). Jesus proclaimed, "This is eternal life: that they may know you, the only true God, and Jesus Christ, whom you have sent" (John 17:3). The more we know God, the more we realize how small we are and how great he is.

Jesus – Alive Forevermore!

Jesus did not stay dead for long. Early Sunday morning, near sunrise, some disciples discovered that the Son of God had risen. They did not see the resurrection itself, but they saw Jesus, alive and well. Over a period of 40 days, they saw Jesus on numerous occasions. Then he rose into heaven.

But Jesus is not taking a vacation. His ministry continues, even in heaven. He serves and leads the church, interceding for us, helping us, preparing us for eternal glory. Christ will return, and after he has subdued every enemy, he will give everything to the Father. Mission accomplished.

Resurrection

Many people have a hard time believing that Jesus rose from the dead. In their experience, dead people always stay dead. They are skeptical of such an extraordinary claim. The disciples must have been mistaken, they say, or else they made it up.

The disciples were skeptical, too. When they went to the tomb, they expected to find a body. When they did not find a body, they first assumed that someone had stolen it. They did not expect a resurrection. It was only when Jesus *appeared* to them that they believed that he was alive again.

Most Jews believed that there would be a resurrection at the end of the age, when everyone would rise for judgment (Daniel 12:2). But a resurrection into glory before the end was just as unexpected as a crucified Messiah. Although Jesus had taught both these ideas (Matthew 16:21; 17:23; Mark 9:9), the disciples didn't understand or believe this (verse 10). They expected him to stay dead.

But if Jesus is the sinless Son of God, then he is unique among the billions of people, and he did not deserve death. We should be surprised if he were *not* resurrected. We also have evidence that gives us confidence that Jesus rose from the dead (as we will cover in a later article).

Many of us also have experiences in our own lives that convince us that God exists, that he sometimes causes miracles, that Jesus is alive and the Holy Spirit is active in his people. This gives us further reason to believe that Jesus is alive.

Significance of the resurrection

The resurrection meant life for Jesus—but a far better life than what he had on earth, the glory that he had with the Father before his incarnation (John 17:5). By his resurrection, he was powerfully revealed as the Son of God (Romans 1:4)—the resurrection declared who he had been all along. The resurrection proves that God will judge the world through Christ (Acts 17:31).

The resurrection also means life for *us*. As Paul says, we will "be saved through his life" (Romans 5:10). If you "believe in your heart that God raised him from the dead, you will be saved" (Romans 10:9). "If Christ has not been raised, our preaching is useless and so is your faith" (1 Corinthians 15:14). Our salvation depends not just on Jesus' death, but also his resurrection (1 Peter 3:21).

Justification, most commonly associated with Jesus' death, is also a result of his resurrection (Romans 4:24-25). Our salvation depends on the entire sequence of the incarnation: Jesus' birth, ministry, death and resurrection.

Our baptism pictures our participation in Jesus' death and resurrection. Rising from the water pictures our new life (Romans 6:4) and it pictures our future: "We will certainly also be united with him in his resurrection" (verse 5). "When he appears, we shall be like him" (1 John 3:2). Our resurrected bodies will be like his (1 Corinthians 15:42-49).

God has "made us alive with Christ...raised us up with Christ" (Ephesians 2:5-6). We were "raised with him" (Colossians 2:12). By faith in Christ, we are spiritually united to him. Our sins are given to him and paid by him, his righteousness and life are given to us, and we join him in his resurrection. "He who raised Christ from the dead will also give life to your mortal bodies through his Spirit, who lives in you" (Romans 8:11). His resurrection is a promise that we will also live again!

Ascension

After Jesus was resurrected, he "gave many convincing proofs that he was alive. He appeared to them over a period of forty days and spoke about the kingdom of God" (Acts 1:3). On the last day, "he was taken up before their very eyes, and a cloud hid him from their sight" (verse 9). He did not simply disappear. He went up bodily into the sky, as a visible indication that he was going into heaven. His post-resurrection appearances had come to an end. (His later appearance to Paul was abnormal—1 Corinthians 15:8.)

As the disciples stared upwards, two angels appeared and told them that Jesus would return "in the same way you have seen him go into heaven" (Acts 1:11). What were the disciples to do in the meantime? They were to wait in Jerusalem until they received the Holy Spirit (verse 4), and then they were to be witnesses for Jesus throughout the world (verse 8). They testified that he is alive, that salvation is available through him.

At the right hand

Jesus did not just go to heaven—he was "exalted to the right hand of God" (Acts 2:33). "God exalted him to his own right hand as Prince and Savior" (Acts 5:31). Being at the "right hand" is a figure of speech meaning "in highest authority." He is exalted above the heavens, ruler of all things (Hebrews 7:27; 1:2).

At least 12 times, Scripture says that Jesus is at the right hand of the Father. These are quotes from or allusions to Psalm 110:1: "The Lord says to my Lord: Sit at my right hand until I make your enemies a footstool for your feet." The picture is that the Father gives Jesus a throne, even while there are enemies to be subdued. God will take care of the enemies; Jesus is secure in his authority. Using the Latin word for "sit," this is sometimes called the "session" of Christ—being seated on his throne.

Ministry

Using his position of power in heaven, Jesus continues working for our salvation. He sends the Holy Spirit to us (John 15:26; 16:7), and the Holy Spirit testifies about Jesus and helps us understand what he taught (John 14:26; 15:26). The Spirit is the way that the Father and the Son live within us (14:18, 23).

Jesus is our Advocate (1 John 2:1). He is like a defense attorney who "speaks to the Father in our defense"—if anyone accuses us, Jesus is there as a perpetual reminder that our sins have already been covered by his sacrifice. It is pointless to make accusations (Romans 8:33-34) — there is no condemnation for those who are in Christ (verse 1).

The risen Christ intercedes for us, to defend us and to give us help. "He is able to save completely those who come to God through him, because he always lives to intercede for them" (Hebrews 7:25). "Because he himself suffered when he was tempted, he is able to help those who are being tempted" (Hebrews 2:18). Because he can sympathize with our weaknesses, we can be confident that he will give us the help we need in our struggles (Hebrews 4:15-16).

The book of Hebrews calls him our high priest, who sacrificed himself for us and now lives to help us (Hebrews 2:17; 3:1). Since our sins have been forgiven through his death, we can approach God with confidence (Hebrews 10:19). "Since we have a great priest over the house of God," we are encouraged: "let us draw near to God with a sincere heart in full assurance of faith" (verse 22).

Jesus is our mediator, who resolves conflicts and brings us to God (1 Timothy 2:5). He ushers us into the throne room of heaven, assuring us that God hears us with favor. This is part of the ongoing ministry of Jesus Christ.

Jesus is also our Shepherd (John 10:11; Hebrews 13:20), implying that he loves, protects and provides for us. Peter brings similar images to mind when he calls Jesus "the Shepherd and Overseer of your souls" (1 Peter 2:25). Jesus watches over us. The book of Revelation tells us that we are shepherded by a Lamb, a gentle guide who sacrificed himself for us (Revelation 7:17). He will supply our needs, because he knows what they are.

God assigned Jesus to be Head of the church (Ephesians 1:22; 4:15), and the church is to submit to his leadership in everything (Ephesians 5:24). He has supremacy over all things (Colossians 1:18; 2:10). Jesus already has all authority on heaven and earth (Matthew 28:18). God has seated him above every power and authority (Ephesians 1:20-22; Colossians 2:10).

Through faith, we join Jesus in his amazing journey. We are crucified with him, we rise with him, we are joined with him by the Holy Spirit. We will be given glory with him and will reign with him forever (2 Timothy 2:11-12). Believe the good news!

Resurrection appearances

Before dawn, Mary Magdalene finds the tomb open and reports the body gone (John 20:1-2). Other women arrive and are told by angels to tell the disciples (Matthew 28:5-7; Luke 24:1-9). They visit the tomb and find it empty (John 20:3-10).

1. Jesus appears to Mary Magdalene (John 20:11-18).
2. Jesus appears to two women (Matthew 28:9-10).
3. Jesus appears to two men on the road to Emmaus (Luke 24:13-33).
4. Jesus appears to Peter (verse 34).
5. Jesus appears to 10 of the disciples (verse 36; John 20:24).
6. One week later, Jesus appears when Thomas is present (John 20:26-29).
7. Seven disciples see Jesus at the Sea of Galilee (John 21:1-22).
8. The disciples meet Jesus on a mountain in Galilee (Matthew 28:16-20).
9. Jesus appears to 500 people (1 Corinthians 15:6).
10. Jesus appears to James at another time (verse 7).
11. Jesus appears to the disciples just before ascending to heaven (Acts 1:6-11).

Adapted from Murray J. Harris, *3 Crucial Questions About Jesus*, pages 107-109.

Michael Morrison

Jesus Was Not Alone

On a small hill just outside of Jerusalem, a troublemaking teacher was killed on a cross. He was not alone. He was not the only troublemaker in Jerusalem that spring day. "I have been crucified with Christ," the apostle Paul wrote (Galatians 2:20), but Paul wasn't the only one with Christ. "You died with Christ," he told other Christians (Colossians 2:20). "We were…buried with him," he wrote in Romans 6:4.

What's going on here? All those people weren't really on that hill near Jerusalem. So what is Paul saying? Just this: All Christians, whether they know it or not, have shared in the cross of Christ.

Were you there when they crucified the Lord? Yes, you were there. We were with him, even though we didn't know it at the time. Perhaps this sounds like nonsense. What does it mean? In modern language, we might say that we *were represented by* Jesus. His death was payment for our sins.

But there is more. We are also represented — and share in — his resurrection! Paul also wrote, "God raised us up with Christ" (Ephesians 2:6). We were there on resurrection morning. "God made you alive with Christ" (Colossians 2:13). "You have been raised with Christ" (Colossians 3:1).

Christ's story is our story, if we are identified with the crucified Lord. Our lives become attached to his life, not only the glory of his resurrection, but also the pain and sorrow of his crucifixion. Can you accept it? Can we be with Christ in his death? If so, then we can be with him in his glory.

Jesus did much more than die and rise. He had a life of righteousness, and we share in that life, too. His righteousness is shared with us. We are not instantly perfect — not even gradually perfect — but we are called to share in the abundant, new life of Christ. Paul ties it all together when he writes, "We were therefore buried with him through baptism into death in order that, just as Christ was raised from the dead through the glory of the Father, we too may live a new life" (Romans 6:4). Buried with him, risen with him, living with him.

A new identity

What is this new life supposed to be like?

Count yourselves dead to sin but alive to God in Christ Jesus. Therefore do not let sin reign in your mortal body.... Offer yourselves to God, as those who have been brought from death to life; and offer the parts of your body to him as instruments of righteousness. (Romans 6:11-13)

When we cast our lot in with Christ, our lives are his. "One died for all, and therefore all died. And he died for all, that those who live should no longer live for themselves but for him who died for them and was raised again" (2 Corinthians 5:14-15).

Just as Jesus was not alone, neither are we. If we identify with Christ, then we are buried with him, and we rise to new life with him, and he lives with us. In our trials and in our successes, he is with us, because our lives belong to him. He shoulders the burden, and he gets the credit, and we get the joy of sharing life with him.

Paul described it in these terms: "I have been crucified with Christ and I no longer live, but Christ lives in me. The life I live in the body, I live by faith in the Son of God, who loved me and gave himself for me" (Galatians 2:20).

Take up the cross, Jesus urged his disciples, and follow me. Identify with me. Accept that your life is united with mine. Let the old be crucified, and let the new life reign in your body. Let me live in you, and I will give you life eternal.

Joseph W. Tkach

Evidence of the Resurrection

Christians, Jews, and atheists agree that Jesus was crucified and buried. The crucial belief for Christianity is that he was also resurrected — as evidence that he is the Son of God, the teacher of truth, the door and the way of salvation, the firstfruits of the resurrection. There is good evidence for his resurrection.

First, most historians agree that the early disciples *believed* that Jesus had risen from the dead. Although at Jesus' death they were dejected and fearful, they were soon dramatically different: They risked their lives repeatedly to preach about Jesus. Even Christians in the second and third centuries (as well as many today) put their lives on the line to preach about Jesus. People sometimes give their lives for erroneous ideas — but only if they think they are true. People do not put their lives on the line for things they don't believe. The disciples never wavered in their belief in Jesus' resurrection. None of them ever changed their story under the pain of persecution. Even agnostic historians can admit that the disciples believed that Jesus had been resurrected.

Now we can consider how dozens of disciples could come to such a conviction. Perhaps the first possibility we could consider is that Jesus didn't really die. Perhaps it wasn't really him on the cross. Maybe Judas led the soldiers to the wrong man, or a substitution was somehow made at the last minute (as some Muslims believe). Is it possible that all the male and female disciples were in such a state of shock that they did not recognize the substitute on the cross? Was it then a coincidence that the tomb was empty, and the disciples thought he had reappeared? All this stretches the imagination so much that this is not seriously considered.

Reconstructing the argument

How did people respond to the claims that Jesus had been resurrected? The initial reaction for almost everyone (including the disciples themselves) was probably "That's preposterous." A more serious response is reported in Matthew 28:11-15:

> While [the disciples] were going, some of the guard went into the city and told the chief priests everything that had happened. After the priests had assembled with the elders, they devised a plan to give a large sum of money to the soldiers, telling them, "You must say, 'His disciples came by night and stole him away while we were asleep.' If this comes to the governor's ears, we will satisfy him and keep you out of trouble." So they took the money and did as they were directed. And this story is still told among the Jews to this day.

Some critics believe that this story was invented by Matthew, but the story is too complex for that. It shows several levels in the argument. It reports not just a distant memory, but a fact that could be verified when it was written: unbelieving Jews were claiming that the disciples stole Jesus' body while the guard slept. Matthew probably included this passage in his Gospel to respond to such a claim, and he probably considered it as the claim most worth refuting. The unbelieving Jews apparently agreed that Jesus' tomb was empty; they made no allegations that Jesus was buried elsewhere, or that the disciples went to the wrong tomb.

To reconstruct the argument:
1. First, the disciples say that the tomb is empty.

2. The unbelieving Jews then say, that's because the disciples stole the body.
3. The believers then say, We couldn't have, because there was a guard.
4. The unbelievers say (rather than denying the existence of a guard), the disciples stole the body while the guard was asleep.
5. Finally, Matthew explains that the guard was bribed to say that this happened while he slept.

The argument assumes that in Matthew's day, the unbelieving Jews talked of a guard at the tomb. It was the first of many attempts not just to deny the resurrection, but to explain the evidence in a different way.

Is it possible that Jesus did not die on the cross — he just went into a coma, and then later revived? Is this historically plausible? Would Roman soldiers botch a crucifixion and take down a body without noticing that the person was still alive? Would this severely injured person then be able to revive, unwrap his own grave clothes, roll away his own tombstone, and convince his disciples that he had good health? Then after 40 days he would never be seen again? No, this borders on the preposterous.

Perhaps the disciples helped Jesus revive. They rolled away the stone, unwrapped the clothes, bandaged the wounds, and told a story about getting their leader back alive out of the grave — a story that turned quickly into a tall tale about resurrection and miraculous appearances, a story that the disciples never tried to set straight. Not only is this historically implausible, it turns the disciples into frauds and deceivers — and yet, as we mentioned above, people do not give their lives for something they know is false. This does not provide a believable explanation for the rise of Christianity, rooted in the early first century in the conviction that Jesus had risen from the dead — and this faith spread first in Jerusalem, where the facts could be investigated most easily!

It is not historically likely that Jesus could have survived the crucifixion. Could the disciples have made up the resurrection? Did they steal the body, hide it somewhere, invent the story of a guard, and then preach a resurrection with conviction? This does not make sense. These fishermen did not make up the biggest lie in history, going against all the facts of life and death as they knew it, going against all religious beliefs of the day, going against Jewish and Roman authorities, risking their lives to tell the story they made up, without any of them ever betraying the conspiracy. No, these people were not sophisticated liars. Their words and deeds do not suggest any such deception. Their behavior matched their message.

We might also observe that the evidence of the empty tomb is indirect. (If it wasn't empty, the Jewish leaders could have stopped the whole problem by producing the body.) Yet according to the Gospel stories, the empty tomb did not convince the disciples. They were convinced only when Jesus appeared, and it is on the basis of the *appearances* that they preached the resurrection. If they had gone to the trouble of stealing the body, surely they would have used the empty tomb as part of their evidence. But they didn't; this tells us that they had what they thought was much better evidence: eyewitnesses of a living Jesus.

As another indirect evidence of the authenticity of their faith, we can observe that the Gospels report that women were the first eyewitnesses of the empty tomb and the risen Christ — and the testimony of women was not accepted in that culture. If the disciples were trying to make up a story, they would have invented witnesses who had more credibility. It is not likely that these fishermen would have been so subtle in creating evidence, and yet be so bold in preaching.

What about the fact that the Gospel stories vary somewhat? If this had been an enormous conspiracy, wouldn't they ensure that the story was told in exactly the same way by everyone? The most believable explanation again is that the disciples genuinely believed Jesus to be resurrected, and each one told it the way he or she remembered it.

Now let's consider another possibility: grave robbers (hoping for riches in the rich man's tomb) got the guards to drink so much wine that they fell asleep; then the robbers took the body and dumped it in the desert. The guards, wanting to cover up their failure and knowing the fears of the religious leaders, made up the story of the angels and the resurrection, and were bribed to blame the disciples. Then the disciples had hallucinations of a risen Jesus.

However, did all the disciples have the same hallucination, several times, against their expectations, against their religious beliefs? Did the hallucination eat and drink, speak, and then suddenly cease 40 days later? This is not the way hallucinations work. The evidence does not match this hypothesis, either.

Let's consider one more idea, that the idea of resurrection was just a religious allegory (sometimes described as a "myth," meaning religious ideas expressed in allegorical stories), and Christianity made a big mistake in taking it literally for almost 2,000 years. There are several problems with this idea. First, the Gospels are not written in a mythological style. The resurrection was understood in a literal way even in the first century, when eyewitnesses of Jesus were still available to either support or refute the story. There was no time for legends to develop. The biblical writers give us history: This is what I saw. This is what it meant. They denounce the idea of myth.

The disciples were not deceived, nor were they deceivers. They just tell us what they saw, and it is clear that they believed that Jesus died and was buried and was resurrected. They believed this because they saw it with their own eyes.

> That which was from the beginning, which we have heard, which we have seen with our eyes, which we have looked at and our hands have touched — this we proclaim concerning the Word of life. The life appeared; we have seen it and testify to it, and we proclaim to you the eternal life, which was with the Father and has appeared to us. We proclaim to you what we have seen and heard, so that you also may have fellowship with us. And our fellowship is with the Father and with his Son, Jesus Christ. (1 John 1:1-3)

The disciples believed that Jesus rose from the dead. The most plausible explanation is that Jesus actually rose from the dead. All other theories are far-fetched and historically unlikely.

When we also take into consideration the need for God to intervene in humanity to save us, and the Old Testament predictions of a suffering servant who would give his life for his people, the explanation that makes the most sense is that the disciples believed that Jesus was resurrected because Jesus appeared to them and told them he was resurrected. That is why they had such a transformation in their beliefs, and why they preached with such conviction. As Luke puts it, by looking at the evidence we "may know the certainty of the things we have been taught" (Luke 1:4).

Michael Morrison

For further reading:

William Lane Craig, *Assessing the New Testament Evidence for the Historicity of the Resurrection of Jesus* (Lewiston, NY: Edwin Mellen, 1989).

N.T. Wright, *The Resurrection of the Son of God. Christian Origins and the Question of God*, volume 3. (Minneapolis, MN: Fortress, 2003).

The Power of the Resurrection

Christians accept the resurrection accounts on faith, but it is a faith sealed by the inward testimony of the Holy Spirit. Faith is not blind, unintelligent trust. Theology has been defined as "faith seeking understanding." Christians worship God with their minds as well as their hearts.

The four Gospels record an event hard to explain away in face of the most obvious evidence – the existence of the Christian church. Something unprecedented happened in Jerusalem in the first century. This forces the question: What kind of history do we encounter in Scripture?

Arthur Glasser calls the Bible "interpreted history." He said, "Its great truths [come] enfleshed in historical events, human experience, and prophetic exposition" *(Kingdom and Mission,* pages 18, 16). Hugh Anderson sheds more light:

> We expect the historian today to be as scientifically accurate as possible in his reporting of facts.... By contrast the historians of Israel viewed history as the sphere of God's activity. Their purpose in telling the story of Israel was to confront men with the sovereign authority of a high and holy God, calling upon them to surrender their lives to Him. (*Historians of Israel,* Vol. 2, pages 26, 28)

The Gospel writers were in that tradition: They were concerned with spiritual meaning and eternal life. Their writings give us history plus interpretation. Matthew, Mark, Luke and John were preachers before they were historians. Nevertheless, the resurrection accounts provide a compelling example of faith meeting understanding. They make sense once the Holy Spirit enables us to believe.

1. First, there is the almost embarrassing honesty of the resurrection accounts. The doubts of Thomas, Peter and the other apostles are freely admitted (Mark 16:9-14). The New Testament is hard on its heroes. Who in the early church could have written such things about prominent church leaders still alive unless those things were true? The transformed lives of the apostles are exactly what we would expect if Christ was resurrected (Acts 4:13).

2. Who among the disciples could invent such a story as that of Jesus of Nazareth? The disciples were often chided for their slowness to believe and their lack of spiritual imagination (Matthew 16:5-12). Could they invent such challenging phrases as: "I am the way and the truth and the life. No one comes to the Father except through me" (John 14:6)?

British Bible scholar C.H. Dodd recorded that as a young man he fretted about the time interval between the events mentioned in the Gospels and when those events were written several decades later. He later changed his mind:

> When Mark was writing...there must have been many people [alive] who were in their prime under Pontius Pilate, and they must have remembered the stirring and tragic events of that time.... If anyone had tried to put over an entirely imaginary or fictitious account of them, there would have been middle-aged or elderly people who would have said... "You are wasting your breath: I remember it as if it were yesterday" (*Tradition: Old and New,* page 41)

Those are wise words. The complexity of the Gospels is part of their fascination.

3. It is hard to account for the Christian faith's sweep across the Roman Empire without a spectacular primary cause. The resurrection was that catalyst.

> One of the compelling proofs of the resurrection is that the crucifixion left the disciples in despair and that, hopeless, they were transformed by their experience of the risen Jesus.... Even more important was the conviction nourished in Christians that by the resurrection Jesus had been vindicated and had been shown to be the Son of God with power. (Kenneth Latourette, *A History of Christianity,* volume 1, pages 58-59)

That power proved invincible. It still is.

Why Jesus Gives Us Hope

The Old Testament is a story of frustrated hope. It begins by telling us that humans were created in the image of God. But it was not long before we humans sinned, and we were kicked out of paradise. But along with the word of judgment also came a word of promise—God said that one of Eve's descendants would crush the enemy (Genesis 3:15). A deliverer would come to rescue the people.

Eve probably hoped that her first child would be the solution. But it was Cain, and he was part of the problem. Sin continued, and it got worse. There was a partial salvation in the time of Noah, but sin continued. There was the sin of Noah's grandson, and then of Babel. Humanity continued having problems, having the hope of something better but never able to achieve it.

Some important promises were given to Abraham. But he died before he received all the promises. He had a child, but no land, and he was not yet a blessing to all the nations. But the promise continued. It was given again to Isaac, and then Jacob. Jacob and his family went into Egypt and became a great nation, but they were enslaved. Even so, God remained true to his promise. With spectacular miracles, God brought them out of Egypt.

But the nation of Israel fell far short of the promise. Miracles didn't help. The law didn't help. They kept on sinning, kept on failing, kept on doubting, kept on wandering for 40 years. But God was true to his promise, and he brought them into the land of Canaan, and with many miracles, he gave them the land.

But that did not fix their problems. They were still the same sinful people, and the book of Judges records some of the grossest of sins. How could this messed-up nation ever become a blessing to other nations? They kept on sinning—falling into idolatry again and again. God finally let the northern tribes of Israel be taken into captivity by Assyria. You'd think that would have made the Jews repent, but it didn't. The people failed time and again, and God let the Jews be taken into captivity, too.

Where was the promise now? The people were right back where Abraham had started from, in Mesopotamia. Where was the promise? The promise was in God, who cannot lie. He would fulfill his promise no matter how badly the people failed.

God let the Jews stay in Babylon for many years, and after that, a small percentage of them returned to Jerusalem, and the Jewish nation became a shadow of its former self. They got a taste of freedom, then a taste of being ruled by Rome. They weren't any better off in the Promised Land than they had been in Egypt or Babylon. They groaned: Where is the promise that God gave Abraham? How are we going to be a light to the nations? How are the promises to David going to be fulfilled if we can't even rule ourselves?

Under Roman rule, the people's hopes were frustrated. Some gave up hope. Some joined underground resistance movements. Others tried to be more religious, more worthy of God's blessing. Everyone longed for God to do something.

A glimmer of hope

God started in the smallest possible way—as an embryo in a virgin. Behold, I will give you a sign, he had said through Isaiah. A virgin will conceive and bring forth a child, and you will name him Immanuel, which means "God with us." But he was first called Jesus — the Hebrew name *Yeshua*, which means, God will save us.

God began fulfilling his promise with a child conceived out of wedlock. There was some social stigma attached to that — even 30 years later the Jewish leaders made snide comments about Jesus' parentage (John 8:41). Who would believe Mary's story about angels and supernatural conception?

God began fulfilling the hopes of his people in a way that they did not recognize. No one would have guessed that the "illegitimate" baby was the answer to the nation's hopes. A baby can't do anything, can't teach anyone, can't help anyone, and can't save anyone. But a baby has *potential*.

Angels told shepherds that a Savior had been born in Bethlehem (Luke 2:11). He was a Savior, but he wasn't saving anyone right then. He even needed to be saved himself. The family had to flee to save the baby from Herod, the king of the Jews.

But God called that helpless baby a Savior. He knew what that baby would do. In that baby were all the hopes of Israel. Here was the light to the Gentiles; here was the blessing for all nations; here was the son of David who would rule the world; here was the child of Eve who would crush the enemy of all humanity. But he was just a baby, born in a stable, his life in danger. But in his birth, everything changed.

When Jesus was born, there was no sudden burst of Gentiles coming to Jerusalem to be taught. There was no sign of political or economic strength — no sign except that a virgin had conceived and had given birth — a sign that no one in Judah would believe.

But God had come to us, because he is faithful to his promises, and he is the basis of all our hopes. The history of Israel shows again and again that human methods do not work. We cannot achieve God's purposes by our own efforts. God does not do things the way we think, but in the way he knows will work. Our way always gets messed up. We think in terms of laws and land and kings and kingdoms of this world. God thinks in terms of tiny beginnings, of spiritual rather than physical strength, of victory in weakness rather than power.

When God gave us Jesus, he fulfilled his promises and brought about everything he had said. But we didn't see the fulfillment right away — all we saw was a baby. Most people didn't believe it, and even those who believed could only hope.

Fulfillment

We know now that Jesus grew up to give his life as a ransom for our sins, to bring us forgiveness, to be a light to the Gentiles, to defeat the devil, and to defeat death itself in his death and resurrection. We can see how Jesus is the fulfillment of God's promises.

We can see much more than the Jews could 2,000 years ago, but we still do not see everything there is. We do not yet see every promise fulfilled. We do not yet see Satan chained where he cannot deceive anyone. We do not yet see everyone knowing God. We do not yet see the end of crying and tears and death and dying. We still eagerly desire the final answer — but in Jesus, we have hope and assurance.

We have a promise, a promise guaranteed by God, ratified by his Son, sealed by the Holy Spirit. We believe that everything else will come true, that Christ will complete the work he has begun. Our hope is beginning to bear fruit, and we can be confident that all the promises will be fulfilled — not necessarily in the way we might expect, but in the way that God has planned.

He will do it, as promised, through his Son, Jesus Christ. We may not see it now, but God has already acted, and God is working even now behind the scenes to bring about his will. Just as in the baby Jesus we had hope and a promise of salvation, so in the risen Jesus we now have hope and promise of completion. That is true of the growth of the kingdom of God, it is true in the work of the church, and it is true in each of our lives.

Hope for ourselves

As people come to faith in Christ, his work begins to grow in them. Jesus said that we must each be born again, and when we come to believe in him, the Holy Spirit overshadows us and begets in us a new life. Just as Jesus promises, he comes to live within us. Someone once said, "Jesus could be born 1,000 times, and it would do me no good, unless he is born in me." The hope that Jesus gives to the world does us no good unless we accept him as *our* hope. We need to let Jesus live in us.

However, we do not yet have the fulfillment of all the promises that God has made. We do not yet have all the life and goodness that he offers. What we have is hope, and a down payment, and a promise of better things to come. What we have now is just a baby in comparison to the glory that God will give us later.

We might look at ourselves and think, "I don't see much here. I'm not much better than I was 20 years ago. I still struggle with sin, doubt and guilt. I am still selfish and stubborn. I am not much better at being a godly person than ancient Israel was. I wonder if God is really doing anything in my life. It doesn't seem like I've made any progress."

The answer is to remember Jesus. Our spiritual beginning may not seem good for much right now, but it is, because God says it is. What we have in us is only a down payment. It is a beginning, and it is a guarantee from God himself. The Holy Spirit in us is a down payment of glory yet to come.

Luke tells us that the angels sang when Jesus was born. It was a moment of triumph, even though humans couldn't see it that way. The angels knew that victory was certain, because God had told them so.

Jesus tells us that the angels rejoice whenever a sinner repents. They are singing for every person who comes to faith in Christ, because a baby has been born. That baby might not perform very well. It might have many struggles, but it is a child of God, and God will see to it that his work is done. He will take care of us. Though our spiritual lives are not perfect, God will keep working in us until his work is done.

Just as there is tremendous hope in the baby Jesus, there is tremendous hope in the baby Christian. No matter how long you have been a Christian, there is tremendous hope for you, because God has invested in you, and he will not abandon the work he has begun. Jesus is evidence that God always keeps his promises.

Five facts about hope

- God made great promises to Abraham, but they were not fulfilled in Old Testament times.
- Because of persistent sin, God let the Jews be taken into captivity.
- God's answer to humanity's problem began in the least expected and least visible way.
- We still do not see the complete answer to all of earth's problems, but we have hope in God's promise.
- Believers do not experience all the promises in this life, but have hope and confidence in Jesus.

Things to think about

- Why did Israel fail to be a light to the other nations?
- Why didn't the Jewish people recognize Jesus as the Messiah?
- What hopes do people have for the world today?
- The lesson of ancient Israel is that human methods do not work. Why do we get so discouraged when our efforts do not work?
- Why do we find it hard to believe that God will finish the work he began in *us*?

Joseph Tkach

Did You Kill Jesus Christ?

Some preachers say that humanity in general and each of us personally is responsible for the death of Jesus Christ. Many sincere Christians have believed this. As a result, many labor under a huge burden of guilt. Particularly in the spring of each year, near the anniversary of his death, the burden is remembered anew.

But are we responsible for the death of Jesus? If we aren't, then who is?

Only one set of shoulders is broad enough and strong enough to bear that burden of responsibility. Those shoulders are not human, but divine. We are responsible for our own deaths: by our sins we have brought death upon ourselves. Our own deaths (Ezekiel 18:4, 20) are the wages we have earned by our sins (Romans 6:23). "You shall surely die!" is what God said (Genesis 2:17).

But Jesus has chosen to die in our place, to make us free from the penalty of our own sins. "I lay down my life for the sheep," he said (John 10:15). He was under no external compulsion to die for us. "I lay down my life…. No one takes it from me, but I lay it down of my own accord" (John 10:17-18). We did not force him to die for us. We did not even ask him to die for us. We were bound up in sin, and we did not know enough to ask for it.

The sacrifice was made at God's initiative. Nothing outside of Jesus compelled him. Only his own nature, his own love, compelled him. The self-sacrifice of Jesus on the cross was the expression within time of the self-giving love that is the nature of God in eternity. Jesus "loved us and gave himself up for us" (Ephesians 5:2)—he gave his life as a sign of his love. His act was designed to create in us a response of love and gratitude and wonder. It was not intended to make us feel guilty every time we think about it.

Consider this: If I were guilty for causing the death of Jesus, what could erase that guilt? To claim the blood of Christ to cover it would incur the same guilt again! I would be forced to the conclusion that the only way to be free of the guilt of Christ's sacrifice would be to die for my own sins, rather than bear the burden of responsibility and guilt that comes along with having him die for them.

Here is a paradox: When we receive his sacrifice as a gift, we are free from responsibility for his death. Our merciful God did not intend that we, his children, carry a burden of guilt through our lives today, or through life everlasting, based on our mistaken notion that by accepting his gift we bear the responsibility for Jesus' death. God intended that we be freed from and remain free from such a sense of condemnation and guilt (Romans 8:5).

Praise God, and thank him that he took the responsibility of giving his Son for us! Praise Jesus, and thank him that he willingly laid down his life for us, and rejoice that he invites us to take advantage of his gift of love without guilt, without reluctance and without condemnation.

Don Mears

Two Truths We Learn From Jesus' Death

Jesus Christ died for us, forgiving all our debts, rescuing us from the slavery of sin, redeeming us from its deadly consequences. He has also been raised for us and lives in us, empowering us to live in him. I am so thankful for what he has done for us! The holy, perfect Son of God gave himself for us to rescue us from our sins. Salvation is truly the best news possible! Let me mention two fundamental truths we can learn from Jesus' crucifixion.

1. First, God hates sin. Sin hurts the people he loves. The cross shows us how ugly sin is. Sin caused the death of God's own Son, and that is another reason he hates sin so much. Sin is the vilest, ugliest thing in the universe — and you and I have done it. We deserve the death that Jesus accepted.

2. Second, the cross shows us how much God loves us. The fact that Jesus, the Son of God, was willing to suffer and die for you and me shows that he loves us with a passion that exceeds and overcomes his hatred of sin. Jesus was willing to pay the price. He was willing to suffer torture and death so that he might conquer sin and reverse its grip on us.

God wants to give you and me and all his children the best gift we could possibly imagine: life with God — life eternal with Father, Son and Spirit — and he wants us to enjoy this forever and ever! No greater blessing could ever exist, and God gives it to us. He so earnestly desires to give us this eternal life that he sent his Son to die so that we might live with him. Oh, what a joy it is!

Can you grasp the enormity of God's love for you? I hope you join with me in praising the God of our salvation — praising in heartfelt joy, in song, in words, and in deeds.

"Christ's love compels us," Paul wrote, "because we are convinced that one died for all, and therefore all died. And he died for all, that those who live should no longer live for themselves but for him who died for them and was raised again" (2 Corinthians 5:14-15). What a powerful message is contained in those two verses!

1. First, we died with Jesus Christ. Christ our Passover lamb has been crucified for us — and our old self was crucified with him (1 Corinthians 5:7; Romans 6:6). Because he died for us, we died with him.

2. How then should we live? What should our response be to this priceless gift? The new self should live — a new creation of Jesus Christ — a new child of God. In him, we put to death the works of the flesh and are clothed in the righteousness of Jesus Christ. By his power, we no longer serve sin, no longer serve ourselves, but now serve our Lord and Savior.

Christ's love compels us, Paul said. Have you understood and experienced that kind of love in your life, the kind of love that compels you to serve the One who died for you? I hope so, because it is the most rewarding life that anyone could ever have.

That's why I rejoice in the opportunity to express faith in my Savior by eating the bread that represents his body, by drinking "the fruit of the vine" that represents the new covenant in his blood (Luke 22:19-20). I rejoice in the opportunity to celebrate not only his death for us, but also that he was resurrected and now lives in us, leading and strengthening us in a life of righteousness through the Holy Spirit.

Paul says our lives are hidden in Christ and that we live for him (Colossians 3:3; 2 Corinthians 5:15).

Can anything be more meaningful, more valuable? I pray that we might renew our commitment to love our Lord with our whole heart and follow him wherever he leads us. I pray that he will bless you with his love, peace and healing touch.

Joseph Tkach

Commemorating the Crucifixion

Almost 2,000 years ago, a Jewish carpenter was condemned as a dangerous religious and political rebel. He was executed in one of the most painful and shameful punishments ever known: flogging and crucifixion. This form of death was a scandal to both Jews and Gentiles.

Nevertheless, Jesus' followers made a point of remembering his death—not just the fact that he died, but also that he died in such a shameful way. In their written stories about Jesus, they devoted lengthy sections to his horrible death. They set aside one day each year as the anniversary of his death.

Why is Jesus' death so important to Christians—and so central to the Christian faith?

Of greatest importance

Jesus' death is listed as of "first importance" in Paul's summary of the gospel message: "What I received I passed on to you as of first importance: that Christ died for our sins according to the Scriptures, that he was buried, that he was raised on the third day according to the Scriptures, and that he appeared…" (1 Corinthians 15:3-5). Paul even characterized his own preaching as "the message of the cross" (1 Corinthians 1:18). "We preach Christ crucified," he said (verse 23).

Jesus' death was predicted in Scripture, and was necessary (Luke 24:25-26; Acts 3:18; 17:3). It was necessary not just for the Messiah to *die*, but to *suffer*, and to be crucified for our salvation. It was an essential part of Jesus' ministry, and an essential part of the gospel. Jesus had predicted his own suffering and death, even his death on a cross (Mark 8:31-32; 9:31; 10:33-34; Matthew 20:19; 26:2; John 12:32-33). He was sure it had to happen the way it did (Matthew 26:54)—it was his purpose, his mission (John 12:27). He had to fulfill the prophecy of Isaiah 53 (Luke 22:37).

Jesus said that his death would be a ransom to save other people (Mark 10:45). At his Last Supper, he said that he gave his body on behalf of other people, and he gave his blood to form a new covenant, the basis of a new relationship between God and humanity, based on forgiveness (Luke 22:19-20; Matthew 26:28). He was, as Isaiah 53 had predicted, an innocent person who suffered and died to ransom the guilty. God laid our sins on Jesus, and he was killed for *our* transgressions to buy *our* freedom.

Jesus not only predicted his death, he also explained its significance for us—and this is why it is good news. He gave his body for us—for our benefit. He allowed his blood to be shed so we would be forgiven. Jesus was the mediator between God and humans. His death enables us to have a covenant with God—a relationship of promise and loyalty. The death of Christ is the *only* way for our salvation. That is why Jesus, even though he knew what pain awaited him, "resolutely set out for Jerusalem" (Luke 9:51). It was the reason he had come.

Publicizing a scandal

The resurrection of Jesus was wonderful news. It was a hope-filled message. Because of that, it would have been easy for the apostles to emphasize Jesus' resurrection and skip over his shameful death. Indeed, we read in Acts that they preached the resurrection—but they also boldly reminded people of the shameful punishment Jesus had received (Acts 2:22-24; 3:13-15; 4:10; 5:30-

31; 7:51-53; 10:37-40; 13:27-30).

Not only did they admit the cross, they also called it a *tree*—a word that would remind Jews of Deuteronomy 21:22-23, which says that anyone who is hung on a tree is under God's curse. By using the word *tree,* the apostles drew extra attention to the shameful way Jesus had died. Why did they emphasize this? Because it was important. The Scriptures had predicted it, Jesus had predicted it, and it was necessary for our salvation.

The cross involves shame as well as pain (Hebrews 12:2). It involves a "curse" (Galatians 3:13-14). Paul did his best not to offend people, but he emphasized the crucifixion even though he knew it was offensive (Galatians 5:11; 3:1; 6:14). The cross was the center of his gospel (1 Corinthians 1:23; 2:2; Philippians 3:18).

Paul gives the spiritual significance of the cross: Jesus redeemed us from the curse of the law by becoming a curse for us. He was made sin for us (2 Corinthians 5:21). He was a sacrifice so that we might be justified, or declared right, so that we might escape the punishment our sins deserve (Romans 3:24-26). He carried our sins on his cross (1 Peter 2:24). "Christ died for sins once for all, the righteous for the unrighteous, to bring you to God" (1 Peter 3:18).

Through the cross, we can be given the blessing promised to Abraham (Galatians 3:14). Through the cross, we are reconciled to God (Ephesians 2:16). Through the cross, God forgives our sins, taking away the written note of debt that was against us (Colossians 2:13-14). Our salvation depends on the cross of Christ.

Since we fail to keep the law perfectly, we fall under its curse (Galatians 3:10). We all deserve death (Romans 3:23; 6:23). Jesus, being sinless, did not need to die, but he willingly died for us. The righteous died for the unrighteous. He received death so that we might receive life.

John Stott writes that the crucifixion shows three truths:

> First, our sin must be extremely horrible. Nothing reveals the gravity of sin like the cross…. If there was no way by which the righteous God could righteously forgive our unrighteousness, except that he should bear it himself in Christ, it must be serious indeed….
>
> Secondly, God's love must be wonderful beyond comprehension…. He pursued us even to the desolate anguish of the cross, where he bore our sin, guilt, judgment and death. It takes a hard and stony heart to remain unmoved by love like that…. Thirdly, Christ's salvation must be a free gift. He "purchased" it for us at the high price of his own life-blood. So what is there left for us to pay? Nothing! (*The Cross of Christ,* page 83)

A memorial of death

The cross was the focus of Jesus' mission as a human. His job was not done until he was crucified. Jesus did not tell his disciples to remember his miracles—they were to remember his *death.* Jesus eliminated many rituals, but he commanded a new one: the bread and wine of the Lord's Supper. He told us to participate in these reminders of his death because his death, and our participation in his death, is vital for our salvation.

We remember Jesus' death not just as something that happened to Jesus—it is relevant for us today. The Lord's Supper looks to the past—Jesus willing gave his life for us—and to the present—his union with us now, and the future—his promise to return. Spiritually, are we crucified with Christ (Galatians 2:20), and on a daily basis, we are to crucify our sinful passions and desires (Galatians 5:24; Romans 8:13). To follow Jesus, we must take up our cross each day (Luke 9:23), willing to deny wrong desires. The Lord's Supper reminds us of what our life is about.

Jesus' death is our pattern for daily living—it is a picture of complete submission to God, a picture of willingness to reject sin and choose righteousness. Jesus died for us, Paul says, so that we should no longer live for ourselves, but instead live to serve Jesus (2 Corinthians 5:15). Since our old self was crucified with Christ, "we should no longer be slaves to sin" (Romans 6:6). Instead, we offer ourselves to God as living sacrifices, willing to serve him (Romans 6:13; 12:1). Because he died for us, we "die to sins and live for righteousness" (1 Peter 2:24).

Jesus' death is evidence that God loves us — it shows us that God cares about us so much that he did something to solve our problem, to rescue us from the pain and death our sinfulness brought upon us (Romans 5:8-10). Since God did not spare his own Son, we can be confident that he will give us everything we need for salvation (Romans 8:32). His love for us becomes an example for how much we should love one another (Ephesians 5:1-2).

The death of Jesus gives us some important freedoms:

- We are no longer prisoners of the law (Galatians 3:23; Romans 7:6).
- We are no longer slaves of sin and passions (John 8:34-36; Romans 6:6-7, 16; Titus 3:3).
- We are no longer enslaved by death or fear (Romans 8:2; Hebrews 2:14-15).
- We have overcome the world and the evil one (1 John 5:4-5; 1 John 2:13-14; Revelation 12:11).

With this freedom, we are to be slaves of righteousness, slaves of Jesus Christ (Romans 6:18). He died for us so we may live for him (2 Corinthians 5:14-15). This is how we should respond to the love of God shown to us in the cross of Christ.

The cross is also an example for us when we suffer. Peter reminds us that when we suffer unjustly, we should remember the example of Jesus, who suffered unjustly for us, setting an example for us (1 Peter 2:19-23). In Hebrews we are told to remember Jesus when we grow weary of our troubles, for he endured great opposition for us (Hebrews 12:2-4). Unjust suffering is part of the Christian calling, and part of the example Jesus set for us. "A servant is not greater than his master" (John 15:20). The Lord's Supper reminds us of what Jesus' life was about, and that we are called to follow him.

When we suffer, we are also encouraged by knowing that a crown of glory awaits us, just as it did for Jesus. When we identify with him in his cross, we will also share in his glory (Romans 8:17-18; 2 Corinthians 4:17).

Many people think that the cross is foolishness, but it shows us the wisdom of God (1 Corinthians 1:17-25). It was a stroke of genius, a brilliant maneuver. It simultaneously shows us how ugly sin is, and how beautiful God's love is, and the extent of his commitment to ensure our salvation. It punishes sin and brings forgiveness. It shows both justice and grace. It breaks the power of sin and death, and gives us power to overcome. The cross gives us visible evidence that our sins have been dealt with once and for all, that our struggles are not in vain, and that a crown of glory awaits us through our Lord and Savior Jesus Christ. It is certainly worth remembering.

Joseph Tkach

Can You Hear the Holy Spirit?

When the church in Antioch gathered for worship, the Holy Spirit spoke to them: "Set apart for me Barnabas and Saul for the work to which I have called them." Does the Holy Spirit speak to us today? Can we hear what he says to us?

People who are led by the Holy Spirit are children of God (Romans 8:14). We should expect the Holy Spirit to lead us, and we want to know how he does it.

In different ways

God works in different ways with different people. He spoke in different ways to Adam, Abraham, Moses, Deborah, Samuel, Elijah, Mary and Paul. He can speak in different ways to us today. The messages given to Philip (Acts 8:29) and Peter are so specific (Acts 10:19) that distinct words may have been involved. But he spoke in a different way at the Jerusalem council (Acts 15). It is only after all the discussion had taken place that the apostles concluded that the Holy Spirit had made the decision for them (verse 28).

Just as the Holy Spirit decides to give different abilities to different people (1 Corinthians 12:11), he works with us in different ways. A person with the gift of miraculous words is likely to hear the Spirit in a different way than a person with the gift of compassion. The Spirit will lead a teacher in a different way than a server, because he has different jobs for different people.

The Spirit shapes us in different ways, and as a result, we value different goals. Someone with the gift of administration will value order and organization; someone with the gift of serving will ask whether people are being helped; someone with the gift of encouragement will focus on peoples' attitudes; people with the gift of generosity will look for needs that they can fill. The Spirit works with us in the way he has caused us to be, according to our interests and values.

For some people, he speaks subtly, in general principles; for others, he must speak with unmistakable details. Each of us must listen in the way that God has made us, in the way that he chooses to deal with us. The important thing is that we listen—that we are ready and willing to hear, and heed, what he says. We should be looking for his leadership rather than ignoring it.

Dangers

There are several dangers in this. First, some people have claimed to hear the Holy Spirit when he didn't really speak to them. They made false prophecies, gave foolish advice, led people into cults and made Christianity look bad. If God spoke to them, they badly misunderstood what he was saying. There is a danger of "hearing" things that God never said. We should be careful, for we do not want to use his name in vain.

A second danger is that some people, afraid of hearing incorrectly, refuse to hear anything at all. But as Dallas Willard has pointed out, we should not "shun the genuine simply because it resembled the counterfeit" (*Hearing God,* page 88). Our Father in heaven does speak to us, and the Holy Spirit leads us, and we will shortchange ourselves if we close our ears.

Hebrews 3:7 says that the Spirit speaks in the words of Scripture, and we should not refuse to follow what he says. He communicates to us today, convicting us of what we should do, guiding us in how we serve God.

A third danger is that some people seek the Holy Spirit for selfish reasons. They want the Spirit to make their decisions for them, to tell them what job to take, which person to marry, when to move and how to live. They want the Holy Spirit to be like an astrologer or horoscope, to save them the trouble of thinking and making decisions.

But God wants us to grow in maturity, to learn through experience what is right and wrong (Hebrews 5:12-14). Many of the decisions we face are not matters of sin and righteousness—they are simply choices. God can work with us no matter which we choose, so he leaves the choice up to us—the Holy Spirit doesn't speak on everything we want him to.

Some people would like to have the Holy Spirit as a conversational companion to keep them company. They want to chat, but the Holy Spirit isn't involved in idle words. He does not call attention to himself (John 15:26), and is often silent because he has already given us enough information and guidance. He wants us to use what he has already given; he has been training our conscience to respond rightly to what faces us. That does not mean that we rely on ourselves, but that we rely on what God has already done in our lives and what he has already taught us.

Scripture

The Holy Spirit speaks to us primarily through the Scriptures that he inspired to be written and canonized. This is our foundation of faith and life. It is the word that everyone has access to, the word that can be studied and discussed most objectively. Often the word that we need to hear has already been written, and the Spirit simply needs to bring it to mind. When Jesus was tempted by the devil, his responses were quoted from Scripture. He had studied and memorized those words, and in each situation the Spirit led him to the appropriate verse.

The Spirit does not bypass our need to think, or our need to read and meditate on his words. If we are not seeking the words he has already given in Scripture, then we should not expect him to suddenly give us new words for new situations. Nor can we expect the random-access method of Scripture skimming to provide good answers for difficult questions. We cannot force, coerce or push the Spirit to speak when he does not choose to speak.

With Scripture, we have the potential for nearly constant communication with God, as we read and pray and live consciously in God's presence. As we pray, we should also listen, for God may use our meditations about Scripture to help us understand what we should do. We have the responsibility to read and study, for the Spirit usually works with words that are already in our minds. He works with our vocabulary, with our ways of reasoning, with the desires and values he has given us.

The devil can use Scripture, too, and the Bible is often misunderstood and misused. But the Bible is still an important means of being led by and hearing the Holy Spirit. Scripture is the standard of comparison for all other words from God. If we think that the Spirit is leading us to do something, our first question needs to be, "Is this in agreement with Scripture?" The Spirit does not contradict himself. He does not tell us to lie, steal, gossip or be greedy, for he has already told us that those things are not godly.

If we think the Spirit is leading us in one direction, we need to check it with Scripture—and the only way we can do that is to know what Scripture says. We need to study it, and since we will never know it all, we need to keep studying it. Memorization can be helpful, but what we need most of all is understanding. We need to see the principles of salvation, of Christian living, of divine love, of the way that God has worked and is working with his people; these will help us understand how he is working with us.

Experience

We can also hear the Holy Spirit through experience. God sometimes changes his methods with us, but most often he works with us in a similar way from one year to another. Through experience, we see how he has answered our prayers and led us in past situations. This will help us recognize his "voice" when he speaks to us in the present. Experience comes through time, submission and meditation. The Spirit helps the humble, not the self-exalting.

We can gain even more wisdom by drawing on the experience of other Christians. The Spirit does not isolate us, but puts us into a church, into a community of other believers. He distributes his gifts so that we stay together, work together and benefit from one another's strengths (1 Corinthians 12:7). In the same way, we can help one another hear the Holy Spirit because we each have different experiences of how God works in our lives.

When a message from God comes to one person, other people are to consider it carefully (1 Corinthians 14:29). They are to consider, for one thing, whether it is really a word from the Lord. The Spirit can speak through the community as well as through certain individuals — the Jerusalem conference is a good example of that. The people learned from their experiences with the Gentiles, saw that those experiences agreed with the Scriptures (Acts 15:15), and through the discussion heard the decision of the Spirit (verse 28).

The Holy Spirit often speaks to people through other people: in worship songs, in small group discussions, in a whispered word of encouragement, in a smile, a picture or a magazine article. There are many ways we can learn from others, to receive godly guidance from others. But this is for each person to discern. Rarely does the Spirit tell one person to give orders to another.

Sermons are a common means of spiritual speech. Those who speak should strive to speak the words of God (1 Peter 4:11), so those who speak in church should strive to listen to God as they prepare the sermons, and those who hear the sermons should likewise listen for the words of the Lord. We need to let our worship services be times of listening, of thinking, of communing with God so that we are letting him change us to be more like Christ. Let us draw near to him, and he will change us.

Circumstances are another experiential means of "testing the spirits." We may have an open door, or all the doors may be closed. Obstacles may test our convictions, or they may be indications that we need to think about whether we have correctly understood the directions. They force us to think again, to seek God again, to check with Scripture, and to check with others who have spiritual maturity.

Responding to the Holy Spirit

If we want to hear, we need to listen. But if we want to hear in the biblical sense, we also need to respond. If we hear his voice, if we believe that God is telling us to do something, then we need to obey. We need to do what he has gifted us to do. We are to submit to God, for everything he says is for our own good. We bring him honor, and we bring ourselves blessings, by doing his will. It begins with listening. Can you hear the Holy Spirit?

Joseph Tkach

Do You Have the Holy Spirit?

Christians sometimes wonder whether they have been given God's Holy Spirit. What are some guidelines we can use in trying to understand our own spiritual state? Since the Holy Spirit is spirit, we cannot feel, touch or sense the Spirit in the way that we might discern a physical object. We can't talk about having the Spirit in those terms.

Our emotions and feelings are part of our spiritual life. But we can sometimes "feel" as though we are charged with the Holy Spirit and at other times "feel" as though we aren't. Both feelings can't be right, because the Holy Spirit does not enter and leave us on a repeated basis. When we are born of God's Spirit, we are a new creation and always have the Spirit within to guide us.

How can we know we have the Holy Spirit? Let's answer a few questions.

- Do we believe in Jesus Christ as our Savior and Lord (Romans 10:9)?
- Are we moved in prayer in ways that sometimes surprise us (Romans 8:26-27)?
- Do we have a desire to obey God in love and bear the fruit of the Spirit (Galatians 5:6-18, 22-25)?
- Do we love others and show them acts of kindness as we have opportunity (James 1:27)?
- Conversely, do we see the need to avoid things that are contrary to God's way (James 1:27; 1 John 2:15-17)?

If we can answer "yes" to these questions, we can have assurance that God's Spirit is leading us. Gradually, as we live in Christ, we will find clear marks of his presence in our thoughts, action and life.

One individual explained the signs of the presence of the Holy Spirit in the following ways, with references to the first letter of John. Spirit-filled Christians have a new:

- desire to please God (2:5).
- assurance of pardon (2:1-2).
- willingness to face opposition (3:13).
- delight in the company of fellow Christians (3:14).
- generosity of spirit (3:17).
- experience of victory over temptations (4:4; 5:4).
- discovery of answers to prayer (3:22).
- understanding of life and set of priorities (5:20-21).

If we see that these factors have been at work in our lives, we should be confident that the Holy Spirit is working in us. We should not deny this evidence of God's work in our lives, as though we are not worthy of it. It is not pride to know we have been born again of God. We should be humbly thankful for God's mercy in bestowing his grace upon us.

Even with God's Holy Spirit we will sin (1 John 1:8-2:5). We will never be perfect in this life. This may cause us to *feel* as though God is not with us. But the things mentioned above will be working in our lives because we do have the Spirit. When we sin, we go to God in prayer acknowledging our sinfulness and our need for his mercy (Luke 18:9-14). *That in itself is a demonstration that we have the Holy Spirit.*

We can always have confidence in the fact that once God begins to work with us and gives us his Holy Spirit, he will never leave us. Despite the ups and downs of life, despite the problems we may have, we can be assured of God's faithfulness. In the words of the apostle Paul: "Being confident of this, that he who began a good work *in you* will carry it on to completion until the day of Christ Jesus" (Philippians 1:6).

Paul Kroll

The Deity of the Holy Spirit

Christianity has traditionally taught that the Holy Spirit is the third Person or Hypostasis of the Godhead. Some, however, have taught that the Holy Spirit is an impersonal force used by God. Is the Holy Spirit God, or simply a power of God? Let's examine the biblical teachings.

I. The deity of the Holy Spirit

Summary: Scripture speaks repeatedly of the Holy Spirit, known also as the Spirit of God and the Spirit of Jesus Christ. Scripture indicates that the Holy Spirit is of the same essence as the Father and the Son. The Holy Spirit is ascribed with the attributes of God, is equated with God and does work that only God does.

A. Attributes of God

1. Holiness: In more than 90 places, the Bible calls the Spirit of God "the Holy Spirit." Holiness is a basic characteristic of the Spirit. The Spirit is so holy that blasphemy against the Spirit cannot be forgiven, although blasphemy against Jesus could be (Matthew 12:32). Insulting the Spirit is just as sinful as trampling the Son of God under foot (Hebrews 10:29). This indicates that the Spirit is inherently holy, holy in essence, rather than having an assigned or secondary holiness such as the temple had. The Spirit also has the infinite attributes of God: unlimited in time, space, power and knowledge.
2. Eternality: The Holy Spirit, the Counselor, will be with us "forever" (John 14:16). The Spirit is "eternal" (Hebrews 9:14).
3. Omnipresence: David, praising God's greatness, asked, "Where can I go from your Spirit? Where can I flee from your presence? If I go up to the heavens, you are there; if I make my bed in the depths, you are there" (Psalm 139:7-8). God's Spirit, which David uses as a synonym for the presence of God, is in heaven and in *sheol* (verse 8), in the east and in the west (verse 9). God's Spirit can be said to be poured out on someone, to fill a person, or to descend — yet without implying that the Spirit has moved away from or vacated some other place. Thomas Oden observes that "such statements are grounded in the premises of omnipresence and eternality — attributes ascribed properly only to God" (*Life in the Spirit*, page 18).
4. Omnipotence: The works that God does, such as creation, are also ascribed to the Holy Spirit (Job 33:4; Psalm 104:30). Miracles of Jesus Christ were done "by the Spirit" (Matthew 12:28). In Paul's ministry, the work that "Christ has accomplished" was done "through the power of the Spirit" (Romans 15:18-19).
5. Omniscience: "The Spirit searches all things, even the deep things of God" (1 Corinthians 2:10). The Spirit of God "knows the thoughts of God" (verse 11). The Spirit therefore knows all things, and is able to teach all things (John 14:26).

Holiness, eternality, omnipresence, omnipotence and omniscience are attributes of God's essence, that is, characteristic of the nature of divine existence. The Holy Spirit has the basic attributes of God.

B. Equated with God

1. Triadic formulas: Several passages discuss the Father, Son, and Holy Spirit as equals. In a discussion of spiritual gifts, Paul puts the Spirit,

the Lord, and God in grammatically parallel constructions (1 Corinthians 12:4-6). Paul closes a letter with a three-part prayer: "May the grace of the Lord Jesus Christ, and the love of God, and the fellowship of the Holy Spirit be with you all" (2 Corinthians 13:14). Peter begins with a three-part formula: "chosen according to the foreknowledge of God the Father, through the sanctifying work of the Spirit, for obedience to Jesus Christ and sprinkling by his blood" (1 Peter 1:2).

The triadic formulas used in these and other scriptures do not prove equality (for example, Ephesians 4:5 puts unequal elements in parallel construction), but they support it. The baptismal formula has a stronger implication of unity — "in the name [singular] of the Father and of the Son and of the Holy Spirit" (Matthew 28:19). The Father, Son, and Spirit share a common name, indicating common essence and equality. This verse indicates both plurality and unity. Three names are given, but all three share one name.

2. Word interchanges. Acts 5:3 says that Ananias lied to the Holy Spirit; verse 4 says that Ananias lied to God. This indicates that "the Holy Spirit" and "God" are interchangeable and thus that the Holy Spirit is God. Some people try to explain this by saying that Ananias lied to God only indirectly, simply because the Holy Spirit represented God. This interpretation might be grammatically possible, but it would still imply that the Holy Spirit is personal, for one does not "lie" to an impersonal power. Moreover, Peter told Ananias that he lied not to humans, but to God. The point that Peter was trying to make is that Ananias has lied not merely to God's representatives, but to God himself, and the Holy Spirit is God to whom Ananias lied.

Another word interchange can be seen in 1 Corinthians 3:16 and 6:19. Christians are not only temples of God, they are also temples of the Holy Spirit; the two expressions mean the same thing. A temple is a habitation for a deity, not a monument to an impersonal power. When Paul writes "temple of the Holy Spirit," he implies that the Holy Spirit is God.

Another type of verbal equation between God and the Holy Spirit is seen in Acts 13:2: "The Holy Spirit said, 'Set apart for me Barnabas and Saul for the work to which I have called them.'" Here, the Holy Spirit speaks on behalf of God, as God. In the same way, Hebrews 3:7-11 tells us that the Holy Spirit says the Israelites "tested and tried me"; the Holy Spirit says that "I was angry…. They shall never enter my rest." The Holy Spirit is equated with the God of the Israelites. Hebrews 10:15-17 also equates the Spirit and the Lord who makes the new covenant. The Spirit who inspired the prophets is God. This is the work of God the Holy Spirit.

C. Divine work

1. Creating: The Holy Spirit does work that only God can do, such as creating (Genesis 1:2; Job 33:4; Psalm 104:30) and expelling demons (Matthew 12:28).

2. Begetting: The Spirit was involved in begetting the incarnate Son of God (Matthew 1:20; Luke 1:35), and the full divinity of the Son (Colossians 1:19) implies the full divinity of the Begetter. The Spirit begets believers, too — they are born of God (John 1:12) and equally born of the Spirit (John 3:5). "The Spirit gives [eternal] life" (John 6:63).

3. Indwelling: The Holy Spirit is the way God lives in his children (Ephesians 2:22; 1 John 3:24; 4:13). The Holy Spirit "lives" in us (Romans 8:11; 1 Corinthians 3:16) — and because the Spirit lives in us, we are able to say that God lives in us. We can say that God lives in us only because the Holy Spirit is in some way God. The Spirit is not a representative or a power that lives in us — God himself lives in us. Geoffrey Bromiley gives a concise conclusion: "to have dealings with the Spirit, no less than with the Father and the Son, is to have dealings with God" ("The New Holy Spirit," in *The New Life*, edited by Millard Erickson, page 23).

4. Sanctifying: The Holy Spirit makes people holy (Romans 15:16; 1 Peter 1:2). The Spirit enables people to enter the kingdom of God (John 3:5). We are saved "through the sanctifying work of the Spirit" (2 Thessalonians 2:13).

In all these things, the works of the Spirit are the works of God. Whatever the Spirit says or does, God is saying or doing; the Spirit is fully representative of God.

II. Personality of the Holy Spirit

Summary: Scripture describes the Holy Spirit as having personal characteristics: The Spirit has mind and will, speaks and can be spoken to, and acts and intercedes for us. These indicate that the Spirit is personal—a Person or Hypostasis in the same sense that the Father and Son are. Our relationship with God, which is accomplished by the Holy Spirit, is a personal relationship.

A. Life and intelligence

1. Life: The Holy Spirit "lives" (Romans 8:11; 1 Corinthians 3:16).

2. Intelligence: The Spirit "knows" (1 Corinthians 2:11). Romans 8:27 refers to "the mind of the Spirit." This mind is able to make judgments — a decision "seemed good" to the Holy Spirit (Acts 15:28). These verses imply intelligence.

3. Will: 1 Corinthians 12:11 says that the Spirit "determines" decisions, showing that the Spirit has a will.[1]

B. Communication

1. Speaking: Numerous verses say that the Holy Spirit spoke (Acts 8:29; 10:19; 11:12; 21:11; 1 Timothy 4:1; Hebrews 3:7; etc.). Oden observes that "the Spirit speaks in the first person as 'I'; 'It was I who sent them' (Acts 10:20).... 'I have called them' (Acts 13:2). None but a person can say 'I'" (*The Living God*, page 200).

2. Interaction: The Spirit may be lied to (Acts 5:3), which indicates that the Spirit may be spoken to. The Spirit may be tested (Acts 5:9), insulted (Hebrews 10:29) or blasphemed (Matthew 12:31), which implies personal status. Oden gathers additional evidence: "The apostolic testimony applied intensely personal analogies: guiding (Romans 8:14), convicting (John 16:8), interceding (Romans 8:26), calling (Acts 13:2), commissioning (Acts 20:28).... Only a person can be vexed (Isaiah 63:10) or grieved (Ephesians 4:30)" (*Life in the Spirit*, page 19).

3. Paraclete: Jesus called the Holy Spirit the *parakletos* — the Comforter, Advocate or Counselor. The Paraclete is active, teaching (John 14:26), testifying (15:26), convicting (16:8), guiding (16:13) and making truth known (16:14).

Jesus used the masculine form of *parakletos*; he did not consider it necessary to make the word neuter or to use neuter pronouns. In John 16:14, masculine pronouns are used even after the neuter *pneuma* is mentioned. It would have been easy to switch to neuter pronouns, but John did not. In other places, neuter pronouns are used for the Spirit, in accordance with grammatical convention. Scripture is not finicky about the grammatical gender of the Spirit, and we need not be either. We use personal pronouns for the Spirit to acknowledge that he is personal, not to imply that he is male.

C. Action

1. New life: The Holy Spirit regenerates us, giving us new life (John 3:5). The Spirit sanctifies us (1 Peter 1:2) and leads us in that new life (Romans 8:14). The Spirit gives various gifts to build the church up (1 Corinthians 12:7-11), and throughout the book of Acts, we see that the Spirit guides the church.

2. Intercession: The most "personal" activity of the Holy Spirit is intercession: "We do not know what we ought to pray for, but the Spirit himself intercedes for us.... The Spirit intercedes for the saints in accordance with God's will" (Romans 8:26-27). Intercession implies not only receiving communication, but also communicating further on. It implies an intelligence, a concern, and a

---

[1] The Greek word means "he or it determines." Although the Greek word does not specify the subject of the verb, the most likely subject in the context is the Spirit. To find a different subject, one would have to backtrack through five verses and six mentions of the Spirit. But this grammatical leapfrogging is not necessary. Since we know from other verses that the Spirit has mind and knowledge and judgment, there is no reason to reject the conclusion in 1 Corinthians 12:11 that the Spirit also has will.

formal role. The Holy Spirit is not an impersonal power, but an intelligent and divine Helper who lives within us. God lives within us, and the Holy Spirit is God.

III. Worship

There are no scriptural examples of worshipping the Holy Spirit. Scripture talks about praying *in* the Spirit (Ephesians 6:18), the fellowship *of* the Spirit (2 Corinthians 13:14), and baptism in the name of the Spirit (Matthew 28:19). Although baptism, prayer and fellowship are involved in worship, none of these verses shows worship of the Spirit. As an opposite of worship, however, we note that the Spirit can be blasphemed (Matthew 12:31).

There are no scriptural examples of praying to the Holy Spirit. However, Scripture indicates that a human can talk to the Spirit (Acts 5:3). If this is done in reverence or request, it is, in effect, praying to the Spirit. If Christians are unable to articulate their desires and they want the Spirit to intercede for them (Romans 8:26-27), they are praying, directly or indirectly, to the Holy Spirit. When we understand that the Holy Spirit has intelligence and fully represents God, we may ask the Spirit for help — never thinking that the Spirit is a separate being from God, but recognizing that the Spirit is the Hypostasis of God interceding for us.

Why does Scripture say nothing about praying to the Spirit? Michael Green explains: "The Holy Spirit does not draw attention to himself. He is sent by the Father to glorify Jesus, to show Jesus' attractiveness, and not to take the centre of the stage" (*I Believe in the Holy Spirit,* page 60). Or, as Geoffrey Bromiley puts it, "The Spirit is self-effacing" (page 21).

Prayer or worship directed specifically to the Holy Spirit is not the scriptural norm, but we nonetheless worship the Spirit. When we worship God, we worship all aspects of God, including the Father, the Son, and the Holy Spirit. A fourth-century theologian explained it this way: "The Spirit is jointly worshipped in God, when God is worshipped in the Spirit" (Ambrose, *Of the Holy Spirit* III.X.82, quoted in Oden, *Life in the Spirit,* page 16). Whatever we say to the Spirit we are saying to God, and whatever we say to God we are saying to the Spirit.

IV. Summary

Scripture indicates that the Holy Spirit has divine attributes and works, and is spoken of in the same way that the Father and Son are. The Holy Spirit is intelligent, and speaks and acts like a divine Person. This is part of the scriptural evidence that led early Christians to formulate the doctrine of the Trinity. Bromiley gives a summary:

> Three points that emerge from this survey of the New Testament data are: (1) The Holy Spirit is everywhere regarded as God; (2) He is God in distinction from the Father and the Son; (3) His deity does not infringe upon the divine unity. In other words, the Holy Spirit is the third person of the triune Godhead….
>
> The divine unity cannot be subjected to mathematical ideas of unity. The fourth century learned to speak of three hypostases or persons within the deity, not in the tritheistic sense of three centers of consciousness, but also not in the weaker sense of three economic manifestations. From Nicaea and Constantinople on, the creeds sought to do justice to the essential biblical data along these lines. (pages 24-25)

Although Scripture does not directly say that "the Holy Spirit is God," or that God is triune, these conclusions are based on scriptural evidence. Based on biblical evidence, we teach that the Holy Spirit is God in the same way that the Father is God and the Son is God.

Michael Morrison

A Theology of the Holy Spirit

Introduction

Seeking to understand and know the Holy Spirit is a wonderful and rewarding endeavor. It ties in with every aspect of the Christian faith and life. But if there was ever a topic we are likely never to get to the bottom of, this one would qualify. The very name of this divine Person, the Holy Spirit, already tells us that we're in pretty deep. But we have a good amount of insight given to us by biblical revelation that can inform our understanding and help us stay away from pure speculation. God has seen fit to reveal himself to us as Father, Son and Holy Spirit and has provided and preserved teaching about the Holy Spirit. Because he wants us to know, trust and worship him, we by faith can dare to pursue understanding on that basis. But we proceed only by God's grace.

In this essay, we will only touch on a few key points that address questions that are, first, foundational to our faith in the Holy Spirit and, second, are of more immediate importance given current discussions and debates. It is our prayer that this essay will also help keep further explorations and other discussions in perspective. It is not possible in a short space to offer anything near a comprehensive view, so regard this as more of a beginning than an ending.

Jesus instructs Nicodemus

I'd like to start by recalling a passage from the Gospel of John. I'm referring to the story of Nicodemus. Jesus is speaking to Nicodemus, trying to explain to him something foundational regarding the nature and work of the Spirit. Jesus says to him, "Very truly I tell you, no one can enter the kingdom of God unless they are born of water and the Spirit." He continues,

Flesh gives birth to flesh, but the Spirit gives birth to spirit. You should not be surprised at my saying, "You must be born again." The wind blows wherever it pleases. You hear its sound, but you cannot tell where it comes from or where it is going. So it is with everyone born of the Spirit. (John 3:5-8)

Nicodemus wants to understand how God works. Jesus tells him that God works with us by the Holy Spirit. But Nicodemus is not satisfied with that answer. He wants to know, if he can, how the Spirit works! Jesus' answer to that "how" question amounts to his saying: How the Spirit works is like trying to talk about how the wind works. We see the effects, but we know very little about it, not even where it was a few moments ago or where it will end up going a few moments later! The Spirit is not predictable or controllable by us. We don't and can't have an answer as to how the Spirit works, the mechanics of it.

Apparently the "how" question is the wrong one to ask. Given Jesus' reply to Nicodemus, we can assume that it's not necessary for us to know, either, even to receive the benefits of the working of the Spirit! Jesus' "no-explanation" answer makes sense. How can we possibly put into words, concepts and ideas something about the Spirit, given that it is like the wind? You can't predict its movement or say much about it except that "it blows where it wills." The Spirit has a mind of his own! I think that's part of our experience. The wind of the Spirit blows where it wills. We did not necessarily see it coming and don't necessarily see where it's going. So it is with the Spirit.

Focus on the biblical teaching

Why not stop right there? In some cases I think

that might be the right thing to do. There is a lot of speculation taking place, especially about how the Spirit works. However, we are given other words and descriptions in biblical revelation that refer to the Holy Spirit. But not surprisingly, they don't tell us how the Spirit works nor especially how to bring the Spirit under our control or how we can influence or predict the working of the Spirit. Rather, most of what we are given relates to the nature and purpose and character of the Spirit, not the mechanics of his working. All sorts of problems can be avoided if we simply pay attention to what biblical revelation actually tells us and resist using what we discover in ways that disregard Jesus' own teaching on the limits of our knowledge of the Holy Spirit's wind-like working.

Sometimes people think the Holy Spirit gets less attention than deserved—the short end of the stick, as we say, or short shrift. The complaint that the Spirit is under-represented can be heard both at the levels of theological discussion as well as at the daily and practical level of church life. That's a perfectly good concern to raise. We should be aware and take to heart all we are told regarding the Spirit. Neglecting any part of biblical witness is not a good idea. Faith seeks whatever understanding of the Spirit we are given, as in any other part of the Christian faith. But we can ask the counter question as well: Is it true that in practice and preaching we don't properly emphasize the Holy Spirit? If so, in what ways do we fail to give the Spirit sufficient attention? And, what measure or criteria can we use to evaluate whether we have under- (or over-) emphasized the Holy Spirit?

Whether we give full attention is best gauged by the norm of biblical teaching. We can look to Scripture to weigh its own emphasis on the Spirit relative to other matters. We can also consider the full range of insights it presents us. Then we can compare our own emphasis and range of teaching to the pattern and proportion found there. While we will not be able to conclude with something like a numerical measurement, I think there will be many indicators in biblical teaching that can greatly assist us in our process of discernment. We can also borrow understanding on this matter from teachers of the church down through the ages, including our present time, as it seems in alignment with biblical revelation considered as a whole.

If there is some kind of deficit, then we'll also need to explore how best to correct that lack. We'll need to discern this issue as well, because there are various ways to correct for it. But some are not as useful or faithful as others. Some purported correctives promoted in recent times have seemed not only speculative but harmful to the health of the Body of Christ. What the Bible teaches can help us discern how best to make any kind of corrective action called for.

What are the basics of revelation about the Holy Spirit?

Recall that any theology built on biblical revelation must seek first and foremost to answer the question of "who" the God of the Bible is, for that is the central concern and controlling topic of the whole Bible. Biblical revelation is not geared nearly as much to answer the questions of how or why, where or when. So our understanding must begin by seeking to know first who the Holy Spirit is.

Let's begin with a review of the most basic truths we have been given about the Holy Spirit. Most fundamentally we are told about the Spirit's relationship with the Father and the Son. Those relationships identify who the Spirit of God is. Who is the Spirit? The Spirit is the Spirit of the Father and the Son. The Spirit is one with the Father and one with the Son. Jesus is conceived by the Spirit, he has the Spirit for us and he ministers in and by the Spirit even in his atoning work on the cross. Jesus and the Father send the Spirit to us. The Spirit takes us to the Father through the Son. By the Spirit we are united to Christ so that we share in his life, life in fellowship and communion with the Father. And we share, by the Spirit, in Jesus' ongoing ministry in the church and in the world.

Notice that what Jesus teaches Nicodemus (and us) fits the overall pattern of revelation about the

Spirit throughout Scripture. Nicodemus wanted to know how a person can be "born again" (or it could be translated, "born from above"). But Jesus' response indicates that such "how" questions can't be answered in connection with the Spirit! Nicodemus is not told how the Spirit blows to bring us new life. Rather, Jesus' answer to his "how" question identifies the "Who" behind the "how." But Jesus does describe in a comprehensive way the effect of the working of the Spirit, namely, bringing us a new kind of life that comes from God. The Gospel of John goes on to shed even more light on the relationship of the Spirit to Jesus and to the Father, which includes the interrelationship of their missions and ministries. These relationships are especially prominent in chapters 13-17. The central concern throughout this Gospel remains their conjoint relationships. They are inseparable, always being together and always working together.

One in being—united in act

Borrowing now from the more developed doctrine of the Trinity, we can say in summary that the three divine Persons of the Trinity are "one in being." This technical phrase helps us remember there are not three Gods, but only one. The Spirit is not a separate God that has his own independent mind, his own action, his own plan, and his own purpose. The Spirit is joined in one being and therefore joined in one mind, action, plan and purpose with the Father and the Son. Even the name "Holy Spirit" indicates to us the unity of the Spirit with Father and Son, since only God has the name "Holy."

The point here is not to let our minds think about the Holy Spirit as an independent operator. That's one of the biggest mistakes people make. Always remember, whatever the Spirit does, wherever the Spirit is at work, that Spirit is the Spirit of the Father and the Son, because they are one in being. They do not act separately, apart from one another. They act out of one shared mind, heart and purpose in unity with each other. St. Augustine famously summarized this in the fourth century: "All the works of God are inseparable."

A number of special phrases have been used down through the ages to convey the oneness or unity of the Persons besides saying that they are "one in being." They are said to "co-exist." They "co-inhere" in one another. They "in-exist" one another or they "mutually in-dwell" one another, they "co-envelop" one another or they "mutually interpenetrate" each other. Their oneness of being has been expressed by saying that the whole God is present in each of the divine Persons. The whole God is present in the Father. The whole God is present in the Son. The whole God is present in the Spirit. That's to say: they're one in being even though they're distinguishable in person. An early creed sums it up this way: the Triune God is a Unity in Trinity and a Trinity in Unity.

Sharing all divine attributes

This means that the Holy Spirit is fully and completely divine and has from all eternity all the attributes that the Father and the Son have. The Spirit is not subordinate or less than the others. All that you can say of the Father, such as being omniscient, holy, omnipotent, eternal, and even being a Creator, can all be said of the Spirit (and can all be said of the Son). Dividing up among the Persons the attributes of God and the actions of God towards creation is ruled out because they are one in being.

That's a hard rule for us to follow because we have developed poor habits of thinking and speaking in the church and likely were never taught otherwise. We also like to divide things up and align certain attributes or actions with the Father and others with the Son or the Holy Spirit. A typical way we do this is by saying the Father creates, the Son redeems and the Spirit perfects or sanctifies. We might think the Father is just and holy in comparison to the Son, who is merciful and gracious. But taking such a division of labor in a strict way would be an inaccurate, even misleading way to speak of God. The distinct Persons of the Trinity do not have separate jobs or wear different hats or play different roles that they accomplish by themselves. God acts as the one being that God is. His being does not fragment in mind, will, purpose or in action.

Therefore, everything you can say about the eternal nature and character of the Father, you can say about the Son and you can say about the Holy Spirit. They are each all-powerful, omniscient, omnipresent, eternal, good, merciful, righteous and holy. They are all to be worshiped together because they're one in being. So we can say of our worship—we worship the Father through the Son and in the Spirit. Or, we pray to the Father, through the Son and in the Spirit. And we proclaim that the Father has redeemed us through the Son and in the Spirit. The whole God is our Savior!

The unity of the being (and therefore of the action, character and attributes of God) is one of the most fundamental things to hold on to and to watch out for when we go on to say other things about the Spirit. We want to avoid talking as if the divine Persons are separate, wear different hats, have divergent purposes or as if they're operating independently of one another. Simply remembering they're one in being will prevent a lot of problems down the theological road.

Next, we'll look at some of the distinctions in the united acts of the Father, Son and Spirit.

A Theology of the Holy Spirit
continued

One in being, distinct in Person

As noted in part one of this series, it's important to avoid thinking that the divine Persons have divergent purposes or that they operate independently of one another. The Triune God is *one in being,* and the three Divine Persons are *one in act.* Whether in creation, redemption or in the perfecting of the creation, the Persons act together as the one God. We see this in the many Scriptures where the Persons are linked in a particular act (work) of God. However, there are times when Scripture shows the Persons working in distinct ways. For example, the Son becomes incarnate in a way that is distinct from the Father and the Spirit. At Pentecost, the Spirit descends and indwells the believing church in a way that is distinct from the Father and the Son.

Even when two or three of the Persons are shown to be joined in a particular act of God, there often is a distinction as to their particular role in that act. Scripture seems to indicate that each Person is involved in a particular way in every act that the Persons do together. Each, from their own "angle," contributes in a unique way to the unified act. We could say that one Person "takes the lead" in certain actions: the Father in creation, the Son in atonement, the Spirit in the perfecting of creation. To speak of such distinctions in this way is fine, so long as we don't think of the Persons as acting separately or as being out of phase with one another in what is a conjoint act. In formal theology this is called the doctrine of *appropriation*. An act can be "appropriated" to the Person of the Trinity who takes the lead, as long as the other two are not regarded as having nothing to do with it, but are co-involved, each in their own way.

We should not think that the distinction, in their contribution to an act external to their triune being, is what *makes* or *constitutes* their being as distinct in their Persons. The error here is to think, for instance, that being the Creator is what makes the Father different in Person from the Son, or that being Incarnate is what makes the Son different in Person from the Father. No, rather the Father is the Father and the Son the Son and the Spirit the Spirit whether or not they perform any actions external to their own triune being. They are distinguished by their internal relationships, not by their external actions. The being of God does not depend on his relationship to something that is external to God, to something that is not God.

As long as we don't leave the Son and the Spirit behind, we can say the Father leads in creation. We can say the Son leads in our redemption. But if we think the Father is absent or has a different view, attitude, purpose or intention for the cross than does the Son, then we have split the Trinity apart, placed them at odds with one another! Even in Jesus' earthly life, we need to remember that he only does what he sees the Father doing. He only says what the Father is saying. They're saying things together. They're doing things together. They're never separate because they're one in being.

It is proper to say the Son takes the lead and that only the Son is incarnate. We can affirm that the Son physically suffers on the cross and not the Father or Spirit. Not being incarnate in our humanity, they cannot physically suffer and die. But if we think the Father was absent or the Spirit was gone on vacation and wasn't around when

Jesus was on the cross, then we've strayed way off the theological path. The Spirit and the Father were present with Jesus, each in their own non-incarnate way. Jesus said, "Father into your hands, I commend my spirit." In the book of Hebrews we read, "How much more shall the blood of Christ, who through the eternal Spirit offered himself without blemish to God, purify your conscience from dead works to worship the living God" (9:14). They're all acting together in Christ's redeeming work. Yes, we can say one leads. But don't let them fall apart just because one is leading.

The Spirit perfects, but he perfects human beings with the perfection that is accomplished by Christ. The Spirit shares with us the holiness and the sanctification of Jesus in our humanity. He doesn't give us a spiritualized or divine perfection, a non-bodily, nonhuman existence. Rather, the Spirit joins us to Christ's glorified human body, mind and soul.

The Spirit makes us to share in Jesus' self-sanctification. The work of the Spirit is not separate from the work of the Son, but the Spirit leads in dwelling in us now. We can talk about the ways the Spirit leads, but we shouldn't think of the Spirit as branching off and saying, "Father and Son, you've done a good job over there, but now I've got to go do something over here that you don't have anything to do with. It's my turn to do my own thing." To think in that way is a mistake. That could happen only if God wasn't one in being and was three beings—*tritheism!* We don't want to go there.

We can distinguish between the various contributions the Father, the Son and the Spirit make by the way they take their lead, but we don't want to separate them or place them in any kind of opposition or in tension with each other. We don't want to say that their differing contributions to what they accomplish together are what make them distinct in Person from all eternity. We can *distinguish* but we should not *separate*. The divine Persons are one in being and distinct in Person, not only in their internal and eternal being, but also in terms of what they do towards creation, in creation, redemption and consummation.

Projecting on God

Why do we get tripped up in this? There are a number of reasons, but one of them is that we tend to think of God in ways we think of ourselves. We start with ourselves and then try to get to our understanding of God. Think of how we usually distinguish ourselves from each other. How do I know I'm not you and you're not me? I note: you have a different body. You're over there and I'm over here. You do this but I do that. You live there but I live here. You think that's funny, but I don't. I want X, but you want Y. We're different in all these ways, and that's how we know we are distinct persons.

So we can project this perspective on God and think that's how the Father, Son and Spirit are distinguished. The Father is over here, the Spirit's over there. The Father wants A and the Son wants B. They each have different jobs to do. We try to distinguish them from each other in the same way we distinguish ourselves. But God is not a creature like we are, so we can't just take the idea of how we distinguish ourselves and apply it in the same way to God. Thinking that way would work only if God were a creature.

Names and relations

The essential way we have been given to distinguish between the divine Persons is by means of their different names: the Father, the Son and the Holy Spirit. The different names reveal a difference of their Persons. That is also why we believe there are three, not four or two. We are given three names, not two or seven. The names we are given are revelatory of real distinctions in God, otherwise they wouldn't be revelatory! They are not just arbitrary words, concepts, ideas, or conventional labels. So we address God in worship, in prayer, by means of these three names. In doing this we follow Jesus' example and instruction. He uses these names in his relationship to the Father and Spirit and directs us to do so as well. For example, he instructs us: "Pray like this: Our Father in heaven…"

Those names also represent and reveal unique relationships. The Father has a different relationship with the Son than the Son has with the Father. The Spirit has a different relationship to the Father than does the Son. The names identify and reveal to us unique relationships. Following biblical teaching, we can also find distinct designations for the different relationships.

Corresponding to the Father is the relationship of begetting to the Son. Begetting is the special term used to describe more particularly how the Son comes from the Father. The Father begets the Son. Begetting indicates a certain kind of relationship. In the early church they recognized that begetting is different from making. What is made is of a different kind of thing than the maker. But what is begotten is of the identical kind of being. So we say that the Son is begotten, indicating a unique kind of relationship to the Father. The Son is distinct from the Father but of the identical kind of being, namely, divine, fully God. The Son doesn't beget the Father and the Father isn't begotten by the Son. They each have a different relationship with each other, and that difference of relationship (which is eternal and internal to God) is what makes them distinct from one another. So we say that the Father begets (is not begotten of the Son) and we say that the Son is begotten (does not beget the Father).

The unique names and relationships identify who the Persons are. They are who they are in relationship with each other. Without the relationships with each other, they would not be who they are. They are not interchangeable. The Father is not the Son, the Son is not the Father. Being the begetter and being the begotten one are different and not reversible. There's a direction to the relationships, and we can't reverse them. We can't say the Son begets the Father. The Son has always been the begotten Son. The Father has always begotten the Son. The Son is eternally the Son, and the Father, eternally Father. That's why we can identify them as the divine Persons of Father and Son.

But the words/names don't explain everything. They represent what we have to go on, and they explain what the names do and don't mean as far as we can tell. In the case of the Father and Son, we have to rule out (or "think away," as Athanasius said) some aspects of the meaning of the words begotten or begetting as used of human creatures. Among creatures these words include the idea of a time sequence. But when it comes to God, the aspect of time doesn't apply. God is eternal and so are the divine Persons. The Father generates (begets) the Son from all eternity. Time sequence doesn't apply to God. There never was a time when the Son was not. The Son was always the begotten Son of the Father, which is to say the Son is eternally the Son and the Father is eternally the Father, begetting the Son. The discipline of theology is to discern where and how words when used to refer to God must be used differently from how they are used of creatures. This task would be impossible if we did not have biblical revelation to lead us.

The Holy Spirit proceeds or spirates

What about the Spirit? There's always been the Holy Spirit, and the Holy Spirit has eternal relationships with the Father and the Son. We use a special word to talk about those relationships. The New Testament gives us a clue as to one word good to use. We say the Holy Spirit *proceeds* from the Father and, or through, the Son (John 15:26). Another word has also been used down through the ages to indicate that unique relationship: "spirates."

These words indicate unique and non-interchangeable relationship. The name and relationship indicate who the Spirit is. The Spirit would not be the Spirit without spirating from the Father and the Son. The Father and Son wouldn't be Father and Son without the Spirit proceeding. The relationship of the Spirit is essential to who the Spirit is and so to who the Triune God is. God wouldn't be God without the Person of the Holy Spirit.

We likely want to ask, "How does that work? How does a 'procession' work in God?" We don't know. We can't say exactly how it is different from begetting or being begotten. Along with the name, Holy Spirit, the word simply indicates that there is a unique kind of relationship of the Spirit with the Father and the Son, one that is different from the relationship of the Son to the Father. It indicates that the Spirit is *from* the Father and *through* the Son in a way that the Son and Father do not proceed from the Spirit and are not the Spirit. With this unique relationship, the Spirit is not interchangeable with the other Persons. It means that the Holy Spirit has always been the Holy Spirit. We affirm in this way that God has always been a Trinity. There never was a time when God was not Triune.

In summary, the three divine Persons eternally exist in unique relationships, and that is what is essential to their being distinct Persons. That's it: they have unique relations. Each one has a different relationship with the others. We don't know how to explain what all that means, but we use unique words because there are unique relations. That's also why we address them according to their unique names that correspond with the relations.

The Father is the Father, not the Son. The Son is the Son, not the Father. The Holy Spirit is the Holy Spirit of the Father and the Son. We have unique names to indicate the unique persons and they have unique relationships and they're not interchangeable. In these ways we honor what we are given by Jesus and through Scripture as if what we are given is revelatory, as if God has actually fulfilled his will and desire to make himself known to us so that we now have accurate and faithful ways to speak about and know God.

When God through Jesus says, to address him as Father, Son and Holy Spirit we're being told something real and accurate about God. We're getting to know God as Jesus knows the Father and Spirit. He's sharing with us his insider knowledge of God so we too can know and trust the whole triune God. Recall John 1:18, "No one has ever seen God, but the one and only Son, who is himself God and is in closest relationship with the Father, has made him known." The triune name identifies who God is, which God we're speaking of, and even what kind of God, God is. God is the Triune God. That's the only God that is or has ever been. God is Father, Son and Spirit. The Father is the Father. The Son is the Son. The Holy Spirit is the Holy Spirit. Don't separate them — they're one in being. In that way we avoid the misunderstanding/heresy that has been called tritheism. But don't collapse them into one Person with no relationships; they're distinct in Person. In that way we avoid the opposite misunderstanding/heresy that has been called modalism.

Endnote: We are attempting to take what we are given in biblical revelation and see what understanding can come of it. There will always be much more, and what we come up with can be further refined, corrected and sometimes even done away with. It's always faith seeking understanding. We do this seeking in fellowship with the rest of the church down through the ages for some additional guidance, inspiration and insight.

The doctrine of appropriation held down through the ages is that the various acts of God towards creation can be appropriated to one or the other of the divine Persons. One way of thinking of this appropriation is to think of one Person "taking the lead" in any particular act of God, such as creation. However, "taking the lead" should not be taken in a temporal way, as if there is a time interval. There isn't. The Persons act as one. There is no temporal before and after in God between the Persons, and no separation of the Persons. They are one in being and one in act. But the kind of oneness they have does not seem to rule out some kind of difference in their united contribution to those united acts as conveyed in biblical revelation.

So saying one "takes the lead" is not meant to prompt the question of "when" the Father did X compared to "when" the Son did X or Y. That would (wrongly) be assuming a temporal order, which is ruled out, as is any idea of the divine Persons acting independently.

The distinction of the Father and Son's

contribution to creation is conveyed in biblical terms by the idea of creation being "through" the Son. "Through" suggests another agent working, one through another. That is, the Father works "through" the Son in creating. The word "through" doesn't make sense if there is only one agent acting, the Son. God speaking creation into existence in Genesis gives the same sense that aligns with what is said in John 1 concerning the Son being the Word of God the Father. God (the Father) and the Word are united and distinct at the same time. The Father speaks—he speaks through his Word (his Son). The result is creation.

It's verses like these that suggest the Father and Son work in a structured or ordered way in creating—and that they don't work separately. The idea of "through" can be represented by the idea of "taking the lead" towards creation; the Father through the Son. But it's not meant to be taken in a temporal way nor should it be taken to mean a separation in act. In that way the more fundamental understandings of the Trinity are at least not undone.

But if the doctrine of appropriation (with its idea of "taking the lead") is found to not be useful, not much is lost if it is left out or made of little use. The doctrine requires careful use because it can be misunderstood.

Gary Deddo

This ends part 2 of a 7-part essay. The remainder of the essay will be in the third volume of our 40-day series. Or you may read it online at https://www.gcs.edu/mod/page/view.php?id=4231

God Speaks to Us!

The Bible is a window. Have you opened it lately?

Almost all American households have one or more Bibles. Yet more than half of the adults in these households do not read their Bibles during an average week, and only 10 or 15 percent do so daily.

"Americans revere the Bible—but, by and large, they don't read it," pollster George Gallup Jr. once observed. This seems to be borne out by what Americans know about the Bible. In one survey, only 42 percent of those interviewed could name five of the Ten Commandments. Only 46 percent correctly named the four Gospels—Matthew, Mark, Luke and John. It is likely that the statistics have gone down since those surveys were taken.

Much more important is how the Bible speaks to our lives. "Until people see the Bible as a practical guidebook for their everyday existence, it will probably continue to remain on the shelf," says Christian pollster George Barna.

So why should we read and study an ancient and (in the minds of many) hard-to-understand book? What could the Bible say that is essential to daily life in the modern world?

For our time

Jack Kuhatschek, in his book *Taking the Guesswork out of Applying the Bible,* openly admits the Bible's bad image—referring to its "age problem." He writes: "People wonder what benefit we can possibly derive from a two-thousand-year-old book written in an obscure corner of the Middle East. In a sense I can't blame them. After all, much of the Bible does seem irrelevant today."

Chapter after chapter, the Bible can seem outdated and irrelevant to our needs. It tells the experiences of people like Noah, Moses and Paul, who lived many centuries ago. They faced problems and questions that don't seem related to our own.

Not only are the human experiences discussed in the Bible ancient, but the cultures, vocabulary and thought patterns are also dated. For example, the book of Revelation is written in what is called "apocalyptic" style. That is not a literary genre familiar to us modern folks, and it seems strange and confusing. This makes it difficult to understand the message of the book—and easy to misinterpret it. But during the first century, apocalyptic writing was a well-known literary genre. The original Christian readers knew this style of writing and how to understand the message Revelation wanted to convey.

What's our view?

We need to see the Bible's books and literary styles on their terms. If we are to grasp the message of any biblical book, we need to hear the word of God coming from its pages in the same way the first readers heard it. We also need to understand the meaning of the story of the lives of Noah, Moses or Paul, even as the first Christians did. Although our culture may be different, we have the same concerns, needs and problems as they did.

God showed his nearness, his saving grace, and his purpose by involving himself in the lives of these individuals. Their past encounters with God help us understand how God deals with us now.

This is the key to becoming motivated to study the Bible. We need to understand it as the book that reveals God and his way. So we should honestly and frankly ask ourselves about our view of the Bible. Do we see it as an oppressive rule book? An out-of-date and irrelevant ancient writing?

Impossible to understand? Filled with boring history in the Old Testament and imponderable theology in the New?

Or do we see the Bible as a book that puts us in touch with God on a personal level? As a book that reveals God's loving and gracious purpose for us?

Our view of the Bible depends on how we perceive our relationship with God. Do we see him as a distant God uninvolved with human affairs? Or do we see him as a living Being who has something important to tell us about himself and his purpose for us—and our future with him? Here are three questions to ponder in our relationship to God and to the Bible:

- Do we believe God is interested in communicating himself and his message to human beings?
- Do we believe God revealed his purpose through prophets (Old Testament) and apostles (New Testament)?
- Do we believe that they faithfully wrote down their revelations from God—and that their writings have been preserved in the book we call the Bible?

God's word to us

In his book *Understanding the Bible,* John Stott asks us: "Do we really believe that *God* has spoken, that *God's* words are recorded in Scripture, and that as we read it we may hear *God's* voice addressing us?" The apostle Paul, speaking of those books that form the Christian Old Testament, said they could make one "wise for salvation through faith in Christ Jesus" (2 Timothy 3:15).

He told his young associate Timothy: "All Scripture is God-breathed and is useful for teaching, rebuking, correcting and training in righteousness, so that the servant of God may be thoroughly equipped for every good work" (verses 16-17).

Peter insisted he had not followed "cleverly devised stories" when he told the church about God's plan of salvation (2 Peter 1:16). He had been an eyewitness of Jesus' work and had seen and talked with the resurrected Christ. Peter promised he would make every effort to provide for the preservation of those truths after his death. These would keep the church within the realm of faith and God's grace (verse 15). Peter also spoke of Paul's letters as Scripture. He said they were authoritative writings that conveyed the words of God about things vital to our salvation (2 Peter 3:15-16).

Do we agree that the Bible contains God's word *to us?* If so, the Bible must matter a great deal as a book that can help us come to know God more intimately. How, then, could the Bible not be a book we would want to read and study on a regular basis? Have *you* read the Good Book lately?

More than reading required

You've probably heard statements like the following: "Simply read the Bible for yourself and do what it says," or "Just read, believe, and obey the Bible." While this approach to Bible reading sounds simple, it's not quite the way that effective study of the Bible proceeds. We need to learn how to correctly interpret what the Bible says on a particular matter before we apply it to our lives. That's because we don't come to the Bible with a clean slate, free of previous opinions. We are not only readers of Scripture, we are, for better or worse, also interpreters.

Our view of what the Bible says on a given matter may be distorted by what we *think* it says. It's easy to fall into the trap of seeing in the Bible something we already believe, but it doesn't teach. "We invariably bring to the text all that we are, with all of our experiences, culture, and prior understandings of words and ideas," write biblical scholars Gordon Fee and Douglas Stuart in their book *How to Read the Bible for All Its Worth.*

That can be dangerous. The authors explain, "Sometimes what we bring to the text, unintentionally to be sure, leads us astray, or else causes us to read all kinds of foreign ideas into the text." To rightly understand the Bible, we also need to understand the kind of book it is. It was written by and for people who lived centuries ago in cultures far different from our own.

The Bible is relevant to all ages. But we must first understand the context or original situation in which a particular portion of Scripture was written. Then comes the need for right interpretation, understanding how a particular passage of Scripture reflects a broad principle applicable to life situations we face. This requires more than a casual reading of the Scriptures.

After rightly interpreting the original intent of the biblical writings, we need to apply them intelligently to our contemporary situation. When we read the Bible, we need to listen to the voice of God coming through his Word, not our own. We should avoid reading into the Bible ideas it doesn't teach.

Help is available to us as we move along our journey of study. Here are two useful books that tell us how to study the Bible:

- *How to Read the Bible for All Its Worth,* by Gordon D. Fee and Douglas Stuart.
- *Understanding Scripture: How to Read and Study the Bible,* by A. Berkeley Mickelson and Alvera M. Mickelson.

Paul Kroll

Five Simple Rules for Bible Study

The Bible is a complex book, but it has a simple message. There's enough wisdom in it for a lifetime of detailed study; and there is also wisdom that beginners can easily find.

If you have never read a 1,000-page book, the Bible may seem difficult and unapproachable. The strange names and strange customs might be intimidating. But perhaps you *want* to read the Bible, despite its difficulties, because you have heard that it can tell you more about the God who made you and who loves you. It can tell you about Jesus, your Savior, and what he did and taught. There's treasure hidden in this book, but you aren't quite sure how to go about finding it.

Here are five simple rules to help you:

1. Start

It is a big book, and nothing will change that. The only way to begin is to begin. The one-mile hike begins with the first step. So start reading! But don't try to read it all at one time. The Bible wasn't designed for fast reading. It is not a novel, a mystery, or a thriller. Rather, it is a collection of different types of writing. Genesis, for example, contains several types of story covering several major characters. Each requires some thought of its own, so don't be in a hurry to rush onward just to say you've done it. Take your time, a little bit each day. Structure your schedule so that you will have some time set aside for this.

Where should you start? Genesis has some interesting stories, and Exodus starts with a great story, but then the story slows dramatically, and most people lose interest by the time they get to Leviticus and Numbers, which are even slower.

It's probably better to start in the New Testament, with the stories of Jesus. Mark is a fast-moving Gospel, and Acts has a great story flow. This will then put Paul's letters in context.

Don't feel obligated to read everything "in order" — the Christians in Rome did fine reading Romans first. Feel free to skip around a bit, reading the Gospel of Luke, then the letter of Hebrews, or whatever. Later, you might want to try an Old Testament book, such as Psalms or Samuel.

When you begin each book, put the date on the first page. That way you'll know which books you've read, and which you haven't. Eventually you'll get to them all — if you keep at it.

You may want to get a modern translation, too. There's nothing especially holy or helpful about 400-year-old English. Try the New International Version, the New Living Translation, or other easier versions.

2. Read

If you read only one sentence, you might misunderstand it. For example, if I shout "Fire!" you might not know whether I am warning you of danger, or telling you to shoot a gun. The word needs a context before you can understand it.

The same is true of sentences in Scripture. For example, "No one is greater in this house than I am. My master has withheld nothing from me except you." To understand this sentence, we need to know who is speaking, who he is speaking to, and why. We need a context.

So if you want to understand what is going on, you need to read *passages,* not lift sentences off the page as if they had independent meaning. Sometimes they do, but most often they do not, and the only way to know whether they do is to read at least a few sentences before and some after, to get a feeling for what the passage as a whole is talking about. Who is talking, who is doing what, and why?

Many modern translations help us see the context by putting the words into paragraphs and giving subtitles for the major sections. These markers are usually a helpful indication of where one subject stops and another starts. The point is to read each verse *in context,* not as a totally independent thought.

3. Ask

Unfortunately, we don't understand everything we read. We don't understand everything in a modern novel or movie, either, but we can nonetheless enjoy the flow of the story. But when it comes to the Bible, people often get troubled when they don't understand everything. After all, it is a message from God, and we are supposed to understand it, and we feel stupid when we don't.

Let's make it clear: Nobody understands all the Bible, even after studying it full-time for 50 years. Nobody understands everything the first time they read it. (Some people *think* they do, but they have a bigger problem!) When it comes to the things of God, we are all a little bit ignorant. So relax. If you don't understand something, ask questions. Ask the Bible. (Talk out loud if you want to, but don't expect to hear voices.)

Ask the Bible: Who is talking here? How does he or she feel? Why are these people doing things this way? Would I probably do the same thing? Are we supposed to take this literally, or is it talking about something else? Is it something good, or something bad? Is there anything in the text to give me clues to help me understand?

Sometimes the answers are clear, sometimes they are not. Sometimes we just have to write a question mark in the margin and move onward. That's just the way the Bible is. Maybe we'll understand it five years later. Maybe a Bible handbook could help us understand. We don't know, but what we know for sure is that we don't understand it right now. That's OK. Sometimes it's just best to move on to another passage. It's OK to have questions.

4. Talk

Often, the things you don't understand, someone else does — and vice versa. So when we have questions about the meaning of the Bible, we can talk about it with other Christians. They may have already studied the same question, and may be able to make it clear.

Or you might want to share something you learned and enjoyed. Perhaps you've seen a proverb that applies to a situation you are in. Perhaps you have read a story of faith that you wish you had. Or maybe it was a glimpse of how great God is. Talk about these things, too, to encourage one another.

The New Testament describes the early church as a fellowship, as a group of people who spoke often to one another about the things of God. They devoted themselves to the apostles' teachings. They enjoyed what they learned, and talked about their joy.

In the modern world, Christians often talk before or after church, or in small groups that meet during the week in homes — small groups that meet for the purpose of praying together, discussing Scripture, and helping one another. One of these groups could help you in your Bible reading. So that's a good step for better understanding: Talk about the Bible with other Christians.

5. Don't stop

Since it's a big book, and since we don't understand it all the first time, it is essential that we keep at it. If you really want to understand how God speaks to us through the Bible, then you need to form a life-long habit of reading, thinking, and talking about the Bible.

We will die before we know it all — there is always more to learn. This should be a motivation to keep at it, not to quit. There are treasures hidden in the Bible, and it takes patience and persistence to seek them out. Some gems we can find right away; others will come to light only after many years. There's always something waiting for us to see.

And we all have to admit it, we aren't getting any younger. We forget things. We forget lessons we once learned, we forget promises we once knew. If we aren't refreshing our memory of Scripture, then we will be slowing losing something we once had. Out of sight, out of mind.

So don't quit — keep reading the Book!

Michael Morrison

Scripture: God's Gift

The Christian church down through the ages has always regarded the Bible as indispensable for its worship, devotion and life. Its very existence is bound up with the Bible. The church would not be what it is without it. Holy Scripture is part of the air it breathes and the food it eats.

I learned of the importance of the Bible as a young child and was encouraged and taught to read it and memorize it. I studied it both on my own and with others—I'm glad I did, now years later. The study of the Bible has always been an essential part of my ministry in serving others, whether it was teaching it, preaching from it, studying it with small groups of other Christians, or referring to it when counseling others. When I attended seminary, my primary focus was the study and interpretation of Scripture. It was so important to me that I was willing to try to learn Hebrew and Greek to see if I could understand Scripture better!

Along the way, I learned that there were various ways the nature and place of Scripture was understood, and various ways to make use of it. Some of these seemed better than others, while some seemed to lead to the misuse of Scripture, or even to making it irrelevant. I read books and took courses to sort out these issues, hoping I could find some wisdom in all this not only to help me, but to pass on to others.

Scripture is so essential to the Christian faith that most denominations have an official statement concerning the importance and place of Scripture. GCI is no exception. These summaries can be a good place to start a reflection on the nature, purpose and right use of Scripture. GCI's statement is brief, to the point and fairly comprehensive:

The Holy Scriptures are by God's grace sanctified to serve as his inspired Word and faithful witness to Jesus Christ and the gospel. They are the fully reliable record of God's revelation to humanity culminating in his self-revelation in the incarnate Son. As such, Holy Scripture is foundational to the church and infallible in all matters of faith and salvation.

Let's explore what's behind this theological summary of our understanding of Scripture. We do so not so we can enter into endless debate or prove ourselves superior to other Christians who might have a different view. And I don't think we simply want a theory about it. We seek understanding of Scripture because we highly value it and want to honor and make proper use of it. We want to handle it well so we can get the most out of it. Holy Scripture itself encourages us to do these very things. We also can remember that others in church history have benefited greatly through a deep understanding of Scripture and how to interpret it. But in the end, I think we want to grasp and use it well because we hope to get to know even better the God of the Bible in whom we put our faith.

By God's grace

Many of us have sung the childhood song that says: "Jesus loves me, this I know—for the Bible tells me so." That's true enough. However there's a different way to sing that verse that is also true: "Jesus loves me, this I know—*so* the Bible tells me so!" This second way is reflected in the GCI statement that the Bible is God's gift to us, a gift of grace and therefore of his love. *Because* God loves us in and through Christ, he has graciously provided us his written Word.

God didn't have to do so, but his love for us, his creatures, has moved him to provide us with his Word in written form. God's love for us comes first, then follows his provision of the Bible. We wouldn't be able to know and love God if God hadn't first loved us and communicated to us through his written Word. God gives us his word in Scripture because he loves us, and he wants us to *know* that he does. We should always remember that the Bible is God's gracious gift of love to us.

God continues to empower his word

That's not the end of it. Human words in and of themselves don't have the capacity to reveal to us the truth and reality of God. Human words are just that, human. They derive primarily from our human experiences. But God is not a creature and can't be simply grasped in creaturely terms, concepts and ideas. Words, when referring to God, don't mean exactly the same thing as when they refer to creation. So we can say we "love," and we can say God "loves." But God's love far exceeds our love. We use the same word, but we don't mean the same thing when we use it of God compared to when we use it of ourselves. Yet our love can be a dim mirror image of God's love. So God has to sanctify, make holy and adequate, our mere human words so we can use them to accurately and faithfully refer to the God of the Bible and not lead us into misunderstandings of God and his ways.

The God of the Bible is active and continually gracious to us by superintending our reading and interpretation of Scripture, helping us to see how they uniquely make God and his ways known to us. He has not become mute since the Bible came into existence. God continues to speak in and through his written Word, enabling it to refer to him and not just to creaturely ideas or realities. The God of the Bible continues to speak his word to us through this gift of written revelation.

If God ceased to be personally involved and stopped empowering the written word to accomplish the miraculous feat of enabling us to know him, then God would not be truly known. We would simply have human and creaturely ideas about God and nothing more. The result would likely be not much better than the ancient Greek and Roman mythological gods.

Inspired by the Spirit

If we ask, "How has God spoken and made himself known to us?" it turns out that this work involves the whole of God, that is, the Father, Son and Holy Spirit. The word "inspired" means "God breathed." The Holy Spirit is identified as the wind or breath of God. By the Spirit of God, certain people down through the ages were called, appointed and specially enabled to speak authoritatively for God. They were "inbreathed" by the Spirit. *How* exactly the Spirit works we do not and cannot know. But we have been told that the Spirit can and has empowered first the prophets of the Old Testament and then the apostles of the New Testament.

The Spirit seems to take into account everything about a particular prophetic or apostolic author and graciously makes use of them. The Spirit incorporates their language, culture and social-political background as well as their own relationship with God into his communicative purposes. The Spirit uses the human elements of the selected prophets and apostles. But the Spirit uses these elements in a way that enables them to refer far beyond creaturely realities. The Spirit takes charge of them in a way that gives those words a capacity to communicate that they could never have on their own.

So by the Spirit, Scripture as a whole serves as a written form of communication that God can continually use to make himself and his ways known to his people down through the ages. If the Spirit was not at work with these individuals, we would not have any authoritative and trustworthy access to God's word. So we can thank God for choosing certain individuals down through the ages and, by his Spirit, inspiring them to speak faithfully for him.

Providential preservation

We have these written words because they have

been preserved for us down through the ages. This too must be regarded as the gracious work and gift of God. Because of his great love for us, the God of the Bible not only kicked things off by selecting and inspiring certain individuals, but also by overseeing them being handed on and finally collected together. We call this form of God's grace his providence.

Apparently an aspect of God's providential oversight also included some inspired editing of preexisting material. God providentially maintained contact with his written word and with the process by which it was canonized (brought together in an authoritative collection). If the God of the Bible wanted us to have a written witness to his Word, then we shouldn't be surprised that God would also have to anticipate and secure its preservation down through the ages (you do, after all, have to be pretty smart to be God!).

God's self-revelation

The gracious gift of revelation as it traces through history does reach a crucial high-point. All the prophetic words prepare for and look forward to the self-revelation of God in Jesus Christ, the Incarnate Son of God. All the apostolic writings look back to the time and place where God himself, as himself, reveals and interprets himself in and through Jesus Christ.

In Jesus, we don't have simply another inspired word about God, but the Living Word of God himself, in person—in time and space and in flesh and blood. So Jesus tells us that he is, himself, the Way, the Truth and the Life. He does not show us a way or tell us about the truth or give us things that lead to life. He himself is these things. Thus God's gracious revelatory work reaches a qualitatively different level with the birth of the Word of God in human form. As it turns out, the written word of God's Spirit-inspired prophets and apostles points to the fulfillment of their own word with the coming of the Living Word.

John the Baptist, as the last of the prophets and representative of them all, serves as an authoritative witness when he points to Jesus as being the Light, the Lamb of God who takes away the sins of the world, the Messiah and the Son of God (John 1:8; 29-34). John proclaimed that Jesus came before him and is the one who baptizes with the Spirit. Therefore John said he must decrease and Jesus increase, for Jesus is the center of the center of God's revelatory work and thus stands at the center of Holy Scripture.

Faithful and infallible

The written word derives its authority and faithfulness from the Father, through the Son and in the Spirit. Because God is the living and speaking God, we have a written word that puts us in touch with the Living Word of God, all by the Spirit. The Bible's authority is established and maintained by a living and real connection of God to the Bible. Scripture can serve as it does because it remains connected to the infallible God. The Bible's authority and faithfulness is not in itself, apart from God, but in its actual, continuing connection with the Father, Son/Word and Spirit. So when we read or listen to the Bible, we can expect to hear the living, triune God speak to us once again.

Part 2A

In the first part of this article, we considered how Scripture is a gift of the living and speaking God. But this gift is not one that becomes separated from the giver. By the Spirit, God spoke through the prophets and then the apostles. But God continues to speak by the same Spirit through those God-breathed written words. If God fell mute, and ceased to actively communicate to us in and through those written words, we would not have a true and authoritative word from God by which he makes himself known. But the living and speaking God of the Bible does not remain at a deistic distance, winding up his Bible and then sending it out to mechanistically convey information about God. The very nature of God is to communicate himself, making himself known, so that we might communicate with him as his children and therefore share in holy loving communion.

One further point, made in part one, confirms this. God's personal act of communication is in and through his Son, the Living Word. The whole of the written words of the prophets and apostles direct our attention to the Living Word, Jesus, the incarnate Son of God. This Jesus is God's own self-communication, his own self-revelation to us. Jesus does not give us words from God — he is himself God's Word to us. He expresses the character of God as a speaking and communicating God. To hear Jesus is to hear God himself speaking to us, directly, in person, face-to-face.

Jesus is at the center of the written word, Scripture. But he is behind all the words, the whole of the Bible, as its source, as the speech of God to us. He is the original Word and the final Word of God, the Alpha and Omega. By the incarnation of the Word of God, the author of the written word of God has come into the play — he has shown up in the person of Jesus. Jesus, as the author, indicates that he is at the center and behind it all. So when the Pharisees attempt to use Scripture (and their interpretation of it against Jesus), he confronts them and says: "You search the scriptures because you think that in them you have eternal life and it is they that testify on my behalf. Yet you refuse to come to me to have life" (John 5:39-40, NRSV throughout). Jesus has to tell them that he is the author [Lord] of the Sabbath (Luke 6:5) and that they are in no place to judge him by their pre-understanding of the Sabbath. When the author of Scripture shows up, we have to stop interpreting Jesus in terms of our pre-understandings of Scripture and interpret the written words in terms of Jesus, the Living Word.

Through his interaction with the men on the road to Emmaus after his resurrection, Jesus instructs us how to approach the written word of God. To help these disciples understand who he was and what he had gone through, this is what he did: "Beginning with Moses and all the prophets, he interpreted to them the things about himself in all the scriptures" (Luke 24:27). Later he explained to them:

> "These are my words that I spoke to you while I was still with you—that everything written about me in the law of Moses, the prophets, and the psalms must be fulfilled." Then he opened their minds to understand the scriptures. (verses 44-45)

Scripture – God's Gift
continued

The written word of God is to be interpreted in the light of the Living Word, because the purpose of the written word is to direct us to the Living Word so that we might know who God is and what he has done for us. When we approach Scripture with Jesus himself as the interpretive key to it all, then we hear the word of God as it was meant to be heard.

Thomas F. Torrance used to explain it this way: It's like reading a murder mystery for the second time. The first time, we're looking for clues as to "who-done-it." But not everything is clear. Some things make sense; others don't. Some things seem significant; others seem trivial. But in a well-crafted murder mystery there will be plenty of clues—so many clues that when it finally is revealed who committed the crime, we are somewhat surprised but also satisfied that it makes sense. We say, "Yes there were clues all along. We just didn't know which ones to pay attention to and didn't see how they 'added up.'"

What would happen if we read the mystery a second time? Now knowing "who-done-it," those early clues would not be irrelevant. Rather, we would see how significant they were. We would be able to sort out the irrelevant clues from the meaningful ones. Those clues would stand out as even more extraordinary. "No wonder suspect A said X. No wonder suspect B did Y." We would see what they mean, how they point to who committed the crime. We would end up valuing those clues as foreshadowings even more than on the first reading.

That's what it's like when properly reading the Bible. Knowing that it all leads to what God has done in Jesus Christ, we don't set that recognition aside. Rather, we interpret the whole of the written word in terms of its center, the Living Word of God. In that way, the whole of Scripture is properly interpreted; the gift of God is properly received.

Another way to say this is that the Bible itself tells us whose Scripture this is. We know who the author is. We know where the Bible came from. It is not anonymous. So here's another analogy: reading the Bible is like reading a letter from someone you know and who knows you, not like getting junk mail from someone you don't know and who doesn't know or care about you. Reading these two types of mail are different experiences, aren't they? Sometimes when I've gotten letters (or emails) from those I know well, as I read what they wrote, I can almost hear their voices. I know how they'd say it. It sounds "just like them." Reading the Bible should be like that. The more we get to know the heart, mind, purpose and attitudes of Jesus, the more we'll hear his voice throughout all of Scripture and see how it points to the Son, and to his mission as the self-revelation of the Father and the Spirit.

When reading and trying to understand Scripture out of the center of knowing whose scripture it is, another aspect of a proper approach becomes apparent. The primary purpose of all Scripture is to reveal to us who this God is. Central to the message of all the biblical writers is to convey to us the nature, character, purpose and attitudes of our Creator and Redeemer God. They want us above all to know not just that some kind of god exists, but which God in particular and what this God is like. They want their hearers to know who God is because the God they know wants to be known and is working through them to accomplish that.

But the revelation that God is accomplishing is not just aimed at abstract, impersonal information. It is knowledge that reveals a God who has created us for relationship, communication and holy love. Knowing this God involves interaction of faith, trust, praise, adoration, worship and therefore fellowship and communion, which includes our following in his ways – our obedience. This interaction is not just a "knowing about" but a knowing in a sense similar to how we hear of Adam "knowing" Eve and conceiving a child. By God's acts of revelation, we come to know deeply who this God is. Love for this God, the worship of this God, trust or faith in this God are our responses to who this God is. True knowledge of God that is accurate and faithful leads to true worship and living trust in God.

Throughout the Old Testament, the most often and widely repeated description of God's nature and character is his "steadfast love." In the Psalms, the Lord's steadfast love is noted nearly 120 times. Psalm 136 proclaims God's steadfast love in the refrain of all its 26 verses. An expanded but slightly more comprehensive description found across the Old Testament echoes what the Lord revealed of himself to Moses: "The LORD, the LORD, a God merciful and gracious, slow to anger, and abounding in steadfast love and faithfulness." The Old Testament prophets constantly held out to their hearers the nature and character of God, the only one worthy of their faithfulness and worship. However, the fullness of what God's steadfast love means does not come into full view until we see it embodied and lived out in the incarnation, life, death, resurrection and ascension of Jesus with his promise to return.

Jesus made inquiring about and knowing who he was of paramount importance. His teachings and actions are designed to raise the question: "Who then is this?" His parables prompted his hearers to inquire more deeply. Jesus confronts his own disciples with this question at two levels: "Who do people say that I am?" and then more pointedly, "Who do you say that I am?" (Mark 8:27, 29). Jesus makes the question of *Who* central. We must do the same if we are to hear the Word of God (Living and written) as it was meant to be heard.

What is disclosed in Jesus and preserved for us in the responses of the apostles and their writings is that God is not just graciously loving towards us, but is Father, Son and Holy Spirit who have their being in triune holy loving from all eternity, before there ever was a creation. Jesus is who he is in his eternal relationship of holy love to the Father and eternal Spirit. That is the deepest level of God's self-revelation, where we discover who God is in God's inner and eternal triune life.

So we should approach our Bible study with our primary goal being listening, and learning from Scripture who our triune God is, as revealed to us in Jesus Christ. We can then rightly interpret Scripture out of that center. This approach means that other questions we might like to ask first, or about which we might be anxious, will be secondary. Scripture, with Jesus at the center, not only provides us with certain answers, it tells us what the right questions are! So the questions of *What?*, *Where?*, *When?*, *Why?* or *How?* must be made relative to the question of *Who?*, for it is the key to all these other questions.

We now have laid out the basic orientation for our understanding of Scripture and how best to approach it. We will consider some further implications for listening to the Word of God in the next part.

Part 3

Guidelines for approaching Scripture reverently with prayer by faith

Scripture is the gift of God, where God has graciously promised to speak to us through his living Word. What, then, are some guidelines for approaching it? The first thing needing to be said is that we must approach it reverently with a desire to be addressed, to hear a word from God. This attitude is probably best demonstrated when we start with prayer to the God of the Bible. In prayer we acknowledge that we look for and anticipate receiving a word from God himself, that is, hearing from the Living Word through the written word by the Spirit. It shows we are ready to listen, to hear. We express in prayer that we want to hear what the Lord has to say to us. We listen as his children, as his sheep, not as one of his advisers, or as an engineer might seek impersonal information about some object or law of physics perhaps to use for some other purpose.

In prayer, we also acknowledge that we depend on the Lord and his grace to speak in a way that we can receive. We listen by faith, as we trust that the Lord does speak and knows how to get through to us. Listening to Scripture as God's holy word is an act of faith in the God whose word it is. We read or listen to Scripture by faith in the grace of God, just as we do in all our responses to God. We listen and study Scripture by faith.

This means that we do not put our trust in our techniques for studying the Bible no matter how simple or how sophisticated they are. We aren't just mining for data, for information, for formulas or principles or for truths that we can possess or use for our own ends or purposes. In prayer we place ourselves before the living Lord trusting that he will make himself known to us and enable us to hear and follow him wherever he takes us. Faithful prayer to the Living God of the Bible is essential for our preparation for listening to Scripture.

God's agenda, not ours

Second, listening to Scripture as God speaking to us means letting it set the agenda for us, according to the nature and purposes God has for giving us the gift of his word. This means that we'll come to Scripture not to give us exactly what we're looking for, such as answers to our current or even pressing questions, but to show us what the right questions are and what issues have priority in God's view. We will not force Scripture to answer questions that it is not designed to answer nor give priority to some concern or issue we have that does not match with the priorities and central matters of Scripture itself. We'll be open to having our mind reshaped to reflect the mind of Christ and what he views as of first-order importance.

The primacy of the WHO? question

What is the central thrust of biblical revelation? It is to make known the identity, character, heart, purpose and nature of God. Scripture is primarily designed to answer the question, "Who is God?" So our primary question in reading and listening to Scripture ought to be, "Who are you, Lord?" That's the first and most important question that ought to be on our hearts and minds as we study Scripture. No matter what passage we're dealing with, our primary concern ought to be: "What is God telling me about himself in this passage?"

We'll need to put in second place our questions of *What*? *How*? *Why*? *When*? And *Where*? Those questions can be rightly answered only by putting the *Who*? question first. In many church settings, the most difficult question needing to be put on the back burner is this: "What am I supposed to be doing for God?" We are so anxious to discover what God wants us to do for him that we often overlook the most foundational aspect of Scripture, which involves revealing, clarifying and reminding us of God's nature, character, heart, purpose and aim. It's far more important to know *who* it is we're obeying, than to attempt to do the right thing. We can't accurately discern *what* God wants us to do, and in what way to do it, unless we act out of knowing and trusting in this God according to *who* he is. Only then will our attitude and motives and the character of our actions match or bear witness to God's own character. Only then will we find that his commandments are not burdensome and that his yoke is easy and his burden is light. So we need to read the Bible and listen to preaching in order to see more deeply into who God is.

The greatest and most damaging deception we can fall into is being misled about the nature and character of God. Being misled or deceived about who God is undermines our faith, which is in turn the foundation of our whole response to God. With our faith or trust in God undermined or twisted, all the rest will collapse: our worship, our prayer, our listening to Scripture, our obedience, our hope and our love for God and for neighbor. Our faith is a response to who we perceive God to really be. When that is properly aligned, then the Christian life is enlivened and energized even under difficult situations. When it is distorted, we then attempt to run the Christian life with ropes tangled around our feet. So being reminded daily of the truth of who God is must be our top priority—matching the priority of the structure and aim of both the written and the Living Word of God.

Jesus Christ, Center of the center

As we do so, we'll have as the center and norm of our knowledge and trust in God all of what Scripture says about Jesus Christ. Oriented to this living Center of the center, we'll want to see how the Old Testament points and prepares us to recognize him. Jesus Christ is God's answer to the *Who* question—in person, in time and space, in flesh and blood—that ancient Israel sought to know. In Jesus Christ, "What you see is what you get." In him the whole God is personally present, active and speaking. Jesus is the interpretive key to all of Scripture, for in him we see and hear the heartbeat of God. We watch and hear the motions of his heart and mind, even his Spirit, the Holy Spirit. The light we find shining forth from the face of Jesus sheds light on all of Scripture, for in him the God of the Bible has revealed himself.

So we ought to read and interpret Scripture in a way that through it all, in one way or another, we come to see how it points towards and finds its fulfillment in Jesus Christ. As noted earlier, we can think of this as a process like reading a murder mystery novel for the second time. The first time through, at the end, we finally come to discover "who done it." The second time through is a much different experience. We can see in a new light how all the clues early on in the mystery pointed to "who done it." We appreciate the clues (and recognize the false leads) even more the second time through. But the clues are not the solution. Their value is how they indicate or are signs pointing to the resolution of the mystery.

This means that central to our study and understanding of the whole Bible should be the person and acts of Jesus. This calls for giving a certain priority to and focus on the Gospels. This does not mean narrowing our attention simply to the words or teaching of Jesus, as some "red letter" Bibles might tempt us to do. Rather, this means placing at center stage all of what the Gospels tell us about who Jesus is. This will include his own words, actions and self-interpretations (think, for example, of all the "I am" statements in John), but also make use of those texts that answer most directly who Jesus is, not only in the Gospels but also throughout the rest of the New Testament.

Who Jesus is in relationship to the Father and the Holy Spirit

As we prayerfully begin to listen to Scripture, concentrating on the *Who* question as answered by God himself in Jesus, we'll find that the primary way Jesus is identified involves his relationship to God the Father and God the Holy Spirit. The answer to the *Who?* question is intrinsically bound up with grasping the nature, character, purpose and aim of Jesus *in relationship* with the Father and Spirit, because Jesus primarily and consistently identifies himself by means of those relationships. He is the one sent from the Father, the one who has been eternally with and eternally loved by the Father. He is the One who has the Spirit and who has come to give us his Holy Spirit.

The highest concentration on the importance of Jesus' relationships with the Father and Spirit comes in the Gospel of John, reaching the apex in John 17. To know Jesus is to know the Father. To know the Father means recognizing who Jesus is. Interacting with Jesus means dealing directly and personally with the Father and the Spirit.

In our Bible study and preaching we must pay attention to the quality and nature of Jesus' relationship and interactions with the Father and Spirit. For he is, in his being, the Son of the Father, one with his Spirit. Pay special attention to anywhere in Scripture where we're given insight into the relationships of the Father, Son and Spirit, for in those relationships we will see and hear most directly, personally and concretely who the God of the Bible is. In returning to that living Center of the center again and again, we'll find our faith nourished and growing with a life of joyful obedience flowing out of it.

With the Center of our prayer, faith, devotion and worship set, as a kind of North Star, everything else regarding listening to and studying the Lord's Scripture gets properly oriented.

Scripture: God's Gift
Part 4

Rules for interpreting Scripture

As I said at the end of part three, "With the Center of our prayer, faith, devotion and worship set, as a kind of North Star, everything else regarding listening to and studying the Lord's Scripture then gets properly oriented." So now, let's explore some of those more general implications that can be expressed as certain kinds of rules, which keep us navigating in alignment with our North Star.

Interpret parts in light of the whole

Jesus is identified in Scripture as the First One and as the Last One. He is also identified as the living Word of God or the *Logos* of God. We could say that Jesus is and speaks both the first word to creation and is and has the last word about creation. Everything was set in motion by him, and the ultimate destiny of everything is established in relationship to him, its rightful inheritor.

Recognizing this about Jesus, our risen and ascended Lord, has implications for our hearing and studying of Scripture. It has been put this way: always interpret the various parts of Scripture (verses, paragraphs, chapters, books, etc.) in terms of the whole of Scripture. No part of Scripture ought to be understood simply on its own, but only in the context of the whole. Some have said that every part of Scripture ought to be interpreted in terms of the fullness of its meaning (its *sensus plenior*).

You may have heard the good advice to not take verses "out of context." The context includes not only the verses immediately surrounding a certain text, but the chapter, the whole book in which it appears and, in the end, the whole of Scripture. Many false teachings down through the ages and even in our contemporary situation come from taking a passage out of context and then concluding what it means on its own. We can then easily substitute our own context for the actual context provided for us by the whole of Scripture. Our context then becomes the interpretive North Star.

There is no substitute for taking a lifetime to study the whole of Scripture, that is, considering "the whole counsel of God." The whole turns out to be not just all the books and verses of the Bible. The whole includes Who is before, behind, surrounding and standing at the end of Scripture. This whole is what the Bible says about who God is. As the *Logos* of all things, including Scripture, Jesus Christ contains it all. So the whole involves all of what we learn through the whole history of revelation preserved in Scripture. Every part must be grasped in a way that it contributes to the whole (of who God is in Christ) and how the whole includes the parts. That "rule" will help us properly hear and interpret the meaning of Scripture as we listen to its various parts, for it all comes from one and the same whole God, Father, Son and Holy Spirit. It ought to all sound like it belongs to one and the same God personally known in Jesus Christ.

Interpret the unclear in light of the clear

Another "rule" that will help us stay oriented to the North Star is to "interpret unclear passages in terms of the clear." Much false teaching has derived from a fascination with the unclear, the obscure, or the opaque passages of Scripture. Teachers can take advantage of those cases because, given the ambiguity of their meaning, lots of meanings can be made to seem plausible.

They're not clear enough on their own to rule out a range of speculative understandings. So someone who can give a logical argument can often be persuasive, often reading in their own meaning. The rule to make use of clear passages to sort through the various options for interpreting the meaning of difficult parts guards against this danger. We especially should not let the unclear passages, and some particular understanding of them, be used to reinterpret the clearer passages!

We can take this rule a step farther. Who or what is the clearest expression of the heart, mind, will and character of God? Jesus Christ. He is the Light of all light. All Scripture, in the end, should be understood in his clear Light. He alone shows us the face of God in person. Let's look at an example. The Pharisees of New Testament times had an understanding of God's Law, the Torah. When Jesus came along, they accused him of violating what they considered the highest priority of that Law, the Sabbath. They had worked out logically what must be implied in keeping the Sabbath. They interpreted Jesus and his actions in terms of their pre-understanding of the Law of God.

How did Jesus respond to their accusations? Did he say, "I came to give you another interpretation of how the Law should be applied"? No, he said, "The Son of Man is Lord of the Sabbath" (Matthew 12:8). The Pharisees gave priority to their understanding of the Law, and interpreted Jesus in terms of it. But Jesus countered by telling them who he was in relationship to the Law and said, "I created the Law, I gave it its meaning, I know how it is to be honored and when it is being violated. Interpret the Law in terms of me, its Lord, not me in terms of the Law. It is my servant. I am not its servant, to be judged by it."

So Jesus puts the Pharisees at a crisis point. Will they recognize Jesus as the Living Lord, the Lord of the Law, or will they continue to use the Law as "lord" to interpret and judge Jesus? What or who is the whole, and what or who is the part? What or who is the clear, and what is relatively obscure? We may not regard the Law as the Pharisees did, but we may have other truths or attitudes or viewpoints that we assume and use to interpret or understand Jesus and who God is. Recognizing Jesus as the Center of the center will challenge us to view everything in terms of his interpretation of things, in his light.

We can sum up: we interpret the parts in terms of the whole and the unclear in terms of the clear, and all in terms of Jesus Christ!

Interpret the Old Testament in light of the New

Another implication is to interpret the Old Testament in terms of the New Testament. This is a good "rule" we can follow and further expand. Jesus is the fulfillment of the revelation and provision of God. He is the self-revelation and the self-giving of God for us and for our salvation. He fulfills all the promises of God set up and signaled in the Old Testament. The promises are to be understood in terms of the fulfillment, not the other way around.

But the Old Testament is about more than the promises themselves. It involves an ongoing relationship and interaction of God with Israel over roughly a thousand years, including interaction with numerous prophets at various points in the history of that relationship. God was taking Israel somewhere and Israel knew it. God had not given them the final word. They looked forward to having his Spirit poured out on all flesh (Joel 2:28) being given to reignite life in the dry bones (Ezekiel 37:5) and having new hearts (Ezekiel 11:19; 36:26). They looked forward to the time of God's peace or shalom, when they wouldn't have to prepare for war anymore and not have blood on their hands (Isaiah 2:4; Joel 3:10; Micah 4:3). They anticipated the completion of the sacrificial worship where they could be in the presence of the living God and then truly live! The Old Testament revelation included the proclamation that there was much more to come, that God was not finished making himself known and providing everything for them. Even at the conclusion of the last words of the prophets, they knew they were not at the end of the story. The climax had not yet been reached.

God's revelation involves a history of interacting with Israel and speaking through selected prophets. This fact means that we should interpret any passage in terms of where it comes in the story as it leads up to or down from God's self-revelation and self-giving in Jesus Christ. This rule of interpretation is especially important for ethical or liturgical directives given to ancient Israel. What God commands of Israel in a particular instance is not God's final or eternal word.

For instance, while the "eye for an eye and tooth for a tooth" saying was far more compassionate than the code of revenge practiced by the surrounding ancient near eastern cultures of the time, it was not God's final word to his people. Rather, the final word is embodied in Christ, who loved his enemies to the end and directed us to do the same. Interpretation should therefore take into account where in the story we find the actions, attitude or instructions given. God fills out and clarifies his revelation through a history of interaction with his people, so not every word in the Bible is God's last word on the subject. Providentially, there are many places in the New Testament where significant change or discontinuity is spelled out, such as keeping of the Sabbath.

This does not mean that everything in the Old Testament will necessarily be radically re-interpreted later on. Some insight or instruction may remain largely unchanged, such as principles we identify as broad moral instructions that are linked to our human nature and take into consideration our fallen condition. About rather permanent and universal features of humanity such as marriage, sexual morality and the relations of parents and children that abide throughout history and across differing cultural contexts, we would expect significant continuity of teaching. The New Testament often does spell out particular continuities and redemptive development of expression.

Even if there are some practical or particular differences, at the level of fundamental principles that reflect God's character, we should expect to see some continuity between earlier and later application of that same principle in the New Testament. There seems to be a redemptive development in the way God's more general purposes are to be applied in the life of the church after the fulfillment of God's will is accomplished in Christ as compared to before this fulfillment. An example would be that although Israel is directed at times to go to war, the Israelites were instructed not to be vengeful and to look forward to a time when their swords would be beaten into plowshares. The Christian church is called to continue along that trajectory to finally be peacemakers and to not regard any human being as their ultimate enemy, but rather forgive and seek reconciliation and restoration.

The issue of slavery seems to fall along the same lines. What was allowed to Israel is no longer to characterize the Christian church. So Paul directed Philemon to emancipate his slave Onesimus (Philemon 16-17). Slavery is a practice that was "passing away." Such instructions given to Israel cannot be directly picked up by the church now without regard for our occupying a different place in the story than did ancient Israel. The God of the Bible is a God of life, not death; a God of freedom, not slavery; a God of love, reconciliation and redemption and not enmity and revenge. While we can find signs of these characteristics in the Old Testament, at times some ambiguity appears along the way in God's history of interaction with Israel. However, we now live to bear witness to the clear and complete fulfillment of God's Word in Christ, not to its foreshadowing and preparation. In this way, we interpret the Old Testament in terms of the New.

There we have several guidelines for properly interpreting Scripture with Jesus Christ the Living Word at the center of the Written Word. In the next two parts of this article (which will appear in the third volume of this collection) we'll continue to offer more guidelines to help us stay oriented to our North Star.

Gary Deddo

Preaching in the Book of Acts: Paul's Sermons

In Acts 11, Luke tells us about some developments in Antioch in Syria. Greek-speaking Jews had been telling Gentiles "the good news about the Lord Jesus." Many Gentiles believed and repented (11:20-21). This was "evidence of the grace of God" (11:23). Through the work of Barnabas and Saul, many people "were brought to the Lord" (11:24). These phrases are descriptive of what the gospel of Jesus Christ does. The believers in Antioch talked about the Messiah *Christos* so much that they became known as the *Christianoi* (11:26).

Paul's first major speech

In Acts 10, the apostle to the Jews (Peter) spoke to Gentiles. We now look at how the apostle to the Gentiles (Paul) spoke to Jews. This illustrates continuity. The message is the same throughout the apostolic history.

Barnabas and Saul were sent on a gospel-preaching journey, and Paul gave a sermon in a synagogue in Antioch in Pisidia. After a brief historical introduction, Paul gets to his point: "God has brought to Israel the Savior Jesus, as he promised" (13:23). Jesus is the fulfillment of the Old Testament promise. (Luke never uses *promise* in the plural. Christ fulfills *the* promise of the Old Testament.)

John the Baptist preached repentance and baptism, but Christ is greater: He brought a message of salvation to both Jews and Gentiles (13:24-26). Paul gives the kerygma message in his own words: In fulfillment of Scripture, Jesus was executed and buried, but God raised him from the dead, and he was seen by many witnesses (13:27-31). This fulfills God's promise (13:32-33).

Paul explains Christ's resurrection further (13:33-37). Because Jesus has been raised, forgiveness is available through him. "Through him everyone who believes is justified from everything you could not be justified from by the law of Moses" (13:39). We cannot be justified by the law of Moses — justification comes only through Christ. (The "law of Moses" will be dealt with again in Acts 15.)

Paul warned the Jews that rejecting the word of God is equivalent to rejecting eternal life (13:46); the implication is that the message Paul preached is about eternal life. The Lord commanded him to bring salvation to the ends of the earth (13:47). Although different words are used, Paul's commission to preach salvation and eternal life is the same as being a witness of Jesus to the ends of the earth (1:8) and the same as preaching the gospel in all the world (Matthew 28:19 and Mark 13:10).

Committed to the grace of God

In Iconium, Paul and Barnabas preached the Lord's grace, and the Lord confirmed that message through miracles (14:3). In Lystra, they preached repentance from idolatry (14:15). On the return trip, they exhorted disciples to remain true to "the faith" (14:22; cf. 13:8). Christianity can be characterized by the one word *faith.* They had put their trust in the Lord and were to be faithful to him (14:23).

They returned "to Antioch, where they had been committed to the grace of God for the work they had now completed" (14:26). The entire journey or commission or work was described as a commitment to the *grace* of God. We see that in 15:40, too, which tells us that Paul and Silas were "commended…to the grace of the Lord." The ministry Paul received from the Lord Jesus was to testify "to the gospel of God's grace" (20:24). Paul committed the Ephesian elders "to God and to the word of his grace" (20:32). That is the message Christ's ministers preach: Faith, repentance, grace, forgiveness, salvation, eternal life through the resurrected Jesus Christ.

Paul's first evangelistic trip demonstrated that God "had opened the door of faith to the Gentiles" (14:27). But not everyone could believe this good news. Some Jews insisted that the Gentile believers ought to become proselytes by being circumcised and accepting the law of Moses (15:1, 5). At the Jerusalem conference, Peter explained that the Gentiles had been given the Holy Spirit upon faith (15:7-8). God accepts people on the basis of faith whether or not they have been circumcised. Gentiles do not need to keep the law of Moses. There is no need to make it difficult for anyone to turn to God (15:19).

God cleansed Gentile hearts (that is, he justified them) by faith (15:9). They are right with God on the basis of faith.[1] Not only are Gentiles saved by "the grace of our Lord Jesus," Jews are, too (15:11). No one can be justified by the law of Moses. The gospel of grace is for everyone.

Paul's next journey

As Paul traveled, he reported the decision of the Jerusalem council, and the churches were strengthened in the faith (16:4-5). Paul went to Philippi and spoke to Lydia. "The Lord opened her heart to respond to Paul's message" (16:14). She believed, and she responded appropriately with baptism and hospitality (16:15). Paul and his group told the people "the way to be saved" (16:17). They told the jailer, "Believe in the Lord Jesus, and you will be saved" (16:31). Paul was preaching a gospel of salvation through faith in Jesus Christ. The jailer believed, and he responded appropriately with baptism and hospitality (16:33-34).

In a Thessalonian synagogue, Paul preached about the messianic promise of the Old Testament and proved that the Messiah "had to suffer and rise from the dead." He proclaimed that Jesus is the Messiah (17:2-3). Hostile Jews accused him of preaching Jesus as a king, and Paul went to Berea, where he was received more favorably. They examined the Old Testament prophecies, and many believed (17:11-12).

Luke is emphasizing that Christianity is rooted in the Old Testament. This is something his Gentile readers would need to know. It is also something Roman officials would need to know when they were asked to judge whether it was legal to preach the gospel. Judaism was legal. Luke records the judgment of Gallio, a Roman proconsul, that Christianity was a branch within Judaism and therefore outside the jurisdiction of Roman courts (18:14-15).

In Athens, Paul preached "the good news about Jesus and the resurrection" (17:18). He preached that we are God's children, that he is patient, that he commands everyone to repent (17:29-30). God "has set a day when he will judge the world with justice by the man he has appointed. He has given proof of this to everyone by raising him from the dead" (17:31). Every human being will be resurrected (and thus have opportunity for eternal life). The proof of this is in the fact that Jesus has been raised from the dead. His eternal life is the key to our eternal lives. Some of the Athenians believed (17:34).

---

[1] Technically, they are right with God on the basis of what Christ has done – that is the objective basis. Their faith is the subjective response to Christ's work, in which a person accepts what Christ has done. Reconciliation is achieved from God's perspective (the objective) by the work of Christ; reconciliation is effected in our lives (the subjective side) by our response of faith and acceptance (2 Corinthians 5:18-20).

Although Christ has paid the penalty of all sin, including the sin of unbelief, and God does not count our sins against us (verse 19), we are not liberated from the sin of unbelief until we actually believe. God has flung the prison doors open, and dismantled the prison walls, but as long as we *think* we are in prison, we still need to be freed.

In Corinth, Paul testified to Jews that Jesus is the Messiah (18:5). Many responded with faith and baptism (18:8). Apollos "had been instructed in the way of the Lord, and he…taught about Jesus accurately" (18:25). But he needed further instruction, presumably in association with Christian baptism. Priscilla and Aquila "explained to him the way of God more adequately" (18:26). What is the "way of God"? Is it a life-style, a behavior? Apollos, a disciple of John the Baptist, would already have had an impeccable life-style. What he needed more adequately was instruction about salvation through Christ. He is the way of God, the way of salvation. Apollos moved to Corinth and helped "those who by grace had believed" (18:27). He not only preached about Jesus accurately, he proved, from the Scriptures, that Jesus is the Christ (18:28).

Meanwhile, Paul was in Ephesus, where he informed more people about Jesus. They were rebaptized and given the Holy Spirit (19:4-6). In the synagogue, Paul argued persuasively about the kingdom of God and preached publicly for two years (19:8-10). Miracles were done, "and the name of the Lord Jesus was held in high honor" (18:17). Many repented of their sorcery, and Paul persuaded many that idols were not gods (18:19, 26). A riot ensued, and Paul moved on.

On his way back to Jerusalem, Paul sailed to Miletus and called for the Ephesian elders (20:17). He gave them a heart-to-heart speech summarizing his work: "I have declared to both Jews and Greeks that they must turn to God in repentance and have faith in our Lord Jesus" (20:21). He had been given the job of preaching the good news about God's grace, and that is what he called preaching the kingdom (20:24-25). The message about the kingdom is actually a message about grace, because it is only by grace that we can be in the kingdom.

We should not be misled by the way the word *kingdom* is used in modern cultures. Rather, we need to see it in its biblical context. The book of Acts shows that "preaching the kingdom" is done by preaching about the Messiah-King and about how humans become part of the kingdom through faith in the King. It is *not* about the details of what Christ will do after he returns. The New Testament does not give such details, and Paul argued for three months with people who knew the Old Testament prophecies. He was not preaching the Old Testament, but something new.

Paul noted that God's grace could build them up and give them "an inheritance among all those who are sanctified" (20:32). He reminded the elders that by "hard work we must help the weak" (20:35). After this farewell, Paul sailed toward Jerusalem knowing that he had many enemies there. From personal experience, he knew their zeal and their willingness to kill. But he told the members in Caesarea that he was ready to die "for the name of the Lord Jesus" (21:13).

Paul a witness to the resurrection

Paul was eventually given Roman protection from his persecutors, and he had several opportunities to explain his message. He had seen and heard the Righteous One, the Messiah, and he had been appointed a witness of what he had seen and heard (22:15). Earlier, Paul had said that others were witnesses of Jesus (13:31); here he says that he is also a witness. In the bright light on the road to Damascus, he had seen and heard the risen Jesus. He believed and was baptized, calling on the name of the Lord (22:16). He gave testimony about him instead of persecuting those who believed in him (22:18-19).

Before the Sanhedrin, Paul summarized his conflict with the Jewish leaders: his "hope in the resurrection of the dead" (23:6). That is a crucial element of the gospel. There will be a resurrection, and the resurrected Jesus is the way in which people can be given eternal life in that resurrection.

The Lord appeared to Paul again, promising that he would not die in Jerusalem but would testify about Jesus in Rome, too (23:11).

Paul told Felix that he had a hope that there would be a resurrection of the dead (24:15). That was the central reason he was on trial (24:21). Felix heard Paul speak not only about faith in Christ

Jesus, but also righteousness, self-control and a future judgment (24:24-25). Here we see that there is an ethical component to the gospel message. Felix, who lacked self-control, did not like the implications of what Paul was preaching about the resurrection of the wicked, and he sent Paul back to jail (24:25).

Two years later, Festus explained to Agrippa that Paul was held in custody because of a religious dispute "and about a dead man named Jesus who Paul claimed was alive" (25:19). The dispute centered on whether Jesus had been resurrected. As Paul told Agrippa, "It is because of my hope in what God has promised our fathers that I am on trial today" (26:6). That promise, that hope, is the resurrection of the dead (26:7-8).

Paul recounted his commission from the Lord, the gospel he had received. Jesus had appointed him to be "a witness of what you have seen of me and what I will show you" (26:16). Paul was sent to the Gentiles "to open their eyes and turn them [i.e., repentance] from darkness to light, and from the power of Satan to God, so that they may receive forgiveness of sins and a place among those who are sanctified by faith in me" (26:18). Paul, always zealous, did as he had been ordered. He preached repentance and good deeds (26:20). He stressed that his message was in complete conformity to the Old Testament, which predicted the suffering and resurrection of the Christ, and the preaching to Gentiles (26:22-23).

To the Jews in Rome, Paul proclaimed that he was chained "because of the hope of Israel" (28:20). The hope of Israel is the resurrection, and Jesus is the first to be resurrected. So Paul, using the Old Testament prophecies, preached for two years about the connection between Jesus and the kingdom of God (28:23, 31). It is a message of salvation given not only to Jews who accept it, but also to Gentiles who listen (28:29).

Resurrection and salvation through the Lord Jesus. That's the gospel according to the book of Acts, both in Peter and in Paul.

Michael Morrison

The Gospel Really Is Good News

When people gather in churches after a disaster, they come to hear words of comfort, encouragement and hope. Yet, try as they might to bring hope to a grieving people, some Christian leaders unwittingly proclaim a message that amounts to despair, hopelessness and fear for people whose loved ones died without having first professed faith in Jesus Christ.

Many Christians are convinced that everyone who did not profess Christ before death, even those who never so much as heard of Christ, are now in hell, being tortured by God—the God the same Christians ironically proclaim as compassionate, merciful, loving and full of grace. "God loves you," some of us Christians seem to be saying, but then comes the fine print: "If you don't say the sinner's prayer before you die, then my merciful Savior will torture you forever."

Good news

The gospel of Jesus Christ is good news. It remains forever, good news, the best news imaginable, for absolutely everybody and everything. It is not merely good news for the few who came to know Christ before they died; it is good news for the whole of creation—even for all who died before they ever heard of Christ.

Jesus Christ is the atoning sacrifice not merely for the sins of Christians but for the sins of the whole world (1 John 2:2). The Creator is also the Redeemer of his creation (Colossians 1:15-20). Whether people know that truth before they die is not the thing that determines whether it is true. It depends entirely on Jesus Christ, not on human action or human response of any kind.

Jesus said, "For God so loved the world that he gave his only Son, so that everyone who believes in him may not perish but may have eternal life" (John 3:16, New Revised Standard Version in this article). It is God who loved the world and God who gave his Son, and he gave him to save what he loved—the world. Whoever believes in the Son whom God sent will enter into eternal life (better translated "the life of the age to come").

The verse does not say that belief has to come prior to death. In fact, it says that believers will not perish, and since even believers die, it is obvious that "perish" and "die" are not the same thing. Belief keeps people from perishing, but it does not keep them from dying. The kind of perishing that Jesus is talking about here, translated from the Greek word *apoletai*, is a spiritual death, not a physical one. It has to do with utter destruction, with being abolished, put an end to, or ruined. Those who believe in Jesus will not come to such a final end, but will, instead, enter into the life *(zoe)* of the age to come *(aeonion)*.

Some enter into the life of the age to come, or kingdom life, while they still live and walk on the earth, but in the grand scheme of things, this happens to only a small percentage of those who make up the "world" (or "*kosmos*") that God loves so much that he sent his Son to save it. What about the rest? This verse does not say that God cannot or won't bring to faith any of those who die physically before believing.

The idea that death is a barrier to God's ability to save, or to his ability to bring a person to faith in Christ, is a human interpretation; the Bible states no such thing. We are told that everyone dies, and then they are judged (Hebrews 9:27). But let us remember that their Judge, thank God, is none other than Jesus, the slaughtered Lamb of God who died for their sins—and that changes everything.

Creator and Redeemer

Where do people get this notion that God is only able to save live people and not dead ones? He conquered death, didn't he? He rose from the dead, didn't he? God doesn't hate the world; he loves it. He didn't create humanity for hell. Christ came to save the world, not to condemn it (John 3:17).

One Christian teacher (and probably many others as well) said that God is perfect in hate as well as perfect in love, which accounts for why there is a hell as well as a heaven. He went on to explain how dualism (the idea that good and evil are equal and opposite forces in the universe) is a false doctrine. But doesn't he realize he posited a dualistic God with his explanation of God holding in tension perfect hate and perfect love?

God is absolutely just, and all sinners are judged and condemned, but the gospel, the good news, lets us in on the mystery that in Christ, God took that very sin and its judgment on himself for our sakes! Hell is real and horrible. But it is precisely that hell, the hideous hell reserved for the ungodly, that Jesus bore in humanity's stead (2 Corinthians 5:21; Matthew 27:46; Galatians 3:13).

All humans are under condemnation because of sin, but the free gift of God is eternal life in Christ (Romans 6:23). That's why it is called grace. In Romans 5:15, Paul puts it like this:

> The free gift is not like the trespass. For if the many died through the one man's trespass [this "many" refers to everybody; there is no one who doesn't bear Adam's guilt], much more surely have the grace of God and the free gift in the grace of the one man, Jesus Christ, abounded for the many [the same "many"—absolutely everybody]. (Romans 5:15)

Paul is saying that as bad as our condemnation for sin is—and it is bad (it deserves hell)—it can't even hold a candle to the grace and the free gift in Christ. God's word of reconciliation in Christ is incredibly louder than his word of condemnation in Adam—the one completely eclipses the other ("much more surely"). That is why Paul can tell us in 2 Corinthians 5:19 that "in Christ God was reconciling the world [that's everybody, the "many" of Romans 5:15] to himself, not counting their trespasses against them…"

So, then, what about the family and friends of those who die without having professed faith in Christ? Does the gospel offer them any hope and encouragement about the fate of their dead loved ones? Indeed, the Gospel of John records Jesus declaring, "When I am lifted up from the earth, I will draw all people to myself" (John 12:32). That's good news, the gospel truth. Jesus didn't lay out a timetable, but he said that he would draw everybody to himself, not just a few who find out who he is before they die, but absolutely everybody.

Then it is no wonder that Paul wrote to the Christians in the city of Colossae that in Jesus Christ, God was pleased, *pleased,* mind you, to "reconcile to himself *all things,* whether on earth or in heaven, by making peace through the blood of his cross" (Colossians 1:20). That's good news. It is, like Jesus said, good news for the whole world, not just for the limited few.

Paul wanted his readers to know that this Jesus, this Son of God raised from the dead, is not just some exciting leader of a new and improved religious concept. Paul is telling them that Jesus is none other than the Creator and Sustainer of all things (verses 16-17), and more than that, he is God's way of fixing everything that has gone wrong with the world from the beginning of history (verse 20)! In Christ, Paul was saying, God has moved once and for all to make good on all his promises that he made to Israel—promises that he would one day act in pure grace to forgive all sins everywhere and make everything new (see Acts 13:32-33; 3:20-21; Isaiah 43:19; Revelation 21:5; Romans 8:19-21).

Only for Christians

"But salvation is only for Christians," some people howl. Yes, of course it is. But who are "the Christians"? Are they only the people who repeat the sinner's prayer? Are they only those who are baptized by immersion? Only those who belong to the "true" church? Only those who are absolved by a duly ordained priest? Only those who have ceased sinning? Only those who come to know Jesus before they die?

Or does Jesus himself, the one into whose nail-pierced hands God has given all judgment, decide who is and is not ultimately to be included among those upon whom he will have mercy? And while he is at it, does he, the one who conquered death and gives eternal life to whomever he wants, decide when he might bring a person to faith, or do we, the all-wise defenders of the true religion, make that determination for him?

Every Christian became a Christian at some point, that is, was brought to faith by the Holy Spirit. But the common assumption seems to suggest, however, that it is impossible for God to bring a person to faith after that person has died. But hold on, Jesus is the one who raises the dead, and he is the one who is the atoning sacrifice, not for our sins only, but for the sins of the whole world (1 John 2:2).

Great chasm

"But the parable of Lazarus," someone will argue. "Abraham says that there is a chasm fixed between his side and the rich man's side" (see Luke 16:19-31).

Jesus did not give this parable as a textbook on the afterlife. After all, how many Christians would want to describe heaven as "Abraham's bosom" with Jesus nowhere in sight? The parable was a message to the members of the first-century Jewish privileged class who rejected their Messiah, not a portrait of the resurrection life. Before we take that further than Christ intended, remember what Paul wrote in Romans 11:32.

In the parable, the rich man was unrepentant. He still saw himself as Lazarus' superior. He still saw Lazarus as existing only to serve his personal needs. Maybe it is not unreasonable to think that the rich man's persistent unbelief is what kept the gulf fixed, not some arbitrary cosmic necessity. Remember, Jesus himself bridges the otherwise impassable chasm from our sinful condition to reconciliation with God. Jesus underscores this point, the point of the parable—that salvation comes only through faith in him—when he says, "If they do not listen to Moses and the prophets, neither will they be convinced even if someone rises from the dead" (Luke 16:31).

God is in the business of saving people, not torturing them. Jesus is Redeemer, and whether we believe it or not, he is awfully good at what he does. He is the Savior of the world (John 3:17), not the Savior of a fraction of the world. "God so loved the world" (verse 16)—not merely 20 percent.

God has ways, and his ways are higher than our ways.

Jesus tells us, "Love your enemies" (Matthew 5:43). Surely we believe he loves his own enemies. (Or do we believe that Jesus hates his enemies while he calls on us to love ours, as if we are supposed to be more righteous than he is, and that his hatred accounts for why there is a hell?) Jesus asks us to love our enemies precisely because *he* loves them. "Father, forgive them, for they don't know what they are doing," Jesus prayed of those who murdered him (Luke 23:34).

Those who continue to refuse Jesus' grace even after they understand it receive the fruit of their own stupidity. There is no place left for people who refuse to enter the Lamb's banquet, except outer darkness (another of the metaphors Jesus used to describe the state of alienation from God; see Matthew 22:13; 25:30).

Mercy to all

Paul makes the amazing assertion in Romans 11:32 that God "has imprisoned all in disobedience so that he may be merciful to all." The Greek words here mean *all*, not some, but *all*. Everyone is disobedient, and in Christ the same everyone is shown mercy—whether they like it or not; whether they take it or not; whether they know it before they die or not.

What can you say to such a marvelous thing, but what Paul says in the next verses:

O, the depth of the riches and wisdom and

knowledge of God! How unsearchable are his judgments and how inscrutable his ways! For who has known the mind of the Lord? Or who has been his counselor? Or who has given a gift to him, to receive a gift in return? For from him and through him and to him are all things. To him be the glory forever. Amen. (verses 33-36)

It seems that his ways are so unfathomable that many of us Christians simply cannot believe that the gospel can be that good. Some of us think we know the mind of God so well that we just *know* that everybody goes straight to hell if they aren't Christians yet when they die. But Paul's point is that the extent of God's mercy is beyond our understanding—a mystery revealed only in Christ: God has done something in Jesus Christ that nobody would ever have guessed in a million years.

In his letter to the Christians at Ephesus, Paul says that this is what God had in mind all along (Ephesians 1:9-10). It was the whole point of God's calling of Abraham, of his choosing of Israel and David, and of the covenants (Ephesians 3:5-6). God is saving even the aliens and strangers (2:12). He is saving the ungodly (Romans 5:6). He really does draw all people to himself (John 12:32). The Son of God has been at work underneath all of history from the very beginning, bringing about the redemption, the reconciliation of all things to God (Colossians 1:15-20). God's grace has a logic all its own, a logic that often seems illogical to religious-minded people.

Only path to salvation

Jesus Christ is the only path to salvation, and he draws everybody to himself—in his way, in his time. There isn't anywhere in the universe except in Christ, since as Paul said, nothing exists that isn't created by him and upheld by him (Colossians 1:15-17). Those who finally reject him do so in spite of his love; it's not that he refuses them (he doesn't—he loves them, died for them and forgave them), but that they refuse him. C.S. Lewis put it this way:

There are only two kinds of people in the end: those who say to God, "Thy will be done" and those to whom God says, in the end, "THY will be done." All that are in Hell choose it. Without that self-choice, there could be no Hell. No soul that seriously and constantly desires joy will ever miss it. Those who seek, find. To those who knock, it is opened. (*The Great Divorce*, chapter 9)

Heroes in hell?

As I listened to Christians preach about the meaning of September 11, 2001, I thought of the firefighters and police officers who sacrificed their lives trying to rescue victims of the attack on the World Trade Center. How can Christians call these people heroes and applaud their self-sacrifice on one hand, but on the other hand declare that unless they confessed Christ before they expired, they are being tortured in hell? Their good works cannot save them, but Christ can.

The gospel declares that there is hope for those who died in the World Trade Center without yet having professed Christ. They will encounter the risen Lord on the other side of death, and he is the Judge—the one with nail marks in his hands—eternally ready to embrace and receive all his creatures who will come to him. He forgave them before they were born (Ephesians 1:4; Romans 5:6, 10). That part is done, just as it was done for us who believe now.

All that remains for them now is to throw down their crowns before him and receive his gift. Maybe some won't. Maybe some are so committed to loving themselves and hating others that they will see their risen Lord as their archenemy. That would be a shame — no, more than that; it's a disaster of cosmic proportions, because he's not their archenemy. Because he loves them anyway. Because he would gather them into his arms like a hen gathers her chicks, if they would only let him (cf. Luke 13:34).

It is safe to say, if you believe passages like Romans 14:11 and Philippians 2:10, that by far most of the people who died in that attack will jump into Jesus' forgiving and merciful arms like a puppy runs to its mother at mealtime.

Jesus saves

"Jesus saves," Christians put on their posters and bumper stickers. It's true. He does. He is the author and finisher of salvation, the beginning and goal of all creation — including all dead people. God did not send his Son into the world to condemn the world, Jesus said. Rather, he sent his Son into the world to save it (John 3:16-17).

Regardless of what some people say, God is out to save everybody (1 Timothy 2:4; 2 Peter 3:9), not just a few. And guess what? He never gives up. He never stops loving. He never stops being who he is, was, and will always be for humanity — their Creator and their Redeemer. Nobody falls through the cracks.

Nobody was created for the purpose of sending to hell. If anybody winds up in hell — the tiny, meaningless, dark, nowhere corner of the eternal kingdom — then what causes them to stay there will be nothing but their own stubborn refusal to receive the grace God has for them. It will not be because God hates them, because he doesn't. It will not be because God is vindictive, because he isn't. It will be because 1) they hate the kingdom of God and refuse his grace, and 2) God won't let them spoil the fun for everybody else.

Positive message

The gospel is a message of hope for absolutely everybody. Christian preachers don't have to resort to threats of hell to coerce people to turn to Christ. They can proclaim the truth, the good news: God loves you. He isn't mad at you. Jesus died for you because you're a sinner, and God loves you so much he has saved you from everything that is destroying you. So why should you keep on living as though this dangerous, cruel, unpredictable and unforgiving world is all you've got? Why don't you come and start experiencing God's love and enjoying the blessings of his kingdom? You already belong to him. He's already paid for your sins. What are you waiting for? He'll turn your sorrow into joy. He'll give you peace of heart like you've never known. He'll bring meaning and purpose to your life. He'll help you improve your relationships. He'll give you rest. Trust him. He's waiting for you.

This message is so good that it bubbles out of us. Paul wrote in Romans 5:10-11: "If while we were enemies, we were reconciled to God through the death of his Son, much more surely, having been reconciled, will we be saved by his life. But more than that, we even boast in God through our Lord Jesus Christ, through whom we have now received reconciliation."

Talk about hope! Talk about grace! Through Christ's death, God reconciles his enemies, and through Christ's life, he saves them. No wonder we can boast in God through our Lord Jesus Christ — we are already experiencing in him what we are telling others about. They don't have to keep on living like they have no place at God's table; he's already reconciled them, they can come on home. Christ saves sinners. It really is good news. It's the best news anybody can hear.

J. Michael Feazell

Sharing Your Faith...
With the Unchurched

By some estimates, 55 to 78 million adults in the United States seem content without attending church (Lee Strobel, *Inside the Mind of Unchurched Harry and Mary,* page 44). Unchurched Harry and Mary are a lot like many Americans today — people trying to fight the traffic, pay the bills and eke out a living in today's uncertain economy. They are "nice" people. They don't throw wild parties, ruin the neighborhood, or threaten others with bodily harm — but they probably haven't been to a church for years, except to attend weddings and funerals. They are the unchurched.

As Christians, we are expected — sometime, somehow — to share our faith with people like Harry and Mary. If Jesus lives in us, then we have little choice. The apostle Paul showed that all Christians participate — to one degree or another — in God's intentions to reconcile the world to himself:

> Therefore, if anyone is in Christ, he is a new creation; the old has gone, the new has come! All this is from God, who reconciled us to himself through Christ and gave us the ministry of reconciliation: that God was reconciling the world to himself in Christ, not counting men's sins against them. And he has committed to us the message of reconciliation. (2 Corinthians 5:17-19)

God has entrusted to us the message of reconciliation. It is hard to think of a bigger incentive to share our faith with the unchurched. "God has reconciled the world in Christ," writes Ralph Martin. "But the task of proclaiming the reconciliation goes on" (*2 Corinthians,* Word Biblical Commentary, page 138).

Paul created a vivid analogy for this part of our Christian job description: "We are therefore Christ's ambassadors, as though God were making his appeal through us.... As God's fellow workers we urge you not to receive God's grace in vain" (2 Corinthians 5:20; 6:1). We are to yield to God, allowing him to make his appeal to this hurting world through people like us. It's a humbling assignment, isn't it? Thankfully, God's Word and real-life Christian examples can help train us for the task.

Evangelism most personal

Charles Swindoll explained personal evangelism:

> The skeptic may deny your doctrine or attack your church but he cannot honestly ignore the fact that your life has been changed. He may stop his ears to the presentations of a preacher and the pleadings of an evangelist, but he is somehow attracted to the human-interest story of how you — John Q. Public — found peace within. (*Come Before Winter,* page 43)

The gospel according *to you* — it's one of the best weapons in your Christian arsenal.

When I was young, I had drifted away from regular church attendance. A preacher forcefully challenged me on some ideas I had. I was stirred to search the Bible, to come to grips with the urgency of the gospel. That produced an upheaval in my life that has had a lasting effect. I remember wanting to share this new conviction with my best friend.

Guess what? Because he was my friend he

listened. He heard me out. And because he had a friend, and she had other friends, eventually a group of seven people who had more or less drifted from active church involvement made a commitment to put God number one in their lives. We've had our ups and downs, but all were affected for the good.

Here's the point: When we are first convicted by the gospel, we are almost bubbling over with enthusiasm for what we have learned. We want to share it with people close to us. We find out fairly soon that some will respond and some won't. It seems that rule number one in sharing your faith with the unchurched is to not be easily discouraged. Even in Jesus' parable of the sower, much seed fell by the wayside (Matthew 13:3-7). As a pastor, I learned that this is normal.

We are best able to influence those closest to us, those with whom we have more credibility than the hit-and-run style of evangelism. But you won't win them all. Jesus was crucified between two thieves. One responded. One did not. Even Paul, probably the greatest missionary in history, didn't always convince the skeptics. "When they heard about the resurrection of the dead, some of them sneered." Thankfully, there were some who said, "We want to hear you again on this subject" (Acts 17:32).

In Acts 28:1-6, we see Paul being regarded first as a murderer and then as a god. That is an insight into real-life evangelism. It is hard to predict how people will respond. But since we care about people and their hurts and fears, we try to stay open to the opportunities God provides for effective witness. "Seize the moment" might have been coined as a slogan for personal evangelism. My challenge has been to learn to build personal evangelism into my Christian walk as an ongoing experience. How about you?

Letters from Christ

Another great principle of sharing your faith is to know the kind of questions you could be asked. The good news is that most things people have on their minds are personal issues. Often it is a personal experience that has turned unchurched Harry and Mary off to Christianity. An abusive minister, a harsh doctrinal stance, above all, a conflict with someone in the church. These are the hurdles in many people's minds.

Here is where your personal example comes into play. Most people you will share your faith with want the gospel according to you. You don't even need to know how to read and write to be an effective ambassador for Christ. It is how we live our Christian lives as employees, neighbors and family members—these are our credentials. The apostle Paul was pleased that his converts were "a letter from Christ, the result of our ministry, written not with ink but with the Spirit of the living God, not on tablets of stone but on tablets of human hearts" (2 Corinthians 3:3).

People open up to people they know. In this unpredictable and uncertain world, we can expect personal and social troubles keyed to the crises of life—a bout with cancer, or the office reaction to a recent disaster, for example. These real-life events can create the seedbed for Christian witness to flower. As Peter wrote, "Always be prepared to give an answer to everyone who asks you to give the reason for the hope that you have" (1 Peter 3:15). Having Christ in us makes us different. Over time, that difference stands out. This is core training in sharing our faith.

Words that help

The best evangelism is intimate, up-close and one-on-one. Perhaps Jane the receptionist will tearfully confide to you that her husband is leaving her for another woman. Or maybe Mark from the shipping department will close your door quietly and break the news he has cancer. These are the real issues of life.

So what do you do? Verbalize your feelings. Make your communication heart-to-heart as well as head-to-head. Tell others you will pray for them. In some situations, it might be appropriate to pray together, asking God for wisdom and healing. Ask for strength and faith and peace, or share a favorite scripture. Perhaps 1 Corinthians 10:13: "No temptation has overtaken you except what is common to mankind. And God is faithful; he will not let you be tempted beyond what you can bear. But when you are tempted, he will also provide a way out so that you can endure it."

There is healing in God's Word. Scripture can calm people. Sometimes that's all that people need when they are caught in the panicky first frightening wave of a crisis. People who share their faith report how these dialogues often go:

- *Question:* "Susan, how does your church explain the killing of those innocent children in the terrorist attack?"
- *Response:* "I can't answer for everything that happens in this crazy world — the Bible says the rain falls on the righteous and the unrighteous. God doesn't promise us clear-cut answers; he offers faith for those who ask."
- *Question:* "Jack, how does your Christian faith help you figure out that big airline crash over the weekend? Still believe in a God of love, do you?"
- *Response:* "Plane crashes and other tragedies trouble us — it might happen to us one day. We make our choices and take our chances. But a Christian always has Someone to turn to when trouble hits."

Be discerning. Go only as deep as the person wants you to go. Most unchurched people are not expecting us to be theologians. It's our personal reaction—the gospel according to you and me— that people want to hear. "Be concise. Be spontaneous. Tell them in your own words what God has shown you," advises one Christian.

God gives us faith to share. Let's remember these basics:

- Be Christlike. Be the kind of person people can respect and confide in. Agree with people as much as possible. Be known for going the extra mile at work and elsewhere (Matthew 5:41). Christ living in you day by day will help you accomplish this. You don't have to be perfect, but you have to be consistently open, honest and concerned.
- Be bold. Don't be afraid to tell people: "I'll be praying for you" or "I have an article that helped me. I'll bring it tomorrow if you want." Offer to pray with them right then and there.
- Follow up. This shows you really are interested. A card or a gift is a concrete way of letting people know you care. Our world is starving for spiritual connection. With God's help we can be ambassadors of healing. God wants us to share our faith with others.

Neil Earle

Heart Trouble

"God doesn't require people to keep old covenant laws," the man said. "He looks on the heart."

That's true—God does not require anyone to keep old covenant laws—but when he looks on the heart, what does he see? Does he see a perfect attitude, a heart that has never sinned? No. When the Bible says that God looks on the heart, it is not giving an easier standard for salvation—it is saying that salvation is a lot harder than the law ever made it out to be.

Jesus illustrated this in the Sermon on the Mount. "You have heard that it was said to the people long ago, 'You shall not murder.... But I tell you that anyone who is angry with a brother or sister will be subject to judgment.... Anyone who looks at a woman lustfully has already committed adultery" (Matthew 5:21-22, 28). In other words, if you think wrong thoughts, you have sinned—you are headed for judgment. If your heart is not totally clean, you've got heart trouble, because God looks on the heart.

Do you deserve eternal joy?

Suppose you are brought to the judge on judgment day, and he asks, "Where should I send you—the place for saints, or the place for sinners?"

What will you say—"I have a saintly heart"? I don't think so. As Paul says, "Everyone has sinned and fallen short." It doesn't matter whether you look on the outside, or look in the thoughts, or look on the heart—everyone has sinned and has a problem.

We can never plead for salvation on the basis of what we did, or what we are, or what our heart is like. No one ever deserves to go to a perfect place, a place where there is no more crying or tears, because none of us is the sort of person who never does anything wrong. We have all let God down; we have all failed to treat others rightly—in the heart if not also in words and deeds. Our hearts fall short every day.

The good news is that Jesus cleanses our hearts—changes our hearts—gives us new hearts (metaphors for the same thing). Even with our new hearts, we still have wrong thoughts, wrong attitudes. But our new heart is the heart of Jesus, and Jesus' heart cannot be stained with sin. "There is now no condemnation for those who are in Christ Jesus" (Romans 8:1).

Satan may accuse us of sin, but the charge doesn't stick, because we have been forgiven, and our old self the sinner died with Christ. We are a new creation in Christ. "The old has gone, the new has come" (2 Corinthians 5:17)!

The gospel, the good news we have in Jesus, is not health and wealth in this age. Faith in Christ is sometimes accompanied by blessings—miraculous healings, financial blessings, better relationships. These blessings, although substantial, are not the good news that Jesus brought, because not every believer gets them. In some cases, faithful Christians experience poverty, sickness and early death because of their faith in Jesus. The time is not yet here when there will be "no more tears" and "no more death." These sorrows still happen to us, just as they happened to Jesus.

Bad news, good news

Jesus brought both good news and bad news. The good news is that God sets the world right. There will be an eternity of joy and fellowship with God. The bad news is that no amount of doing good will ever qualify us to be part of that world. We've got heart trouble.

The good news is that eternal life is a gift. It cannot be earned—it must be given to us, based on what Christ has done for us in his life, death, resurrection and ascension to heaven. In the Sermon on the Mount, Jesus said, "Blessed are the merciful, for they will be shown mercy" (Matthew 5:7). They don't earn salvation by showing mercy—they still need mercy. The good news is that it will be given to them.

That is why sinners can enter the kingdom of God ahead of law-abiding religious leaders. Eternal joy is not based on self-made people who rely on themselves for moral strength. Rather, the ones who know their need for mercy are the ones who understand and embrace the mercy of God. If law-abiding, clean-living people recognize their need for Christ, that's great. But sometimes such people don't admit their need, because they believe they are doing fairly well on their own. But fairly well is not good enough. When we come to the day of judgment, "I did fairly well" is not a good excuse.

We have *no* excuse—but we do have a Savior. When we come to judgment, our only valid response will be to trust in the mercy and grace of Jesus Christ. Our answer, our hope of salvation, can never rest in ourselves, can never rest in our own hearts. It must always rest in Jesus Christ. Our lives are hidden in him (Colossians 3:3) so that when God looks at us, he sees the righteousness of Christ (1 Corinthians 1:30).

It is good that wrongs will be righted, that evil will be eliminated, that an eternity of perfection will come. But that news will do me no good unless I listen to the gospel, the good news that tells me how I can participate in that wonderful world. Jesus has good news for people with heart trouble. He brings us grace, and he gives us everything we need for salvation, so we can live forever with him.

Joseph Tkach

How Baptism Pictures the Gospel

Rituals were a prominent part of Old Testament worship—there were annual rituals, monthly rituals and daily rituals. There were rituals for birth and rituals for death, rituals of sacrifice, rituals of cleansing, rituals of ordination. Faith was needed, but rituals were prominent.

The New Testament, in contrast, has two basic rituals: baptism and the Lord's Supper—and there are no detailed regulations for either observance. Why these two? In a religion in which faith is primary, why have any rituals at all?

The primary reason is that both the Lord's Supper and baptism picture the gospel of Jesus Christ. They rehearse the fundamental elements of our faith. The Lord's Supper reminds us of the Lord's death, his life now, which we share in, and his promise to return. It is a reminder that our salvation is based on the life and death of Jesus Christ.

Pictures the gospel

How does baptism picture the central truths of the gospel? The apostle Paul wrote:

> Don't you know that all of us who were baptized into Christ Jesus were baptized into his death? We were therefore buried with him through baptism into death in order that, just as Christ was raised from the dead through the glory of the Father, we too may live a new life. If we have been united with him like this in his death, we will certainly also be united with him in his resurrection. (Romans 6:3-5)

Baptism pictures our union with Christ in his death, burial and resurrection. These are the primary points of the gospel (1 Corinthians 15:3-4). Our salvation depends on his life, death and resurrection. Our forgiveness—being cleansed of sin—depends on him; our Christian life and future depend on him.

Baptism symbolizes the death of the old self—the old person was crucified with Christ—died with Christ—buried with Christ in baptism (Romans 6:8; Galatians 2:20; 6:14; Colossians 2:12, 20). It pictures that we are identified with Jesus Christ—he united himself with humanity. We accept that his death was "for us," and "for our sins." We acknowledge that we have sinned, that we have a tendency to sin, that we are sinners who needed a Savior. We acknowledge our need to be cleansed, and that this cleansing came through the death of Jesus Christ.

Baptism is one of the ways that we confess Jesus Christ as our Lord and Savior. We are saved by what he did, not by the way we responded. Therefore, the emphasis in baptism should be on what Jesus did, not on our faith or acceptance. The only reason that we can show our response of faith is because he is already committed to us. Baptism

---

From our Statement of Beliefs:

The sacrament of baptism proclaims that we are saved by Christ alone and not through our own repentance and faith. It is a participation in the death and resurrection of Jesus Christ, in which our old selves have been crucified and renounced in Christ and we have been freed from the shackles of the past and given new being through his resurrection. Baptism proclaims the good news that Christ has made us his own, and that it is only in him that our new life of faith and obedience emerges. Grace Communion International baptizes by immersion.

(Romans 6:3-6; Galatians 3:26; Colossians 2:12; Acts 2:38)

is not a memorial of *our* faith — it is a memorial of Jesus' faithfulness toward us.

Raised with Christ

Baptism pictures wonderful news—we have been raised with Christ to live with him (Ephesians 2:5-6; Colossians 2:12-13; 3:1). In him, we have a new life, and are called to live a new way of life, with him as Lord leading and guiding us out of sinful ways and into righteous and loving ways. Baptism reminds us that faith involves a change in the way we live, and that we cannot make this change in ourselves — it is done by the power of the risen Christ living in us. Christ has united himself to us in his resurrection not just for the future, but for life right now. This is part of the symbolism.

Jesus did not invent the ritual of baptism. It developed within Judaism, and was used by John the Baptist as a ritual to show repentance, in which the water symbolized cleansing. Jesus continued this practice, and after his death and resurrection his disciples continued to use it, but with a more profound meaning. Baptism dramatizes the fact that Jesus has given us a new basis for life, and a new basis for our relationship with God.

Paul saw that since we are forgiven or cleansed through the death of Christ, baptism pictures his death and that we (even before we were alive) are participants in his death. Paul was also inspired to add the connection with Jesus' resurrection. As we rise from the baptismal waters, we picture Christ raising us to a new life — a life in Christ, with him in us.

Peter wrote that baptism saves us "by the resurrection of Jesus Christ" (1 Peter 3:21). However, baptism itself does not save us. We are saved by God's grace, through faith in Jesus Christ. Physical water removing physical dirt cannot save us, this verse reminds us. Baptism saves us only in the sense that it is "the pledge of a good conscience toward God." It is a visible representation of trusting in Christ — that is, trusting that *he* has cleansed our conscience and forgiven us. We are saved by what he has done, not by what we do.

Into one body

We are baptized not only into Christ Jesus, but we are also baptized into his body, the church. "We were all baptized by one Spirit into one body" (1 Corinthians 12:13). That is why people cannot baptize themselves—it should be done within the context of the Christian community. There are no secret Christians, people who believe in Christ but no one knows about it. The biblical pattern is to confess Christ before other people, to make a public acknowledgment of Jesus as Lord, to become part of a community of believers.

Baptism is one of the ways in which Christ may be confessed, in which a person's friends may see that a commitment has been made: Christ's commitment to us in his death, and our commitment to him as a response. It may be a joyous occasion in which the congregation sings hymns and welcomes the person to the family. Or it may be a smaller ceremony in which an elder (or some other authorized representative of the congregation) welcomes the new believer, rehearses the significance of what is being done, and encourages them in their life in Christ.

Baptism recognizes that a person has already repented of sin, already accepted Christ as Savior, already begun to grow spiritually — is already a Christian. We are simply catching up to what Christ has already done for us. Baptism does not make a person a Christian—it recognizes that they already are a Christian. Baptism is usually done soon after a person has come to believe in Christ as Savior, but occasionally it may be done much later.

Teens and children

When a person has come to faith in Christ, he or she may be baptized. This may be when the person is old, or when young. A young person may explain faith differently than an older person does, but young people may have faith nonetheless. Teenagers and younger children may have genuine awareness of sin, genuine trust that Christ has paid for their sins, and awareness that their life is united with Christ, and they may be baptized.

Will some of them eventually change their

minds and fall away? Perhaps, but that happens with adult professions of faith, too. Will some of those childhood conversions turn out to be mistaken? Perhaps, but that happens with adults, too. There are no guarantees about what humans will do — the guarantee comes in what Christ has already done for us. That is what we can celebrate with certainty.

If the person has faith in Christ, then the person may be baptized. It is not our practice, however, to baptize minors without the consent of their parent or legal guardian. If the minor's parent objects to baptism, then the child who has faith in Jesus is still a Christian, even if he or she has to wait until later to be baptized.[1]

In our denomination, we generally baptize by immersion. That was most likely the practice in first-century Judaism and in the early church. Immersion pictures death and burial better than sprinkling does. Sprinkling pictures cleansing, but not death. Nevertheless, for those who were baptized by sprinkling, we might say that the old person died with Christ, whether or not the body was properly buried. The old life is dead, and the new life is here, and that is what is important.

We do not make the method of baptism an issue to divide Christians. The important thing is that we remember that Christ has done the real work of salvation, and we are simply responding to what he has done. We give up on our own self-centered approach to life and begin to let him guide us by his Spirit.

Salvation does not depend on the exact method of baptism (the Bible doesn't give us many details on procedure, anyway) nor on the exact words. Salvation depends on Christ, not on the depth of the water. If a person has faith in Christ, that person is a Christian, no matter what kind of baptism was done. A Christian who was baptized by sprinkling or pouring is still a Christian. If such a person wishes to become a member of our denomination, we do not require a new baptism. Christianity is based on faith, not on performance of a ritual.

Occasionally people baptized in infancy wish to become members of our fellowship. Is it necessary for us to re-baptize them? If they have only recently come to a point of faith and commitment, it may be appropriate to baptize them. In such cases, baptism would emphasize to them that the old self has died with Christ.

If people were baptized as infants and have been living as adult Christians for many years, with good fruit, then they do not need another baptism. If they request it, we may do it, but we do not need to quibble about ceremonies of decades ago when Christian fruit is already evident. We can simply praise the grace of God. The person is a Christian whether or not the ritual was done in the "right" way or "right" time.

Sharing the Lord's Supper

For similar reasons, it is permissible for us to share the Lord's Supper with people who have not been baptized in the manner we are accustomed to. If people have faith in Jesus Christ, they are united to him and have been baptized, one way or another, into his body, and they may share in the bread and wine, even if they do not agree with us on every point of doctrine.

We should not get sidetracked by arguments about detail. We have our beliefs and practices, and we love those who have other beliefs. We focus on the larger picture, provided by the apostle Paul: Baptism pictures our old self dying with Christ, our sins being washed away by what he did, and Christ raising us up to new life in him and in his church. Baptism is a reminder that we are saved by the death and life of Jesus Christ. It is the gospel in miniature drama — the central truths of the faith being portrayed in the actions.

Joseph Tkach

---

[1] We may also baptize infants. See https://www.gci.org/articles/infant-baptism/

Too Much Grace?

Some people are worried that we emphasize grace too much. The suggested corrective to this worrisome tendency is to counter-balance it with teaching on obedience or righteousness or other obligations mentioned in Scripture, especially those in the New Testament. I think I might have something useful to say about 1) the nature of grace, and 2) our response to grace.

A legitimate concern

People who worry about extending "too much grace" often have a legitimate concern. Some people hold the idea that living by God's grace means that it doesn't matter what we do, given that we are saved by grace and not by works. According to this view, grace means no obligations, no rules, and no expected or required patterns of relationship. Grace means that pretty much anything goes, since it's all forgiven beforehand. This view sees grace as a free pass—carte blanche permission to do whatever one wants. Most persons I know who hold this view, or something like it, don't go quite this far—they seem to know that there are some limits. However, some hold an extreme, and I believe unbiblical, view of grace.

Living without or against any laws or rules is known as *antinomianism*. This problem has been written and preached about throughout church history. The Christian who was killed by the Nazis, Dietrich Bonhoeffer, called it "cheap grace" in his book *The Cost of Discipleship*. Antinomianism is addressed in the New Testament. Paul referred to it in when addressing the accusation that his emphasis on grace was encouraging people to "continue in sin in order that grace may abound" (Romans 6:1). Paul's reply was short and direct: "By no means!" (verse 2). A few sentences later he repeats their charge against him and answers it: "What then? Should we sin because we are not under law but under grace? By no means!" (verse 15).

But what's the real problem and solution?

There is no ambiguity in Paul's response. Those who might want to argue that grace means "anything goes because it's all covered" are mistaken. What's gone wrong? Is the problem really "too much grace"? And is the solution to counter-balance grace with something else? Is that how Paul and the rest of the New Testament writers understood the problem? Was that how they sought to remedy it? I think the answer to both questions is clearly, "by no means!" The whole of the New Testament revelation, founded in Jesus Christ himself, identifies the nature of the problem and its solution differently.

Rather than the problem being "too much grace," the real problem is a misunderstanding of both grace and obedience. Ironically, those who worry about "too much grace" hold the same misunderstanding about grace as those who have no worries at all and so go merrily on their way without giving further thought to living a life of faithfulness to Jesus Christ and the instructions given in the New Testament. Their misunderstanding of grace trips them up and undermines their ability to live a life of joyful obedience in the freedom of Christ—a freedom and joy that both Paul and Jesus talk about.

It took me many years to get to the bottom of this issue, and I didn't get there without a lot of help from others who I learned from, some in person and others through their writings. So let me try to lay out what I found.

The problem is not too much grace, nor is the solution to counter-balance grace with an equal insistence on obedience, works or service. The real problem is thinking that grace means God makes an exception to a rule, a requirement or an obligation. That is a common, everyday misunderstanding of grace. If grace involved merely allowing for exceptions to rules, then yes, a lot of grace would simply yield a lot of exceptions. If God is *all* gracious, then we could expect that for *every* obligation or responsibility, God would make an exception. The more grace, then the more exceptions to obedience. The less grace, the fewer exceptions allowed. A nice clean proportion. If we have to allow some room for grace in this scheme, then the question is where to put the balance between grace and requirements: 25/75? 50/50? 75/25?

Such a scheme perhaps describes the best that human grace can achieve. But this approach pits grace against obedience. It puts them at odds with one another—always pushing and pulling one another; back and forth, never really settling down, since they fight against one another. Each one undoes or negates the other. They are in perpetual contradiction with no hope of ever getting along. When people assume that "this is just the way things have to be," they experience this tension within themselves. Externally their lives might look like a teeter-totter, tipping now on one side and then the other. But fortunately such a scheme does not represent God's kind of grace. The truth about grace sets us free from this false dichotomy.

God's grace in person

Question: How does the Bible define grace? Answer: Jesus Christ himself is God's grace to us. Paul's benediction ending 2 Corinthians refers to "the grace of our Lord Jesus Christ." Grace is what God freely gives us in his incarnate Son, who in turn, graciously communicates to us God's love and restores us to fellowship with God. What Jesus does towards us reveals to us the nature and character of the Father and the Holy Spirit. Scripture tells us that Jesus bears the stamp of God's exact character (Hebrews 1:3). "He is the image of the invisible God" and "all the fullness of God was pleased to dwell" in him (Colossians 1:15, 19). Whoever who has seen Jesus "has seen the Father" and if we know him we will know the Father (John 14:7, 9).

Jesus explains that "I only do what I see the Father doing" (John 5:19). He tells us that only he knows the Father and he alone reveals him (Matthew 11:27). John tells us that this Word of God, who has existed from the beginning with God, took on a human existence and has shown us "the glory as of a father's only son, full of grace and truth" (John 1:14). In contrast, "the law was given through Moses; grace and truth came through Jesus Christ." "From his fullness we have all received, grace upon grace." This Son who has existed in the heart of God from all eternity "has made him known" (John 1:14-18).

Jesus is God's grace to us—revealing in word and in action that God himself is full of grace. Grace isn't just one of the things God happens to do every now and then. Grace is who God is. God gives us his grace out of his own nature and character. He does not give out of a dependence on us, nor does he give because we somehow obligate him to extend his good gifts to us. God gives grace because he has a giving nature. That means that God gives us his grace in Jesus Christ, freely. Paul calls grace a free gift from God (Romans 5:15-17; 6:23). In his letter to the Ephesians he memorably declared: "By grace you have been saved through faith, and this is not your own doing; it is the gift of God — not the result of works, so that no one may boast" (2:8-9).

All that God gives us, he gives out of his own goodness. God, who is light and in whom is no darkness, gives himself to us freely—in the Son, by the Spirit. That freely-given life is, for us, both temporal and eternal.

Was God always gracious?

Unfortunately it has often been explained that God originally agreed to give of his goodness (to Adam and Eve and then to Israel) only if his creatures fulfilled certain conditions (obligations) that he set out for them. If they didn't, he would not extend much of his goodness to them. He especially would not extend forgiveness and eternal life.

This erroneous viewpoint sees God has having a contractual, "if you-then I" relationship with his creatures. That contract has conditions or obligations (rules or laws) that humanity must meet in order to receive what God is offering. According to this view, God's primary concern is conformity to his rules. If we don't measure up, God will withhold his best from us. Worse than that, he will give us something that is not good, that leads to death, not life; now and in eternity.

This erroneous view sees Law as the deepest thing about God's nature and thus the most fundamental aspect of God's relationship with his creatures. He wills what he wills and blesses only upon our fulfillment of certain obligations. This God is a contract God who has a legal and conditional relationship with his creatures. He conducts that relationship in a slave-master way. Grace, God's freely giving of his goodness and blessing, is far from the essence of this God. From this perspective, Jesus is viewed as only a minor footnote—an insignificant aspect of who God is. Jesus is an exception to God's rule and will, nature and character.

If law actually was the most fundamental feature of God's relationship to us, then grace would be an exception to the law. But law is *not* the most basic way that God relates to us now, and it never has been. God is not fundamentally sheer will or law. This is most clearly seen looking at Jesus, who shows us the Father and sends us the Spirit. It is clear when we hear from Jesus about his eternal relationship with the Father and Spirit. Jesus tells us that his nature and character is identical to that of the Father's nature and character.

The Father-Son relationship is not one of rules, obligations or the fulfilling of conditions in order to earn or deserve benefits. The Father and Son do not have a legal relationship with each other. They have not drawn up a contract with each other where if one fails to complete their part the other will not fulfill their part. The idea of a contractual, law-based relationship between the Father and the Son is an absurdity. The truth, revealed to us in Jesus, is that their relationship is one of love, faithfulness, self-giving and mutual glorification.

As we read Scripture carefully, it becomes clear that God's relationship with his creation and even with Israel is not contractual—it is not one of conditionality. An important point to remember, one that Paul is clear about, is that God's relationship with Israel was not fundamentally one of law, of an if-then contract. God's relationship with Israel began with a covenant, a promise. The Law of Moses (the Torah) came in 430 years after the inauguration of the covenant. Given that timeline, law could hardly be regarded as the foundation for God's relationship with Israel.

In the covenant, God freely pledged himself and his goodness to Israel. It had nothing to do with what Israel could offer God (Deuteronomy 7:6-8). Abraham was a moon worshipper when God made his pledge to bless him and make him a blessing to all the nations (Genesis 12:4). A covenant is a promise. It is freely chosen and freely given. "I will be your God and you shall be my people" said God to Israel (Exodus 6:7). God's pledge of blessing was unilateral—it was established from his side alone. God gave the covenant as an expression of his own nature, character and being. Its establishment with Israel was an act of grace!

The early chapters of Genesis make it clear that God does not act according to some kind of contractual agreement. First, creation itself was an act of free giving. "It was good, even very good." Eve was a gift of grace to Adam. So were the garden and their good purpose in creation. Was not God's pursuit of them and giving them an opportunity to repent following their disobedience an act of grace? Consider also God's provision of animal skins for their clothing. Even their expulsion from the Garden to prevent them from taking of the tree of eternal life in their fallen state, was an act of grace. God's protection and provision for Cain can only be regarded in the same light. We also see grace in God's protection of Noah and his family and in his pledge of the rainbow. All these are of grace—freely given gifts of God's goodness. None of them are rewards for fulfilling some kind of even minimal legal contractual obligation.

Grace as unmerited favor?

It is often said that grace is God's *unmerited favor*. Strictly speaking, this is true — but given what we think it implies, it is just barely true. What is false about it is the assumption (almost always lurking in the background) that God originally intended for us to merit his favor. That is utterly false. God did not originally plan on us meriting his favor, but then gave up as he saw us fail. God did not abandon "Plan A: Merited Favor" for "Plan B: Unmerited Favor." No—God never, from the foundations of the earth, wanted a contractual, conditional relationship with us. He never wanted a master-slave relationship.[1] Rather, he wanted all along for his children to have a relationship with him that mirrored as much as possible the relationship God the Father has with his Son in the Spirit.

God always freely gives of his goodness—of himself—to his creatures. He does so because of who he is, eternally and internally as Father, Son and Holy Spirit. Everything they do towards creation is an overflow of their inward life together. It mirrors, reflects and therefore gives glory to who God is. A legal and contractual relationship with God would not give the triune creator and covenant-making God glory, but would obscure it, even deny it. It would make God into a mere idol. Idols always enter into contractual relationships with their appeasers because they need their worshippers just as much as the worshippers need them. They are mutually dependent, so they use one another for their own self-centered ends. The only question is which "side" will win. The outcome of that competition largely depends on which side is strongest, more powerful, and slightly less dependent than the other. But such a relationship is exactly what the God of the Bible repudiates. God is no idol and does not want the kind of contractual, conditional relationship with his people that idols demand. Idols must be appeased, but not the God of Israel and of our Lord Jesus Christ.[2]

The smidgen of truth hidden under the saying that grace is God's unmerited favor is that we don't merit it. But the implication almost always accompanying that idea is false! God's favor or blessing (his freely-given goodness) was never meant to be merited. You can "unmerit" God's blessing, but you can't merit it and you never could. For if God extended his goodness to us because we merited it, that action would not be motivated by God's own nature and character. The goodness would not be freely given by a good God. Favor earned is not favor freely given. It is not grace!

---

[1] An even worse explanation is that God wanted us to believe the falsehood that he wanted a conditional relationship with us, where we merited his favor, so that when we failed (which he knew we would), we would come to see that we couldn't merit it. Thus it turns out that he never did really want a conditional relationship with us although we were led to believe that he did.

[2] See for example Isaiah 1 and 66 and Hosea 4-14 for God's complaint about sacrifices given to God to appease him as if he were an idol.

Too Much Grace?
continued

The graciousness of grace demonstrated

Grace does not come into play only when there is sin, making an exception to some law or obligation. God is gracious whether there is or is not sin. God does not need sin to be gracious. However, grace continues when there is sin. God continues to freely give of his own goodness to his creatures even when they don't merit it.

Even when we sin, God remains faithful because he is faithful, just as Paul says: "Though everyone be faithless, God will remain faithful" (2 Timothy 2:13). Because God always is true to himself, he persists in extending his love and in pursuing his holy purposes for us even when we rebel and resist. This constancy of grace shows the depth of God's freedom — the freedom to be good toward his creation. "For while we were still weak, at the right time Christ died for the ungodly…. But God proves his love for us in that while we still were sinners Christ died for us" (Romans 5:6, 8).

The special character of grace shines forth when it shines out in the darkness, so we most often speak of grace in the context of sin. There is nothing wrong with that. But the problem comes when we think God's favor was originally to be earned in a legal arrangement with him. Sin can't stop God's free giving of his goodness. He remains constant in character, nature and purpose. God is not dependent on us to remain true to himself. We cannot make God freer that he is, nor by our rejection of it can we take from him his freedom to be gracious.

So God is gracious without sin and God is gracious with sin. God is faithful in being good to his creation and maintaining his good purposes for creation. We see this most fully in Jesus, who cannot be stopped from completing his atoning work by all the forces of evil arrayed against him. Those forces cannot prevent him from giving up his life so that we could have life. No amount of pain, suffering and humiliation could deter him from carrying out his holy, loving purposes to reconcile humanity to God.

God's goodness does not require evil to be good. But when it comes upon evil, goodness knows just what to do with it: overcome it, conquer it, and vanquish it. There is no such thing, then, as too much grace. Next, let's consider how we respond to God's grace.

So why the law (or any other commands)?

Given what we saw about grace, how then do we regard the Old Testament Law and Christian obedience under the new covenant? If we remember that God's covenant is a unilateral promise, the answer more easily falls into place. A promise calls for a response from the one to whom it is made. However, the fulfillment of the promise does not depend on this response.[1] There are only

---

[1] The idea of an inheritance conveys the same sort of understanding. The giving of an inheritance does not depend on its reception. It is given, and therefore possessed in a certain way, even before it is received. Found in the practices of Israel, the idea of an inheritance is used to speak of God's ultimate blessings at numerous key points in the New Testament. See Galatians 3:18; Ephesians 1:11; Colossians 3:24; Hebrews

two options here: to trust (or have faith or to believe) in the promise or not. The Law of Moses (the Torah) described for Israel much of what trusting God's covenant should look like during its pre-fulfillment stage (prior to Jesus Christ). God graciously provided for Israel ways to live within his covenant (as it was expressed in the old covenant). The Law of Moses also described ways that were distrustful of God's covenant promises to Israel. But what the Torah did not do is prescribe how Israel might earn God's favor and blessing—it did not define how to get God to make a promise and then how to keep him faithful to it.

The Torah was freely given by God to Israel. It was meant to help Israel. Paul calls it a "tutor" (Galatians 3:24-25). It should be regarded as a good gift of God's grace to Israel. The Law is given inside and under the old covenant, which was the covenant of grace in its phase as promise (awaiting the fulfillment in Christ under the new covenant).

What difference does the response to grace make? It is at this point that confusion often arises. If we are to benefit from the promise, we must live on the basis of trusting it. This is what is meant by "living by faith." We see faithful living exemplified by Old Testament "saints" in Hebrews 11.

There are consequences for not living out of a trust in the promise. Distrust in the covenant and in the God of the covenant severely limits a person's experience of the covenant benefits. The Israelites' distrust cut them off from the source of their life—their sustenance, health and fruitfulness. Distrust blocked their relationship with God to the point where they were unable to receive much of anything from God. God did not want that, because he is gracious! Thus in Scripture we find warnings describing the dire consequences of living in ways that deny God's faithfulness to his word of promise, thus preventing his people from receiving the freely-given grace of God. Instead of blessings, what his faithless people receive is sometimes referred to as "curses."

But even such warnings given to his people can be regarded as gifts of God's grace. If God did not care about Israel and would just as soon cancel his covenant, there would be no reason for him to warn them at all. He'd just let them go and be done with it. There are consequences of living as if you weren't in the covenant, but canceling the covenant is not one of them. Ignoring the covenant does not undo it or nullify it, nor does it make God change his mind and go back on his promise. God cannot be tempted to be unfaithful to his promise.

God's covenant, Paul tells us, is irrevocable. Why? Because God is faithful and will keep his covenant even when it costs him dearly! God will never go back on his word; he cannot be forced to act uncharacteristically towards his creation or his people. Even in our distrust of the promise, we cannot make God to be untrue to himself. This is what is meant by God doing things "for his own name's sake."

Israel's disobedience resulted in bad (even dire) consequences. But all of these occurred within the covenant, under God's grace. God never abandoned Israel and he never went back on his covenant promises. From time to time, God renewed his covenant with Israel, always leading up to the fulfillment of the covenant in Jesus Christ.

Grace makes no exceptions!

It's important to realize that God makes no exceptions to his good purposes and holy aims for his people. Because he is faithful, God will not give up on us. Instead, he loves us to perfection—the perfection of his Son. God intends to glorify us so that we perfectly trust and love him with all that we are and have, and so live out our trust in God's graciousness to the full. Doing so means that our distrusting hearts will be done away with so that our lives perfectly reflect our trust in God's freely given goodness. God's perfect love will love us to completion by justifying us, sanctifying us and finally glorifying us. "He who began a good work in us will bring it to completion" (Philippians 1:6).

Would God be gracious to leave us less than

9:15.

whole? What if heaven were filled with individuals for whom exceptions were made: allowing for a lack of faith here, a failure of love there, a bit of unforgiveness here, some bitterness and resentment there, a mite of jealousy here and a mote of selfish pride there? What would that be like? It would be just like it is here and now, but forever! Would God really be gracious to leave us in such an "exceptional" condition for all of eternity? No, he would not! In the end, God's grace allows for no exceptions to his ruling grace, to the rule of his love, to the sovereignty of his loving will—because otherwise he would not be gracious.

Where does obedience come from?

So where does obedience come from? It arises out of a trust in God's faithfulness to his covenant purposes fulfilled in Jesus Christ. The only obedience that God is interested in is the obedience of faith (Romans 1:5; 16:26)—faith in God's constancy, in God's faithfulness to his Word, faithfulness to himself. Obedience never was and never is an attempt to fulfill conditions to get God to be faithful, to make God more likely to be good, to get God to be gracious. Obedience is our response to grace. Paul is clear on this in one place especially. He tells us that Israel's failure was not that she did not fulfill certain legal conditions of the Torah, but that she "did not strive for it on the basis of faith, but as if it were based on works" (Romans 9:32). Paul, a law-keeping Pharisee, came to realize the astounding truth that God never wanted him to work up a righteousness of his own through keeping the law. What good would that be even if it were possible (which it is not)? Compared to the righteousness that God intended to give him by grace, compared to having a share in God's own righteousness given to him in Christ, it would be garbage (or worse!).

All along, God intended to share his own righteousness with his people as a gift of grace. Why? Because God is gracious! (Philippians 3:8-9). So how do we receive this freely given gift? By trusting God for it, by having faith in his promise to provide it. Trying to work for that gift—trying to meet certain legal conditions, trying to conform to specified obligations in order to earn God's blessings, actually indicates distrust. It indicates unbelief in God's grace.

The obedience that God is looking for is motivated by faith, hope and love for God. The obligations that are described for us throughout Scripture are those of grace. They are not conditions of grace. If we believe in God's promises, and trust in their fulfillment in Christ and then in us, we will want to live in, under and by those promises, as they are true and trustworthy. If we are not living in a way that expresses trust in God's grace—his being good to us even when we don't deserve it—then we're not trusting in God's grace!

The obedient life is a trusting life. A disobedient life is one that is not trusting or perhaps does not (yet) want what is promised. Only obedience that arises out of faith, hope and love gives God glory, for only that kind of obedience bears witness to the truth of who God is, as revealed to us in Jesus Christ.

God will continue to be gracious to us whether we receive or resist his grace. Part of his graciousness will be to resist our resistance to his grace! That's the nature of God's wrath, as he says "No" to our "No" to him in order to reaffirm his "Yes" to us in Christ (2 Corinthians 1:19). God's "No" is just as strong as his "Yes," because it is an expression of his "Yes." Those who resist God's grace will not experience the benefits of living by faith. However, they will not, by that unbelief, stop God from being true to himself, will not stop him from being gracious.

How should we answer those who say that they can do whatever they like since we're under grace and not law? We should say that we're surprised they have such little understanding of grace! Living a lawless life, devoid of trust in God, is not receiving grace at all. Instead, it is resisting grace, refusing to live in it. Presuming upon grace is not receiving it but rejecting it. Few of its benefits will be experienced that way.

As we disciple people in the way of Jesus, we

should help them to not reject grace by misunderstanding or pridefully resisting it. We should exhort them to not presume upon grace. Instead we should help them live in the grace that God is extending to them right now. We should help them know that no matter what they do, God will continue to be true to himself and true to his good purposes for them. We will help them trust that because God loves them and because he is gracious in his own nature, character and purpose, he will resist our resistance to grace so that one day we might fully receive and thus live by his grace and so gladly take on all the joyful obligations of grace, knowing the privilege it is to be a child of God with Jesus Christ as our elder brother.

Gary Deddo

Is Jesus the Only Way of Salvation?

People sometimes object to the Christian belief that salvation is given only through Jesus Christ. In our pluralistic society, tolerance is expected, even demanded, and the concept of freedom of religion (which permits all religions) is sometimes misinterpreted to mean that all religions are somehow equally true.

All paths lead to the same God, some say, as if they have traveled all of them and have returned from the destination. They are not tolerant of the "narrow-minded" people who believe in only one way, and they object to evangelism, for example, as an insulting attempt to change the beliefs of other people. Yet they themselves want to change the beliefs of those who believe in only one way.

Other religions

Most religions are exclusive. Orthodox Jews claim to have the right path. Muslims claim to have the best revelation of God. Hindus believe that they are right, and Buddhists believe what they do, not surprisingly, because they think it is right. Even the pluralists believe that pluralism is more right than other ideas.

All paths do not lead to the same God. The different religions even describe different gods. The Hindu has many gods, and describes salvation as a return to nothingness—a different destination than the Muslim emphasis on monotheism and heavenly rewards. Neither the Muslim nor the Hindu would agree than their paths eventually lead to the same destination. They would fight rather than switch; the Western pluralists are seen as condescending and uninformed, an offense to the people that the pluralists do not want to offend.

We believe that the Christian gospel is correct, while at the same time allowing people to reject it. Faith requires that people have liberty not to believe. Although we affirm the right for people to believe as they decide, this does not mean that we think that all faiths are true. Allowing other people to believe as they wish does not mean that we have to quit believing what we do.

Biblical claims

Jesus' earliest disciples tell us that he claimed to be the one and only path to God. He said, in effect, If you don't follow me, you are not doing the will of the Father, and you will be rejected on the day of judgment (Matthew 7:21-27). If you reject me ("deny me before others"), you will be rejected (Matthew 10:32-33). People who reject Jesus probably would not want to be with him in eternity, anyway.

Jesus said that God "has entrusted all judgment to the Son, that all may honor the Son just as they honor the Father. He who does not honor the Son does not honor the Father, who sent him" (John 5:22-23). Jesus claimed to be the exclusive means of truth and salvation. People who reject him are also rejecting God, because God is just like Jesus.

"I am the light of the world," he said (John 8:12). "I am the way and the truth and the life. No one comes to the Father except through me. If you really knew me, you would know my Father as well" (John 14:6-7). People who claim that there are other ways to salvation are wrong, Jesus said.

Peter was equally blunt when he told the Jewish leaders, "Salvation is found in no one else, for there is no other name under heaven…by which we must be saved" (Acts 4:12).

Paul also said that people who did not know Christ were "dead in your transgressions and sins" (Ephesians 2:1). They had no hope, and despite their religious beliefs, they did not have God (verse 12). There is only one Mediator, he said—only one way to get to God (1 Timothy 2:5). Jesus was the ransom that everyone needed (1 Timothy 4:10). If there were any other set of instructions, or any other path that offered salvation, then God would have provided it (Galatians 3:21).

It is through Christ that the world is reconciled to God (Colossians 1:20-22). Paul was called to spread the gospel among the Gentiles. Their religion, he said, was worthless (Acts 14:15). The book of Hebrews says: Christ is not just better than other paths — he is effective whereas they are not (Hebrews 10:11). It is an all-or-nothing difference, not a difference of one being a little better than the others.

The Christian teaching of exclusive salvation is based on what Jesus said, and what the Scriptures teach. This is tightly linked to who Jesus is, and our need for grace.

Our need for grace

The Bible says that Jesus is the Son of God in a unique way. As God in the flesh, he gave his life for our salvation. Jesus asked if there might be some other way, but there was none (Matthew 26:39). Salvation comes to us only through God himself entering the human world to suffer the consequences of sin, to free us from sin, as his gift to us.

Most religions teach some form of works as the path of salvation — saying the right prayers, doing the right things, hoping it will be enough. They each teach that theirs is the right way. They teach that people can be good enough if they try hard enough. But Christianity teaches that we all need grace because we cannot be good enough no matter what we do or how hard we try.

It is impossible for both ideas to be true at the same time. The doctrine of grace teaches, whether we like it or not, that no other paths lead to salvation. We either rely on what we do, or we rely on what God has done in Jesus Christ.

Future grace

What about people who die without hearing about Jesus? What about people who lived before Jesus was born, or in a land thousands of miles away? Do they have any hope?

Yes — precisely because the Christian gospel is the gospel of grace. People are saved by God's grace, not by pronouncing the name "Jesus" or having special knowledge or special formulas. Jesus died for the sins of the whole world, whether they know it or not (2 Corinthians 5:14; 1 John 2:2). His death was an atoning sacrifice for everyone — past, present, future, Palestinian or Peruvian.

We are confident that God "wants everyone to come to repentance" (2 Peter 3:9). Although his ways and times are often unknown to us, we nonetheless trust him to love the humans he has made. Jesus said: "God so loved the world that he gave his one and only Son, that whoever believes in him shall not perish but have eternal life. For God did not send his Son into the world to condemn the world, but to save the world through him" (John 3:16-17).

We believe that the resurrected Christ has conquered death, and therefore not even death can prevent him from leading people to trust him for salvation. We don't know the hows or whens, but we can trust him. Therefore we can believe that one way or another, he urges every person who ever lived, or who will ever live, to trust in him for salvation. That might be before they die, at the point of death, or even after they die. At the last judgment, if some people turn to Christ in faith when they at last learn what he has done for them, then he will not turn them away.

But no matter when people are saved, or how well they understand it, it is only through Christ that they can be saved. Well-intentioned good works will never save anyone, no matter how sincerely people believe that they can be saved if they try hard enough. The reason that we need grace, and Jesus' sacrifice, is because no amount of good works, no amount of religious deeds, can ever save anyone. If such a path could have been devised, then God would have done it (Galatians 3:21).

If people have sincerely tried to attain salvation by working, meditating, flagellating, self-immolating or any other humanly devised means, then they will learn that their works have not earned them anything with God. Salvation is by grace, and only by grace. The Christian gospel teaches that no one can earn it, and yet it is available to all.

No matter what religious path a person has been on, Christ can rescue them from it and set them on his own path. He is the only Son of God, who provided the only atoning sacrifice that everyone needs. He is the unique channel of God's grace and salvation. This is what Jesus taught. Jesus is exclusive and inclusive at the same time—the narrow way and the Savior of the entire world—the only way of salvation, yet available for all.

God's grace, shown most perfectly in Jesus Christ, is exactly what everyone needs, and the good news is that it is freely given to all. It's great news, and it's worth sharing.

Joseph Tkach

Parable of the Lost Son

The parable of the prodigal son (Luke 15:11-32) is perhaps better named the parable of the lost son, since it is designed to go with the parables of the lost sheep (verses 3-7) and lost coin (verses 8-10). Some have even called it the parable of the prodigal father, because of the father's extravagance. Even today, after centuries of teaching about God's grace, the father's willingness to forgive his runaway son is shockingly generous.

This is Jesus' longest parable: 22 verses. Let's go through the parable, noting its story, its organization and its lessons.

Historical background and observations

1. Return of the lost son — verses 11-24

A. The younger son leaves — verses 11-16

"There was a man" — This is a standard introduction to a parable. "Who had two sons" — The first parable in this chapter had one of 100 getting lost, the second parable one in 10, this parable has one out of <u>two</u> becoming lost. The sequence emphasizes the magnitude of the lost son. To lose half your sons would be a tragedy, and regaining half would likewise be a greater cause for rejoicing.

"The younger son" — There's no mention of a wife, so he would probably have been 18-20. His youth isn't emphasized, but younger sons may be more likely to be foolish and older sons more likely to look down on a brother. Figuratively, the older son represented the Pharisees and the younger son represented the people Jesus was reaching (verse 1). In the early church, the older son may have been seen as corresponding to the Jews and the younger son to Gentiles.

"Give me my share of the estate" — Inheritances were normally given only when the father died. The son's demand for an early distribution was unusual and frowned upon – it's as if the son had said, "I wish you were dead." He valued the money more than he did the relationship. Traditionally, firstborn sons were given twice as much as other sons, but we don't know if this was always done in Jesus' day. If so, the younger son would have received one third of the estate. The amount isn't stressed. Nor are we told how the property was turned into cash. Such details are ignored because they aren't part of the point.

"Divided his property" — Early distribution of the estate normally meant that the father continued to receive the benefits of the estate as long as he lived. (The father could therefore kill the fattened calf without asking the older son, who owned it.) The younger son didn't just receive surplus property; it was part of the father's source of income. (The word for property is *bios*, meaning "the resources which one has as a means of living."[1]) If a son sold land, the new owner could not use it until the father died. Again, such details are ignored because they are not part of the point. "Between them" — The older son also received his share.

"Not long after that" — His departure was probably not surprising. His desire for the inheritance indicated he wanted to strike out on his own rather than continue being part of the family. He was insulting the family as well as injuring it. "A distant country" — A Gentile country. Many

---

[1] J. Louw and E. Nida, *Greek-English Lexicon of the New Testament*, volume 1, page 560, 57.18.

Jews lived in Gentile areas. "Squandered his wealth in wild living" — Not only did he waste the money, he sinned in the process. However, his sins aren't specified. Luke doesn't emphasize the sinning as much as he does losing the money. This is consistent with Luke's interest in possessions and poverty. Perhaps the prodigal son was trying to make friends by spending money on them.

"Spent everything...began to be in need" — His poverty is emphasized, not any deficiency in character. Luke is emphasizing his lostness, not his guilt. "To feed pigs" — He had an unclean occupation, abandoning religious scruples, but still the emphasis seems to be on his poverty (hunger, verse 16) rather than sin.

"He longed to fill his stomach with the pods" — He *wished* he could eat the carob-tree pods, but humans can't digest them. As a servant, he would have received some pay. Jesus is painting a hypothetical, not an actual story, to emphasize the son's desperate plight. "No one gave him anything" — He received no alms (one of Luke's interests). His former friends did not help him.

B. The son decides to return — verses 17-20

"When he came to his senses" — This pivotal verse changes the direction of the story. "When" (rather than "it so happened that") implies that his sanity was inevitable. The word "repentance" is not used. "My father's hired servants" — He contrasts himself, a hired servant of a Gentile, to his father's servants, who had plenty to eat. "Food to spare...starving to death" — Though the setting of the story is sin and repentance (verses 1-2), the story itself emphasizes financial need rather than moral corruption. "Starving" is another exaggeration. If he had been near starvation, he would not have had the strength to travel back home.

"Set out and go" — Literally, "rising up, I will go." This was a translation of an Aramaic idiom for go immediately. But "arise" may also hint at a rising in state of life.

He then prepared a speech he would use to get a job with his father. "Sinned against heaven" — "Heaven" is a euphemism for God — used perhaps because the father represents God in the story. Specific sins aren't mentioned except in the accusations of the older brother (verse 30). "And against you" — He acknowledged his affront to the family.

"No longer worthy to be called your son" — This could be in a legal and a moral sense: He had no rights for further inheritance, and his behavior had not been up to family standards. He assumed that his relationship to his father was based on the work that he did – he had to be worthy. "Make me like one of your hired servants" — He was willing to <u>earn</u> his keep by serving the family (which would have meant serving his older brother, too).[2]

C. The father receives him — verses 20-24

"While he was still a long way off, his father saw him" — Some commentators say this implies that the father was continually watching for the return of his son. However, the text says nothing about watching, nor does it add a word like "when" to imply inevitability. It says: "The son being yet far off, his father saw him." The father was very willing to have a reconciliation — acting while the son was far away shows that, without any need to add the idea of watching.

"Compassion...ran" — These words emphasize the father's enthusiasm. In ancient societies, it was considered undignified for an older man to pull up his robes to run. His actions, representative of God's feelings for repentant sinners, show enthusiastic acceptance, love and joy. "Kiss" — Perhaps a sign of forgiveness (cf. 2 Samuel 14:33). The son didn't finish his speech, perhaps because he was cut short by his father.

"Best robe...ring" — Both robe and ring may allude to Joseph's promotion to authority (Genesis 41:42). Robes were given to honored guests; the ring was a signet ring, indicating authority. "Sandals" — Servants did not wear sandals; only family members did.

---

[2] "Hired men" is *misthioi*, contract laborers, probably farmhands, not the *douloi*, household bondservants, mentioned in verse 22.

"Fattened calf" — Meat was eaten primarily on festivals, and calves would be fattened for such feasts, so this may hint that a celebration of restoration is more important than a religious festival. The celebration corresponds to the "rejoice" of the parables of the lost sheep and coin.

"This son of mine was dead" — In what way was he dead? Here are two possibilities: 1) The father heard about the famine, hadn't heard from his son in a long time, and thought he had died. 2) Perhaps he counted him metaphorically dead because he had become as a Gentile. Some Jews conducted funerals for children who married Gentiles. But the father doesn't seem to be the type to disown his son.

2. Conflict with the older son

A. The older son comes home — verses 25-27

So far, this parable has been parallel to the first two parables; the lost has been found and there is rejoicing. The parable could have stopped at this point, and still be a good parable. However, Jesus uses the older son to introduce an additional lesson in the parable. Perhaps this is where our attention should be directed, because it is what is new and different.

In some ways this is two parables in one, both parts ending with the statement about dead and alive, lost and found. Both sons are lost — one who left home (like the sheep that was lost in verse 4) and one who was lost even while at home (like the coin in verse 8). Both the "sinners" and the Pharisees were separated from God — the first ones are visibly lost, the others still live at home — but both are welcomed when they turn to God.

The older son's arrival on the scene is odd; normally a servant would have been sent to get him at the start. But in the parable it is as if the older son found out about the party by accident. Some commentators say this implies the son was out of touch with his father, estranged in attitude or too addicted to work. This seems to read too much into the story; he may have simply been working at the far end of the estate.

The older son is contrasted to the younger: The younger starts the story by leaving home; the older starts by returning. The younger then decides to go home; the older refuses to enter. The younger wants to be his father's servant; the older son resents being a servant. The younger son admits guilt; the older one insists on his innocence.

The servant describes the younger son as "safe and sound," or in health; this is less dramatic than the father's comment about dead and alive. The servant is matter-of-fact; the father is overjoyed.

B. Complaint of the older son — verses 28-30

The older son "became angry" — in contrast to his father's compassion — and he did not want to go in despite knowing his father's will. In contrast to the older son's unwillingness to come in, the father went out, just as he had done for the younger son. "Pleaded with him" — The father eagerly desired for the older son to share his joy. Normally a son would do what his father said to do; here the older son is disobedient. The older son had inherited his father's estate, but not his attitude of mercy.

"Look!" — The older son starts abruptly, hinting of disrespect, frustration and impatience. "I've been slaving for you" — The verb is *douleun*, related to *doulos*, servant. His relationship to his father was based on work, not love. "Never disobeyed" — until now.

"You never gave me even a young goat" — Yet a goat is of lesser value than a calf. But the father would have given a goat if the son had asked (verse 31). The son felt unappreciated and unrewarded; his complaint suggests that he had a long-smoldering resentment. He complained about the extra given to the younger — similar to the workers in the vineyard who complained about a days' wage being given to those who worked only one hour (Matthew 20:12).

"This son of yours" — The older brother doesn't say "my brother"; it is as if he no longer claims him. "Squandered" — Literally, "devoured," an ironic word for a man who was starving. "Your property" — This continues the emphasis on physical possessions. The younger son had wasted part of the family estate, failing in his duty to provide for his father. "With prostitutes" — Did the older son really know how his brother had spent the money? Perhaps the financial waste had begun before the son left home, or perhaps some reports had come back from the far country. Both are possible, but the story says nothing about it. This suggests that the older son (perhaps like the Pharisees) was making an unsubstantiated accusation.

C. Response of the father — verses 31-32

"My son" — The usual word for "son" in this parable is *huios;* here it is *teknon,* "child," a term of affection. "Everything I have is yours" — The older son will get the entire inheritance. Some commentators speculate about the legal status of the property rights and whether the younger son could have inherited something, but the parable says nothing about it. Inheritance details are not the point; acceptance or reconciliation is. Older sons inherited twice as much as other sons because they had a responsibility to the family. The older son would have had a duty to take care of a brother who fell on hard times. But the older son was not willing to accept this responsibility; he (like the younger son!) simply wanted the property.

"We had to celebrate" — The word *edei* is used, meaning "it was necessary." Rejoicing about the return of a lost person isn't an option — it is a necessity. "This brother of yours" — Not "my son," but "your brother." The father reminded the older son of his family responsibility. The implication is that it is necessary for *him* to rejoice — and by extension, for the Pharisees to rejoice at what Jesus was doing.

What this parable teaches us about God

The context helps us understand the lessons of the parable. Verses 1-2 tell us that sinners and tax collectors were being taught by Jesus. Pharisees criticized Jesus — not for teaching such people, but for eating with them, which was a sign of social acceptance. The Pharisees tried hard to be righteous, and they were disturbed that Jesus accepted people who hadn't been trying hard. Perhaps they were worried that Jesus was making it too easy on people, and his acceptance might encourage others to be lazy.

Jesus then gave the parables of the lost sheep and the lost coin, both concluding that God rejoices about each sinner who repents. "There will be more rejoicing in heaven over one sinner who repents than over ninety-nine righteous persons who do not need to repent" (verse 7). There's no such thing as a person who has no need for repentance, but the Pharisees weren't yet aware of that. There would be rejoicing for them, too, if they would accept it.

The parable of the lost son continues the theme of rejoicing and adds to it. The first half of the parable illustrates rejoicing over a sinner who returned; the second half more directly addresses the situation Jesus faced: criticism about his willingness to be with sinners. By telling the parable the way he did, Jesus chides those who do not rejoice about the sinners' interest in being taught (figuratively, they were returning to God).

In the first two parables, the lost were found by searching. But the younger son was found by waiting. The spiritually lost were already coming to Jesus. They had been spiritually dead and were now showing interest — they wanted to be taught by Jesus. Jesus received them and ate with them. His reception would have encouraged them to obey as much as they knew and to continue to listen to him for more instruction in God's way.

But the parable is not just about Jesus in the first century; it is also a timeless message about God the Father. He rejoices over (cf. the celebration) and honors (cf. the robe, ring and sandals) every sinner who repents. He doesn't wait for a full and formal apology; he perceives the attitude and comes toward us.[3] This theme of joyful acceptance, similar to that of the first two parables of this

---

[3] Theologically, people do not start coming toward God unless they are led by the Holy Spirit. The Father has been seeking (illustrated by the first two parables in this chapter) before the people "come to themselves" and desire to return.

chapter, dominates the first part of this parable. This lesson is illustrated by the father: He is always ready to welcome a returning child.

The parable shows that sinners can confess and return to God. Since God is gracious, sinners can return to him with confidence that he will warmly welcome them. But in the parable, poverty is more prominent than sin. Unlike the first two parables, the word *repent* is not used; only superficial reasons are given for the son's return. As Jesus spoke to the Pharisees, encouraging sinners to return was not the main issue; the main issue was what to do about sinners who were already willing to return.

The parable shows that God's people should rejoice at a) the willingness of sinners to turn to God and b) the willingness of God to receive them. This is the lesson of the second half of the parable, illustrated by the father's correction of his older son. This theme addresses the setting of the three parables, the Pharisees' criticism of Jesus' reception of sinners. The parables of the lost sheep and lost coin and the first half of the parable of the lost son are preparatory to this point.

These themes are timeless. God rejoices over each person who repents, and so should we. We need not kill a calf for repentant persons (Jesus didn't; the parable illustrates the attitude of rejoicing, not the specific actions we should take). We need to accept repentant[4] sinners to social fellowship (cf. eating with them, verse 2) and religious instruction (cf. allowing them to listen, verse 1). This parable does not say we should *seek* outcasts (that is shown better by the parables of lost sheep and lost coin), but that we should be happy when they come to us to be taught.

Jesus' story shows that it is ungodly to refuse to rejoice about repentance. The Pharisees, by insisting on a too-strict standard of righteousness, were being unrighteous. They, too, needed to repent.

Epilogue

The parable ends without revealing what the older son did. Would the hard-hearted son change his mind and rejoice about his brother's return? For the situation in Jesus' day, either response was still possible — it was up to the Pharisees. Would they rejoice with Jesus? The book of Acts shows that some did and some did not.

Similarly, the parable does not reveal what the younger son did. Did he abuse his second chance? That also reflects the situation Jesus was in. Would the tax collectors and sinners continue in their repentance? It was not yet known. Nevertheless, it is appropriate — no, necessary — to rejoice at their first change of heart, rather than waiting for some probationary period.

Michael Morrison

---

[4] This does not mean that people must conform to all our expectations before we will have anything to do with them (that was the attitude of the Pharisees). In the context, their repentance is shown not by impeccable behavior, but simply by their willingness to be with and to be taught by Jesus. They were turned in the right direction, even though they were not very far along on the journey.

Responding to God With Worship

We respond to God with worship, because worship is simply giving God what is fitting. He is praiseworthy, not only for his power but also for his gentleness. God is love, and all that he does is done in love. This is praiseworthy. We praise love even on a human level, don't we? We praise people who give their lives to help others. They did not have enough power to save their own lives, but what power they had, they used to help others—and that is praiseworthy. In contrast, we criticize people who had the power to help but refused to do it. Goodness is more praiseworthy than power is, and God is both good and powerful.

Praise deepens the bond of love between us and God. God's love for us is never diminished, but ours for him often grows weak. In praise, we rehearse his love for us and, in effect, fan the fire of love for him that the Spirit has started within us. It is good for us to remember and rehearse how wonderful God is, for that strengthens us in Christ and increases our desire to be like him in his goodness, which increases our joy.

We were made for the purpose of praising God (1 Peter 2:9), of giving him glory and honor—and the better we are in harmony with God's purpose for life, the greater joy will be ours. Life is more satisfying when we do what we were made to do: honor God. We do that not only in worship, but also in the way we live.

A way of life

Worship is a way of life. We offer our bodies and minds as living sacrifices (Romans 12:1-2). We worship God when we share the gospel (Romans 15:16). We worship God when we give financial offerings (Philippians 4:18). We worship God when we help other people (Hebrews 13:16). We say that he is worthy of our time, attention and loyalty. We praise his glory, and his humility in becoming one of us for our sakes. We praise his righteousness and his mercy. We praise him for the way he is.

This is what we were made for, to declare his praises. It is right that we praise the One who created us, the One who died and rose to save us and give us life eternal, the One who now works to help us become more like him. We owe him our allegiance, and our love.

We were made to praise God, and this is what we will do eternally. John was given a vision of our future: "I heard every creature in heaven and on earth and under the earth and on the sea, and all that is in them, singing: 'To him who sits on the throne and to the Lamb be praise and honor and glory and power, for ever and ever!'" (Revelation 5:13). This is the right response: awe at the awesome, honor for the honorable, and allegiance to the trustworthy.

Five basic principles

Psalm 33:1-3 tells us, "Sing joyfully to the Lord, you righteous; it is fitting for the upright to praise him. Praise the Lord with the harp; make music to him on the ten-stringed lyre. Sing to him a new song; play skillfully, and shout for joy." Scripture tells us to sing, shout, to use harps, flutes, tambourines, trumpets, cymbals—even to worship with dancing (Psalms 149-150). The picture is of exuberance, unrestrained joy, and happiness expressed without inhibitions.

The Bible gives us examples of spontaneous worship. It also gives us examples of very formal approaches to worship, with stereotyped routines that stay the same for centuries. Both approaches to worship can be legitimate, and neither one can claim to be the only authentic way to praise God.

Let me review some of the broader principles involved in worship.

1. We are called to worship

God wants us to worship him. This is a constant we see from one end of Scripture to another (Genesis 4:4; John 4:23; Revelation 22:9). Worship is one of the reasons we are called: to declare his praises (1 Peter 2:9). God's people not only love and obey him, but they also do acts of worship. They make sacrifices, they sing praises, they pray.

In Scripture, we see a wide variety in the way that worship can be done. In the law of Moses, many details were given. Specific people were assigned to do specific actions at specific times in specific places. The who, what, when, where and how were spelled out. In contrast to that, we see in Genesis very few rules about how the patriarchs worshipped. They did not have a designated priesthood, were not restricted to a certain place, and were told little about what to offer or when to offer it.

In the New Testament, we again see very little about the how and the when of worship. Worship activities are not restricted to a certain group of people or a certain place. Christ did away with the Mosaic requirements. All believers are priests and continually offer themselves as living sacrifices.

2. Worship only God

Despite the great variety in worship styles, we see a simple constant throughout Scripture: Only God should be worshipped. Worship, to be acceptable, must be exclusive. God requires all our love—all our allegiance. We cannot serve two gods. Although we may worship him in different styles, our unity is based on the fact that it is him we worship.

In ancient Israel, the rival god was often Baal, a Canaanite deity. In Jesus' day, it was religious tradition, self-righteousness and hypocrisy. Anything that comes between us and God— anything that might cause us to disobey him—is a false god, an idol. For some, it is money. For others, it is sex. Some have a bigger problem with pride, or with concerns about what other people may think of us. John mentions some common false gods when he writes,

> Do not love the world or anything in the world. If anyone loves the world, the love of the Father is not in him. For everything in the world—the cravings of sinful man, the lust of his eyes and the boasting of what he has and does—comes not from the Father but from the world. The world and its desires pass away, but the man who does the will of God lives forever. (1 John 2:15-17)

No matter what our weakness is, we need to crucify it, kill it, put all false gods away. If something distracts us from obeying God, we need to get rid of it. God wants people who worship only him, who have him as the center of all life.

3. Sincerity

The third constant about worship that we see in the Scriptures is that worship must be sincere. It does no good to go through the right motions, sing the right songs, meet on the right days and say the right words, if we don't really love God in our hearts. Jesus criticized those who honored God with their lips, but who worshipped in vain, because their hearts were not close to God. Their traditions (originally designed to express love and worship) had become obstacles to real love and worship.

Jesus also stresses the need for sincerity when he says that worship must be in spirit and in truth (John 4:24). If we say that we love God when we actually resent his commands, we are hypocrites. If we value our freedom more than we do his authority, we cannot worship him in truth. We cannot take his covenant on our lips and cast his words behind (Psalm 50:16-17). We cannot call him Lord and ignore what he says.

4. Obedience

Throughout Scripture, true worship includes obedience. This includes God's words concerning the way we treat one another. We cannot honor God when we dishonor his children. "If anyone says, 'I love God,' yet hates his brother, he is a liar. For anyone who does not love his brother, whom he has seen, cannot love God, whom he has not seen" (1 John 4:20-21). It is similar to Isaiah's scathing criticism of people who perform worship rituals while indulging in social injustices:

> Stop bringing meaningless offerings! Your incense is detestable to me. New Moons, Sabbaths and convocations—I cannot bear your evil assemblies. Your New Moon festivals and your appointed feasts my soul hates. They have become a burden to me; I am weary of bearing them. When you spread out your hands in prayer, I will hide my eyes from you; even when you offer many prayers, I am not listening. (Isaiah 1:11-15)

As far as we can tell, there was nothing wrong with the days the people were keeping, or the kind of incense and animals they were bringing. The problem was the way they were living the rest of the time. "Your hands are full of blood!" he said (verse 15)—and yet the problem was not just with those who had actually committed murder.

He called for a comprehensive solution: "Stop doing wrong, learn to do right! Seek justice, encourage the oppressed. Defend the cause of the fatherless, plead the case of the widow" (verses 16-17). They needed to get their interpersonal relationships in order. They needed to eliminate racial prejudice, social class stereotypes, and unfair economic practices.

5. In all of life

Worship should make a difference in the way we treat one another seven days a week. We see this principle throughout Scripture. How should we worship? Micah asks the question and gives the answer:

> With what shall I come before the Lord and bow down before the exalted God? Shall I come before him with burnt offerings, with calves a year old? Will the Lord be pleased with thousands of rams, with ten thousand rivers of oil? Shall I offer my firstborn for my transgression, the fruit of my body for the sin of my soul? He has showed you, O man, what is good. And what does the Lord require of you? To act justly and to love mercy and to walk humbly with your God. (Micah 6:6-8)

Hosea also stressed that relationships are more important than the mechanics of worship: "I desire mercy, not sacrifice, and acknowledgment of God rather than burnt offerings" (Hosea 6:6). We are called not only to praise, but also to do good works (Ephesians 2:10). Our concept of worship must go far beyond music, days and rituals. Those details are not as important as the way we treat our neighbors. It is hypocritical to call Jesus Lord if we do not also seek his sense of justice, mercy, and compassion.

Worship is much more than outward actions—it involves a change of behavior, rooted in a change of heart, produced in us by the Holy Spirit. Instrumental in this change is our willingness to spend time with God in prayer, study and other spiritual disciplines. The transformation does not happen by magic—it happens through time spent in fellowship with God.

Paul's expansive view of worship

Worship involves all of life. We see this in the letters of Paul. He uses the terminology of sacrifice and worship in this way: "I urge you, brothers and sisters, in view of God's mercy, to offer your bodies as a living sacrifice, holy and pleasing to God—this is your true and proper worship" (Romans 12:1). All of life is to be worship, not just a few hours each week. If our entire life is devoted to worship, this will definitely include some time each week with other Christians!

Paul uses more words for sacrifice and worship in Romans 15:16 when he speaks of the grace God had given him "to be a minister of Christ Jesus to the Gentiles. He gave me the priestly duty of proclaiming the gospel of God, so that the Gentiles might become an offering acceptable to God, sanctified by the Holy Spirit." Preaching the gospel is a form of worship.

Since we are all priests, we all have the priestly

duty of proclaiming the praises of the One who called us (1 Peter 2:9) — a worship any believer can do, or at least participate in by helping others preach the gospel. When Paul thanked the Philippians for sending him financial support, he used words for worship: "I have received from Epaphroditus the gifts you sent. They are a fragrant offering, an acceptable sacrifice, pleasing to God" (Philippians 4:18).

Financial help given to other Christians can be a form of worship. Hebrews describes worship given both in words and in works: "Let us continually offer to God a sacrifice of praise — the fruit of lips that confess his name. And do not forget to do good and to share with others, for with such sacrifices God is pleased" (Hebrews 13:15-16).

We are called to worship, celebrate and glorify God. It is our joy to be able to declare his praises, to share the good news of what he has done for us in and through our Lord and Savior Jesus Christ.

Joseph Tkach

Five facts about worship

- God wants us to worship, to respond to him with praise and thanks.
- Only God is worthy of our worship and total allegiance.
- Worship should be sincere, not a performance.
- If we respect and love God, we will do what he says.
- Worship is not just something we do once a week — it involves everything we do.

Things to think about

- What characteristic of God do you feel most thankful for?
- Some Old Testament sacrifices were completely burned up — nothing left but smoke and ashes. Have any of your sacrifices been like that?
- Spectators cheer when their team scores a goal or wins a game. Do we respond to God with equal enthusiasm?
- For many people, God is not very important in day-to-day life. What do people value instead?
- Why does God care about the way we treat other people?

Church: Some Assembly Required

Just across the road from our home is a beautiful church. Many of our neighbors go there on Sunday morning to worship. My wife's parents were married in that church, and her great grandfather donated the land on which it is built. I like the worship service. It is dignified and meaningful, and the congregation shares my preference for traditional hymns and music. The pastor is a good friend, and from time to time he has asked me to stand in for him. The people good-naturedly appreciate my clumsy attempts to handle the unfamiliar liturgy, and some have told me they wish I would come more often.

So why, most Sundays, do we make a round trip of about 100 miles to attend "our" church in the big city? That is the closest congregation of the denomination in which I have membership and am ordained. But it is not just a matter of brand loyalty. I feel more or less at home in most Christian churches, and I believe they are valid places to worship. The styles might be different, but I suspect that we are more concerned about styles than God is. Wherever and whenever Christians gather together in his name, Jesus said he would be there, too. Then why do I drive to my relatively distant congregation instead of just walking across the road?

Does it matter?

I think about this sometimes as I make the Sunday morning drive. Does it matter where we go? Are we at liberty to just pick a church out of convenience? Or even to go nowhere? Many people feel it is acceptable to watch a church service on television, never committing themselves to regular assembly. Others say that just talking about God and religion with friends at work or at an informal gathering from time to time is all the "church" they need.

But the Bible places a high importance on belonging to a congregation — and not just belonging, but supporting and participating in its life and work. One reason is that a congregation provides the opportunity for fellowship and joining in worship and communion. Another reason is that a congregation also requires *accountability*, something that, ironically, is often put forward as an excuse for *withdrawing* from regular congregational worship, and even leaving a church. We don't like accountability. It implies restriction, discipline, correction and expectations about our time and money — things we resist.

There are often some disagreeable aspects of congregational life. We tend to get ourselves bogged down in distracting details and stir them into the church mix. But the primary thing God is concerned about is our relationships. Jesus taught that lasting, productive relationships, based on mutual love and respect, are the substance of Christian life. Human societies and organizations rarely put the highest priority on this; they have different agendas. But a congregation of fellow believers should be a safe place to nurture, maintain and, if necessary, repair relationships. To deny ourselves this environment is to miss out on a key aspect of the central dimension of our Christian lives.

I am not suggesting that regular church attendance makes us more righteous, or that to stay away is unforgivable. My long commute to worship does not make me more acceptable to God. Nevertheless, I think he does want me to have a strong commitment to my not-so-local congregation, and I do not take it lightly. The extra effort is definitely more worth than it is trouble.

The early church

People tend to interpret the scriptures about congregational worship in terms of our modern situation. But those instructions were not written against a backdrop of what has become the world's largest religion with over two billion adherents and a bewildering variety of sects, groups and denominations. We need to see what was written in the context of the first-century church.

After the initial surge, the church settled down to a slower growth pattern. The typical congregation in New Testament times seems to have been a relatively small number of people meeting in homes or public places. Some congregations were in contact with one another, and there is evidence of some rudimentary organization and central authority. But most of the time the churches were on their own.

Paul himself seems to have been the linking factor in the churches he founded. Most of his letters have the flavor of a personal, intimate communication to people he knew rather than that of a large, general audience. He never dreamed that his words would be endlessly dissected and analyzed 2,000 years later in churches on continents he did not even know existed. He wrote to people he knew, gathered in little groups around the Mediterranean Sea.

Unlike today, where we have many choices, the early believers were a small minority, struggling to exist in what was often a hostile environment. With enemies, physical and spiritual, waiting to pounce, unity and harmony within the group were vitally important. That is why Paul and the other founding fathers focused their letters so much on *koinonia*, or community.

God's building

One of Paul's favorite analogies was to see the congregation as a building that was a work in progress (1 Corinthians 3:9). "God is building a home," he reminded the church at Ephesus.

> He's using us all — irrespective of how we got here — in what he is building. He used the apostles and prophets for the foundation. Now he's using you, fitting you in brick by brick, stone by stone, with Christ Jesus as the cornerstone that holds all the parts together. We see it taking shape day after day — a holy temple built by God, all of us built into it, a temple in which God is quite at home. (Ephesians 2:19-22, *Message Bible*)

In such a building, every part is needed. "From him the whole body, joined and held together by every supporting ligament, grows and builds itself up in love, *as each part does its work*" (Ephesians 4:16, NIV). This does not imply an easy-going "come when you feel like it" approach, does it?

These first Christians were, like us, frail and flawed human beings. Like us, they had their politics and quarrels. So how to handle such problems is often discussed. For example, when two long-standing members of the congregation at Philippi had a serious disagreement, Paul urged them publicly to settle their differences:

> I urge Euodia and Syntyche to iron out their differences and make up. God doesn't want his children holding grudges. And, oh, yes, Syzygus, since you're right there to help them work things out, do your best with them. These women worked for the Message hand in hand with Clement and me, and with the other veterans — worked as hard as any of us. Remember, their names are also in the book of life. (Philippians 4:2-3, *Message Bible*)

Was Syzygus successful? Let's hope so. Paul valued both Euodia and Syntyche, and did not want to lose either of them. So Paul urged them to reconcile quickly, for the good of the whole group.

The early church was taught to see membership in a congregation as a privilege and a responsibility. It was not a "useful option" or an "added benefit" to take advantage of if and when one felt like it. The instructions have the feeling of "this means you, so listen up" rather than "here are some general principles that you might want to think about in your planning meetings." Hebrews 10:25 was an urgent warning to "not giving up meeting together" because of a trend that needed to be nipped in the bud.

Breaking up is hard to do

Members who persisted in unacceptable or disruptive conduct might eventually have to be denied fellowship — but only as a last resort, after all other efforts to reconcile had failed. Even then, it was not done out of revenge or punishment, but as a last-ditch effort to bring the erring member to their senses. To be barred from fellowship was a serious matter. You couldn't just shrug your shoulders and find another church that would have you. There was nowhere else to go.

Does this mean there is never a reason to leave a congregation? No. A church that is controlling and abusive does not deserve your membership, and you are better off out of it. But most congregations are not like that. They are just a group of imperfect believers struggling with the trials of life. Membership in a group like that should not be discarded lightly. In our modern world, nearly every relationship is fraying—marriage, family, neighbors, friends. What should be strong committed relationships have become casual and negotiable. Sadly, that includes membership in a congregation.

Reasons for leaving a congregation often sound righteous—a disagreement over a doctrine or a change of worship style. But often, the *real* reason is hurt feelings and wounded pride. We draw ourselves up, puff out our feathers and say, "Here I stand, I can do no other." But what we mean is, "Here I go, I can't stand the others." The result is that people who were once friends now cross the road rather than pass the time of day.

If we are having difficulty with relationships in our church, it is all the more reason to stay and try to work things out. Jesus and his apostles urged their people to solve problems quickly. They knew that, if left to fester, hurts and grudges could spread to others and eventually destroy the *koinonia*, the fellowship. How much stronger, more robust and more influential would the Body of Christ be today if we would commit ourselves to working out differences rather than endlessly splitting and dividing?

A lesson from persecution

Some years ago I met a man in eastern Europe who published a small Christian magazine on an underground press in his basement. The Communist rulers of his day ruthlessly suppressed Christianity, and this man had endured years of prison and persecution. As he drove me around his city, he showed me a dramatic account of what life had been like under Communism.

We stopped in front of a pile of rubble. "We built a church here, but they bulldozed it," he told me. We drove on, and after a few minutes, he stopped again and said, "We started a new church here, but they knocked this one down too." He drove us to another site, and another and another, each time repeating the story.

"Finally," he said, "once the authorities realized that European Communism was collapsing, they began to relax the restrictions a little." They summoned the Christian leaders and told them they had permission to meet. There were two conditions. One was that they had to all meet together at a time and a place that the government chose. Second, the government would appoint the pastor. The man selected was not the best speaker, nor the most educated. But it did not matter. Catholics, Baptists, Orthodox, Pentecostals and even Jehovah's Witnesses would share a common service. "We were so happy to be able to meet that our differences did not matter."

Then, when the Communist government finally fell apart, Western evangelists rushed in. Soon the group broke up into the various sects and denominations again. That brief moment of harmony has been replaced with competitive congregations glaring at each other due to their different teachings. "We appreciate the freedom, and we do have our different religious traditions," explained my friend as he showed me yet another demolished building. "But in some ways we were never happier than when we had no choice but to get along together."

No one wants persecution. But today, where we have freedom of worship, many of us use that freedom *to reduce our commitment.* Then we wonder why our witness is not as effective as it could be.

A place of safety

A church should be a safe place where there is genuine interaction—sharing the fun, pain, hope, joy, forgiveness and reconciliation of life. You can't experience that as a lone wolf, any more than you can experience baseball, basketball or soccer by chasing balls all by yourself. Real living must be experienced in community and fellowship.

Bryan Leech's popular hymn, "We are God's People" puts it nicely:

We are a temple, the Spirit's dwelling place,
Formed in great weakness, a cup to hold God's grace;
We die alone, for on its own, each ember loses fire:
Yet joined in one the flame burns on
To give warmth and light, and to inspire.

I suppose that's why on most Sunday mornings my wife and I drive out of our little country town and head up the highway to the big city. I'm sure we could find rich and meaningful fellowship with any group of believers, but we find that our long-term friendships and shared history outweigh the convenience of proximity. We've been through good times and hard times with our church. We've shared hopes, joys, pains and sorrows, disappointments and successes. We feel a commitment there, and despite the long miles and significant tread wear, we would not have it any other way.

John Halford

Leadership in the Church – An Examination of Eight Words

The New Testament mentions a wide variety of leaders in the church: apostles, prophets, evangelists, pastors, teachers, bishops, elders and deacons. What are these offices? Are they commanded for the church today? Let's examine the evidence, starting with the titles given in Ephesians 4:11: "Christ himself gave the apostles, the prophets, the evangelists, the pastors and teachers."

Apostles

The word "apostle" is sometimes used for the highest rank of church leadership. However, the word had a different meaning before the church existed. It originally meant "one who has been sent" — an ambassador or representative. This general meaning is seen in some New Testament uses.

Jesus used the word in a general sense when he said that a "messenger" is not greater than the one who sends him (John 13:16). Similarly, Paul referred to some apostles whose names were not given; the NIV calls them "representatives" (2 Corinthians 8:23). The general function of an *apostolos* was to represent someone else. When Paul called Epaphroditus an *apostolos*, he may have meant that Epaphroditus was a messenger of the church at Philippi (Philippians 2:25).

Jesus, who was sent by the Father, was an apostle (Hebrews 3:1). The 12 disciples, who were sent by Jesus, were also apostles (Mark 3:14, etc.). The disciples are not in the same category of authority as Jesus, but the same Greek word is used. The focus is on the function, not rank. Barnabas and Paul were also sent out, and they were called apostles (Acts 14:4, 14).

The disciples and Paul used the term *apostolos* as the name of their leadership office in the church (Acts 15:23; Romans 11:13; Galatians 1:1; etc.). Authority came with the sending — a messenger sent by Jesus Christ had an authoritative understanding of that message.

James may have been an apostle, too — in one verse he is distinguished from the apostles, and in another he is included (1 Corinthians 15:7; Galatians 1:19). Similarly, Timothy is excluded sometimes (2 Corinthians 1:1; Colossians 1:1) and included once (1 Thessalonians 2:6) — but in this latter verse Paul may have been using the term in a general sense of messenger or representative.

The reference in Romans 16:7 is debated. Some say that Andronicus and Junia were apostles; others say that the verse simply means they were esteemed highly by the apostles. Even if they were apostles, however, it is likely that they were messengers rather than having a permanent position of authority in the church. (If they were apostles in the same sense that Paul was, it is odd that we know almost nothing about them, either from the Bible or from church history.)

Some people falsely claimed to be apostles (2 Corinthians 11:13; Revelation 2:2). Paul facetiously called them "super-apostles" (2 Corinthians 11:5; 12:11). Although he was the least of the apostles, he was not inferior to the self-proclaimed apostles (1 Corinthians 15:9). God appointed some people to be apostles (1 Corinthians 12:28; Ephesians 4:11). This was part of the foundation of the church (Ephesians 2:20; 3:5).

What role did apostles have in the church? The Twelve and Paul were instrumental in beginning the church. Soon after Jesus ascended to heaven, the disciples said that a requirement for their "apostolic ministry" was to have been with Jesus during his ministry (Acts 1:21-25). These apostles not only preached, but also exercised some administrative leadership. They laid hands on deacons whom the people had chosen (Acts 6:6) and they made decisions with the elders (Acts 15:22).

Paul mentioned some of his qualifications to be considered an apostle: seeing the Lord and raising up churches (1 Corinthians 9:1). His converts were the "seal" of his apostleship — evidence that he had been sent, at least to them (verse 2). He noted characteristics that marked an apostle: "signs, wonders and miracles" (2 Corinthians 12:12). An apostle preaches the gospel as a faithful messenger of the Lord. He is an official representative of Jesus Christ, more exclusive and authoritative than elders.

Prophets

Isn't a prophet somebody who predicts the future? That may be one meaning of the word, but that's not the only way the word is used. When the Samaritan woman perceived that Jesus was a prophet (John 4:19), it was not because of a prediction about the future, but because of a revelation about the past and present. When the guards told Jesus to prophesy (Matthew 26:68), they were asking for a revelation about the present, not the future.

On the Mount of Olives, Jesus made some predictions about the future. But even before that, the people considered him a prophet (Matthew 21:11). It was because of his teaching and his miracles (Luke 7:16; 24:19; John 6:14; 7:40; 9:17). Moses had predicted such a prophet — "a prophet like me" (Acts 3:22-23) — and Moses was known much more for teaching than for prediction. Jesus was a prophet like Moses, speaking the words of God. The role of a prophet might include predicting the future, but it didn't necessarily require predictions.

God appoints prophets in the church (1 Corinthians 12:28; Ephesians 4:11). In the early church, some prophets made predictions (Acts 11:27; 21:10). Others served in encouraging and strengthening (Acts 15:32). In Antioch, they worked with teachers (Acts 13:1). Philip's four daughters prophesied (Acts 21:9). Paul referred to a prophetic message that accompanied Timothy's ordination (1 Timothy 1:18; 4:14). On the Day of Pentecost, when people spoke in tongues, Peter said it fulfilled a scripture about men and women prophesying (Acts 2:17-18; cf. Acts 19:6). God was causing them to speak.

Paul listed prophecy as one of the gifts of the Holy Spirit (1 Corinthians 12:10). A prophet is "spiritually gifted" (1 Corinthians 14:37). Paul urged the Corinthians to desire the gift of prophecy (verses 1, 39) — but, judging by the way that Paul used the word, this rarely means predicting the future. "Everyone who prophesies speaks to people for their strengthening, encouragement and comfort…. The one who prophesies edifies the church" (1 Corinthians 14:3-4). Prophecy is also for instruction (verse 31). God inspires prophetic messages to build and help the church.

Prophecy, although a very helpful gift, has limitations. "We know in part and we prophesy in part" (1 Corinthians 13:9). Prophecies will cease (verse 8). Love is much more important (verse 2). Every Christian should love, but not every Christian has the gift of prophecy. "We have different gifts, according to the grace given us" (Romans 12:6).

Paul gave some instructions about how prophetic speaking should be done decently and in order. In keeping with social custom, women were told to cover their heads when prophesying, and men were told they should not (1 Corinthians 11:4-5). Instead of everyone speaking at once, people should take turns (1 Corinthians 14:29-31). If God inspires a second person to speak, the first person should stop (verse 30). The result of such prophecies would then be "that everyone may be instructed and encouraged" (verse 31).

In summary, prophets help the church by comforting, edifying, encouraging, instructing, strengthening and sometimes by predicting.

Evangelists

Some people use "evangelist" as an administrative rank, but Paul was probably not describing a church-government hierarchy in Ephesians 4:11. Although the apostles had more authority than prophets did, Paul does not use this verse to say that. He does not say that prophets had authority over evangelists, or that evangelists had authority over pastors and teachers. He is not prescribing a hierarchy.

Paul seems to be concerned with order only in 1 Corinthians 12:28, where he numbers the first three gifts: "first of all apostles, second prophets, third teachers." However, we do not have any evidence that prophets exercised any administrative authority over anyone — and the category of evangelist is not even mentioned in this verse.

In most of Paul's lists of spiritual gifts (Romans 12:6-8; 1 Corinthians 12:8-10), he does not seem to be concerned about which gift is most important. Even in verse 28, after the first three gifts are numbered, Paul does not attempt to rank the gifts. Indeed, he argues against that idea, saying that a person's gift doesn't make anyone more important than others. Every gift is given for the common good; every person should use his or her gift to serve others. In Ephesians 4:11, Paul is saying that Christ puts all types of leaders in his church for the same reason: to equip the saints for the work of ministry.

What is an evangelist? The New Testament uses the word only three times, which in itself suggests that the word is not a formal title in the church. Philip was called an evangelist (Acts 21:8). That means he did evangelism — he preached the *euangelion,* the gospel (e.g., Acts 8:5-40). But there is no evidence that he had any administrative authority.

Paul exhorted Timothy to "keep your head in all situations, endure hardship, do the work of an evangelist, discharge all the duties of your ministry" (2 Timothy 4:5). Paul was not conferring a formal title on Timothy — nor is there evidence that Timothy ever had a formal title like that. Paul was simply listing things for him to do. "The work of an evangelist" was evangelism — preaching the gospel. A deacon such as Philip could do the work of an evangelist; so could an apostle, such as Paul, or a pastor, such as Timothy. Paul said "do the work of an evangelist" as a way of exhorting Timothy to do evangelism.

In Ephesians 4:11, Paul says that God gives evangelists to the church. God gives us people who can preach the gospel with extra effectiveness. People gifted at evangelism do not have to be ordained or be given administrative authority. Ordination and administration involve other gifts, which may or may not be present in someone with the gift of evangelizing. If administrative duties are assigned to people who do not have a gift for handling them, then those duties would decrease their ability to use their true gifts.

Pastors

The word *pastor* appears only once in the NIV (Ephesians 4:11). The Greek word is usually translated "shepherd." Luke 2:8 uses the word in its literal meaning: "There were shepherds living out in the fields nearby, keeping watch over their flocks at night." Shepherds take care of sheep.

"Shepherd" is often used metaphorically for spiritual leadership. Jesus considered himself a good shepherd (John 10:11-14). The people were "like sheep without a shepherd" (Matthew 9:36). His own disciples were "sheep of the flock" (Matthew 26:31; Luke 12:32) — but Jesus had other sheep, too (John 10:16). He is the great shepherd, and we are the sheep of his pasture (Hebrews 13:20; 1 Peter 2:25).

Jesus, using the verb for shepherding, told Peter to "take care of" his sheep (John 21:16). Paul told the Ephesian elders that the Holy Spirit had made them overseers of a flock; he exhorted them to shepherd the church (Acts 20:28). Peter also told elders to shepherd the flock, serving as overseers (1 Peter 5:2).

How should pastors "shepherd" their flocks? The verb has a range of meanings. On one end of the spectrum, it can mean to rule with great power, as Christ will when he returns (Revelation 2:27;

12:5; 19:15). Christ "will separate the people one from another as a shepherd separates the sheep from the goats" (Matthew 25:32). However, Christ will also be a shepherd of great gentleness: "The Lamb at the center of the throne will be their shepherd [note the irony of a lamb being the shepherd]; he will lead them to springs of living water. And God will wipe away every tear from their eyes."

Church pastors are told to imitate Jesus' gentle style: Serve willingly, Peter admonishes, "not greedy for money, but eager to serve; not lording it over those entrusted to you, but being examples to the flock" (1 Peter 5:2-3). This is the kind of leaders Christ wants in his church. "The good shepherd lays down his life for the sheep" (John 10:11).

Teachers

Jesus is the perfect example of every category of church leader. He is an apostle, a prophet, an evangelist, a shepherd, an overseer, a servant and a teacher. He called himself a teacher, his disciples called him teacher, the crowds called him teacher, even his enemies called him teacher. "Teacher" is the Greek equivalent of "Rabbi" (John 1:38; 20:16).

One of Jesus' chief activities was teaching. He taught not only his disciples, but also the crowds — in the temple, in synagogues, in towns and villages, on mountains and at the lakeside. "I have spoken openly to the world," Jesus said. "I always taught in synagogues or at the temple" (John 18:20).

Jesus commanded his disciples to teach (Matthew 28:20), and they did. "Day after day, in the temple courts and from house to house, they never stopped teaching and proclaiming the good news that Jesus is the Christ" (Acts 5:42). Paul taught in Ephesus "publicly and from house to house" (Acts 20:20). He called himself a teacher, and he told Timothy to teach (1 Timothy 2:7; 4:11-13; 2 Timothy 1:11; 4:2).

Paul told the Colossians to teach one another (Colossians 3:16). People who have been in the church a long time should be able to teach (Hebrews 5:12). If they have a gift for teaching, they should teach (Romans 12:7). Although every member may teach, not everyone has the position of "teacher" (1 Corinthians 12:29). James warns us, "Not many of you should presume to be teachers… because you know that we who teach will be judged more strictly" (James 3:1). God appoints teachers in the church (1 Corinthians 12:28); he gives teachers to equip the saints (Ephesians 4:11).[1]

The Holy Spirit teaches (Luke 12:12; John 14:26; 1 Corinthians 2:13; 1 John 2:27). Scripture teaches (Romans 15:4; 2 Timothy 3:16). Overseers should be able to teach (1 Timothy 3:2). Paul warned Timothy, "Watch your life and doctrine [teaching] closely" (1 Timothy 4:16).

We are frequently warned about false teachers and false teachings. Jesus warned about the teachings of the Pharisees; later, some of them taught that Gentiles had to be circumcised (Acts 15:1). John warned about idolatrous and immoral teachings (Revelation 2:14-15; 2:20-24). Keep away from false teachers, Paul warned (Romans 16:17). "If anyone comes to you and does not bring this teaching, do not take him into your house or welcome him" (2 John 10).

Using the word for "teaching," Paul warned about "every wind of doctrine," "human commands and teachings," and "things taught by demons" (Ephesians 4:14; Colossians 2:22; 1 Timothy 4:1). "The time will come when people will not put up with sound doctrine. Instead, to suit their own desires, they will gather around them a great number of teachers to say what their itching ears want to hear" (2 Timothy 4:3). "Do not be carried away by all kinds of strange teachings"

---

[1] The Greek construction in Ephesians 4:11 implies that *pastors* and *teachers* are two descriptors of the same people. There is one article for apostles, one for prophets, one for evangelists, and only one for "pastors and teachers." One of the primary functions of a pastor is teaching. We see in Acts 20:28 and 1 Peter 5:2 that pastors are overseers, and we see from 1 Timothy 3:2 that overseers must be "able to teach." The titles overlap.

(Hebrews 13:9).

What should be taught? The way of God (Matthew 22:16). Obedience to Jesus' commands (Matthew 28:20). The word of God (Acts 18:11). The Lord Jesus Christ (Acts 13:12; 18:25; 28:31). A way of life in Christ Jesus (1 Corinthians 4:17). The teachings given by Paul (2 Thessalonians 2:15; 2 Timothy 2:2). The elementary truths of God's word (Hebrews 5:12). Specific doctrines (Hebrews 6:2). The true faith (1 Timothy 2:7). The truths of the faith (1 Timothy 4:6). The gospel (2 Timothy 1:11). "You must teach what is in accord with sound doctrine" (Titus 2:1).

Teachers play an important role in the church. As a simplification, evangelists bring people into the church, and teachers build on that foundation to help members in the church to minister according to their spiritual gifts. The categories overlap — evangelism frequently includes teaching (as seen in the ministry of Jesus and the sermons in Acts), and teaching must include the gospel — but in general, evangelism is targeted at nonmembers, and teaching is targeted at members.

That concludes our survey of the terms found in Ephesians 4:11. We will now look at bishops, elders and deacons.

Leadership in the Church
continued

Bishops

In many denominations, a bishop supervises all the churches in a region. The bishop often leads the largest congregation in the largest city in the region. Hierarchical churches (Eastern Orthodox, Roman Catholic, Anglican, Methodist, etc.) assign a bishop to each region to have authority over the pastors and churches in that region. Each city or region has only one bishop.

However, the New Testament does not reveal this particular structure. There was more than one bishop (NIV: overseer) in Ephesus, and more than one in Philippi (Acts 20:28; Philippians 1:1). Near Ephesus, Paul sent for the elders, called them all bishops, and told them to be pastors of the church (Acts 20:28). In Philippi, Paul greeted the bishops and deacons without mentioning pastors or elders (Philippians 1:1). Bishop, pastor and elder are overlapping terms.

When Paul wrote to Timothy, he listed qualifications for a bishop (1 Timothy 3:2) but not for an elder, even though Ephesus had elders (1 Timothy 5:17), and presumably Timothy would ordain elders. Paul left Titus on Crete to ordain elders (Titus 1:5). The qualifications for elders are brief (verse 6) and blend right into qualifications for bishops (verses 7-9). It seems that, although Paul used a different term in verse 7, he was talking about the same type of church leader as in verse 6. Why would Paul tell Titus about the qualifications of a bishop if Titus' only commission was to ordain elders? This again suggests that bishop is another name for an elder.

Although the terms bishop, elder and pastor may have suggested slightly different leadership functions, there was a great deal of overlap in these titles. The difference, if any, between such functions was never spelled out. Paul does not seem to be concerned about what the leaders were called, and he does not detail what they did.

In the original hierarchy, Paul was over Titus and Timothy, and they had authority over the elders, who had some authority over other members. A similar hierarchy exists in some denominations today, with denominational leaders providing supervision over pastors, and pastors supervising elders in the churches. This provides accountability at all levels.

Just as pastor is a functional title, describing the shepherding role that church leaders have, bishop is also a functional title. The Greek word is *episkopos*,[1] which comes from the words *epi* (over) and *skopeo* (see). A bishop is an overseer, a supervisor, someone who watches over others (Acts 20:28). This implies both care and authority. A shepherd watches over the sheep. Jesus Christ is both "Shepherd and Overseer of your souls" (1 Peter 2:25). Peter told elders to be shepherds, "serving as overseers" (1 Peter 5:1-2). Again, we see that the titles overlap.

What do overseers do? Judging by the qualifications, they must set a good example, both inside the church (1 Peter 5:2-3) and in society (1 Timothy 3:7). Since they must be able to teach (verse 2), teaching must be one of their functions.

---

[1] As the word moved from Greek to Latin to English, it was changed to *episcopus*, then *biscopus*, then *biscop* and then *bishop*.

They must take care of the church in much the same way that they manage a family (1 Timothy 3:4-5). They are "entrusted with God's work" (Titus 1:7). They should "encourage others by sound doctrine and refute those who oppose it" (verse 9). They must teach, rule, encourage and refute (cf. 2 Timothy 4:2). "Whoever aspires to be an overseer desires a noble task" (1 Timothy 3:1).

Elders

"Elder" is the most common translation of *presbyteros,* which means "older one." The prodigal son's older brother was a *presbyteros,* "the older one" (Luke 15:25). Patriarchs and prophets were *presbyteroi,* which the NIV translates as "ancients" (Hebrews 11:2). The 24 elders in heaven are also *presbyteroi* (Revelation 4:4, etc.). Jewish religious leaders were often called elders. The word was used within the Christian community, too (Acts 11:30; 15:2, etc.). Peter and John called themselves elders (1 Peter 5:1; 2 John 1; 3 John 1).

Since *presbyteros* can refer to an older man or to a church leader, we have to look at the context to see which is meant. Since 1 Timothy 5:1-2 deals with younger men, older women and younger women, it appears that *presbyteroi* in verse 1 refers to older men, not to church leaders. Titus 2:2-3 also seems to be about older men and older women. They need to be taught basic things that church leaders should already know. Verses 4-6 then address younger women and younger men, so the context shows that Paul is dealing with older men as an age group, not church leaders.

Paul and Barnabas appointed elders in each of the churches they founded (Acts 14:23). Paul told Titus to appoint elders in every town in Crete (Titus 1:5). In both cases, the churches were young and probably small. Nevertheless, more than one elder was appointed in each church. In Jerusalem, elders seem to have had a ruling function in conjunction with the apostles (Acts 15:6, 22-23; 16:4; 21:18), just as the Jewish elders had a ruling function when they met as the Sanhedrin. Paul referred to "the elders who direct the affairs of the church" (1 Timothy 5:17).

What does it mean to "direct" the church? The Greek word is *proistemi,* which comes from root words meaning "to stand before." This word is used to say that elders and deacons should "manage" their own households (1 Timothy 3:4-5, 12), which should be done with self-sacrificial love. The NIV translates this word "leadership" in Romans 12:8. 1 Timothy 5:17 tells us that elders helped direct the church, but only some of the elders were preachers and teachers. All preachers[2] were elders, but not all elders were preachers.

The extent and limits of elders' authority is not spelled out in the New Testament, but they do have authority. Members are told, "Have confidence in your leaders and submit to their authority, because they keep watch over you as those who must give an account. Do this so that their work will be a joy, not a burden" (Hebrews 13:17). "Respect those…who are over you in the Lord and who admonish you. Hold them in the highest regard in love because of their work" (1 Thessalonians 5:12). "The elders who direct the affairs of the church well are worthy of double honor" (1 Timothy 5:17).

Because elders have a leadership position, they sometimes become the object of a disgruntled person's anger. For that reason, Paul told Timothy, "Do not entertain an accusation against an elder unless it is brought by two or three witnesses" (1 Timothy 5:19). If the accusation is true, it must be dealt with publicly: "Those who sin are to be rebuked publicly, so that the others may take warning" (verse 20).

Although elders have authority that should be obeyed, they should not use their authority for self-service. Peter told them to serve "as overseers — not because you must, but because you are willing, as God wants you to be not greedy for money, but eager to serve; not lording it over those entrusted

---

[2] Paul here seems to equate preachers and teachers. In Ephesians 4:11, he seems to equate pastors and teachers. He also seems to equate pastors with bishops. Although different gifts may be involved, the gifts often overlap. Paul does not use any one title consistently.

to you, but being examples to the flock" (1 Peter 5:2-3). Like overseers and pastors, they are to take care of the flock (1 Timothy 3:5). They anoint the sick and pray for healing (James 5:14). "They keep watch over you as those who must give an account" (Hebrews 13:17).

However, many of the functions of elders are not restricted to elders. The New Testament tells members to serve one another, teach one another, instruct one another, edify one another, admonish one another and submit to one another. The elders serve in all these areas to build others up, teach right doctrines, promote spiritual maturity and equip the saints for works of ministry. Elders preach and direct the church with concern for the spiritual well-being of the members; they work to bring out the most in the other members.

Deacons

The word *diakonos* means "assistant" — someone who works to help others. The word is used in a general sense to describe apostles, preachers, servants and other workers. It is used in a more specialized meaning in Philippians 1:1 and 1 Timothy 3:8-13 to denote an office in the church.

The word *diakonos* and the verb *diakoneo* often mean manual labor. 1 Peter 4:11 makes a contrast between those who serve by speaking and those who serve (*diakoneo*). Those who have been given a gift of (manual) ministry (*diakonia*) should use that gift (Romans 12:7). The seven men of Acts 6:3 have often been understood as deacons (although they are not explicitly given that title), because they served by *diakoneo* — waiting on tables (verse 2). Physical service has traditionally formed the core of the duties of a deacon.

We are given a list of qualifications for deacons, but not a list of their duties. The qualifications suggest that deacons *may* have had some teaching and ruling functions. "They must keep hold of the deep truths of the faith" (1 Timothy 3:9). This concern for doctrinal accuracy may have simply been part of the concern for a good example (verse 8), but it may also suggest that deacons helped teach.

Deacons must manage their children and households well (verse 12). The same qualification was given for bishops in verse 4, with the explanation given that bishops must manage the church (verse 5). If the same rationale applies to deacons, it implies that deacons helped direct the church. However, the New Testament does not mandate the specific duties of deacons. The church today is free to assign duties based on current needs.

Summary

The New Testament church had various leaders, who served members through the word and through physical services. Speaking ministries include preaching, teaching, instructing, edifying and admonishing. Physical ministries included food distribution and other internal needs of the church. Leaders also had a role in directing or managing the church, and they were to be obeyed and respected.

All service, whether in speaking, serving or decision-making, should be done for the benefit of those being served. God puts people in the body as he wishes, all for the common good. He has given leadership roles to help the church function in its upward, outward and inward responsibilities.

Ephesians 4:11-16 gives an overview:

- "It was he who gave some to be apostles, some to be prophets, some to be evangelists, and some to be pastors and teachers" — God has given various leaders to the church.
- "To prepare God's people for works of service" — leaders exist to prepare God's people for helping others. Leaders inform, encourage, train and organize to bring out the most in others.
- "So that the body of Christ may be built up" — the result of this is that the church becomes stronger. Works of service help build and unify the church.
- "Until we all reach unity in the faith and in the knowledge of the Son of God and become mature, attaining to the whole

measure of the fullness of Christ" — this process continues until the church reaches maturity, which means unity in faith and the knowledge of Christ, as measured by the standard of Christ himself. Although the goal is never attained in this life, it is still the goal the church is working toward.

- "Then we will no longer be infants, tossed back and forth by the waves, and blown here and there by every wind of teaching and by the cunning and craftiness of people in their deceitful scheming" — maturity in Christ gives us doctrinal stability. We know where the anchor is.
- "Instead, speaking the truth in love, we will in all things grow up into him who is the Head, that is, Christ" — maturity in Christ comes from combining doctrinal accuracy with love.
- "From him the whole body, joined and held together by every supporting ligament, grows and builds itself up in love, as each part does its work" — it is from Christ that the church grows, and the church is held together by its members, who work together in love to build the church.

Church growth comes as each member does his or her work of service, everyone according to 1) the needs of the church, 2) the place in the body God has given them, and 3) the spiritual gifts he has given them. Leaders and laity work together for the same purpose: maturity in Christ.

Lifetime or temporary?

Christians sometimes view the pastoral ministry as a lifetime calling. This is not necessarily true; there is no verse that requires it. God calls every member to serve, but the way in which he wants us to serve may change through the years. God may call a person to serve as a pastor for several years, to serve as a professor for a few more years and then to serve as a business manager for a while. The person might serve as a pastoral supervisor, and then as an assistant pastor a few years later, depending on the needs of the church and changes in the person's family, health or other personal circumstances. The person might serve as a full-time employee or as a self-employed or retired elder.

Due to changing circumstances in their lives, pastors may sometimes need to resign from the pastoral role entirely, depending on what they understand God to be calling them to do. They may need to minister (serve) as laypersons rather than as elders. People who see leadership solely in terms of authority might view this as a demotion, but when ministry is seen in terms of service, a resignation may be seen as a spiritually mature response to God's call to serve in a new way. On the other hand, a resignation could also be a refusal to serve in the way that God wants. Ministers must make their own decisions, without peer pressure or fear of criticism.

Michael Morrison

New Life in Christ

Dietrich Bonhoeffer, a leader in the German Confessional Church, was arrested by the Gestapo in April 1943. A year later, he was jailed in Berlin's Tegel prison. He was hanged by the Nazis at Flossenbürg concentration camp only two weeks before the camp was liberated by Allied armies.

Christians in crisis

But on April 30, 1944, Bonhoeffer was still very much alive, though imprisoned. He was mulling over the significance of what it meant to be a Christian in such trying times. Nazi Germany was testing Christian discipleship in a direct and crushing way. We in today's Western society have not been tested in the same way.

Bonhoeffer had seen a tragic appeasement among Christians in Nazi Germany. Most church leaders and their flocks had gone along with the pagan and anti-Christian sentiments at the heart of Nazism. Only a few had spoken out, like those Germans who formed the Confessing Church. Bonhoeffer's Christian faith as a member of this group was on the line, and so was his life.

When Bonhoeffer sat down to write a letter to his friend Eberhard Bethge on that day in 1944, the meaning of the Christian faith was uppermost on his mind. "You would be surprised, and perhaps even worried, by my theological thoughts and the conclusions that they lead to," he wrote. "What is bothering me incessantly is the question: what Christianity really is, or indeed who Christ really is, for us today" (*Letters and Papers From Prison*, edited by Eberhard Bethge, page 279).

Christianity in Germany had become, in Bonhoeffer's view, nothing more than pious talk and a sterile repetition of creeds. Those who call themselves Christians "do not in the least act up to it," he wrote. Bonhoeffer was dismayed at the many German Christians who had sold out.

What about us?

What happened to Christianity in Nazi Germany should send chills through us who call ourselves Christian. But it's easy for those of us who live in democratic and nominally Christian nations to take Christianity for granted. Well more than half of Americans call themselves Christian. Some even consider the practice of Christianity be patriotic. It seems easy to be a Christian.

We may not be forced to face human tragedy and madness in the profound way Bonhoeffer and his community, the Confessing Church, did. But we can be overcome by the world in more subtle ways. For this reason, we all need to ask ourselves a basic question: What is Christianity? When we say, "I am a Christian," what do those words mean for us who were born into a Christian world?

The word *Christ* is the foundation and basis of the words *Christian* and *Christianity*. It is logical to assume that Christ would also be the foundation and basis of Christianity, and of each Christian's life. But as Bonhoeffer asked, who is Christ for us today? Where does he fit into our Christianity?

Today, Christianity is often defined by specific religious practices. It's about such things as going to church, ceremonies of various kinds, and giving some financial support. But you don't have to be a Christian to listen to preaching, to go through rituals, or to give money to a church or charity.

Christianity emphasizes correct beliefs, creeds and doctrines. Biblical truth is important to faith. But is Christianity only about believing? Is it about doing good and being a certain way? Christianity for many is primarily about being moral and doing good. That's commendable. However, people of other religions—Buddhism, Hinduism, Islam and

Judaism, to name a few—also try to live good, law-abiding lives. Christianity has no monopoly on morality.

For many, Christianity is a cause to get involved—to change the world through politics. But is cause-Christianity transforming the world, or is it selling out by putting its faith in the political world? Much of what passes for Christianity falls under the five Cs: causes, ceremonies, churchgoing, conduct and creeds. But is it enough to define the Christianity of the Bible?

Perhaps we can see by now that it's a bit harder to discover what the Christian faith should be about. So what *should* it be about?

Chipping to Christ

There's an old story about a sculptor who had just finished a magnificent horse in marble. When asked how he was able to sculpt such an exquisite piece, he replied, "I just chip away everything that doesn't look like a horse." In a similar way, we need to chip away everything that passes for Christianity but is not an essential part of it. If we use our hammer and chisel properly, we can discover what the Christian faith looks like at its fundamentals.

Let's begin by offering a basic proposition: Christ is Christianity, or Christ = Christianity. That is the good news the Gospel of John proclaims. John records Jesus as telling his disciples: "I am the way and the truth and the life" (John 14:6). According to the apostle John, Jesus Christ kept insisting that *he* was whatever true religion might be. "I am the resurrection and the life," he told Martha (John 11:25).

Since Jesus is the way, that means Christianity ought to be *the way*. Since Jesus is the truth, that means Christianity ought to be *the truth*. Since Jesus is the life, that means Christianity ought to be the way to *life* eternal.

Misunderstood Messiah

The simple solution to finding true Christianity, then, would be to follow Jesus Christ, and to become Christ-like. But it's not as simple as it sounds. We can't just *decide* to do it.

The apostle Peter thought he knew what it meant to be a dedicated and zealous Christian—a follower of Christ, which the word implies. To him, faith was having a religion of dedication and zeal. When challenged on his ability to be a Christian, Peter said: "Lord, why can't I follow you now? I will lay down my life for you" (John 13:37). Jesus said Peter didn't know what he was talking about—and that he would fail. Peter soon did (Mark 14:66-72).

Philip, another disciple, said something about Jesus showing them the Father. "That will be enough for us," he said (John 14:8). Perhaps Christianity was only a mystical experience for Philip. Thomas, the doubting disciple, was befuddled about the center or way of Christianity. "Lord, we don't know where you are going, so how can we know the way?" he asked (verse 5).

Jesus wasn't that easy to understand. He announced a message that turned common beliefs upside down — and gave them a surprising dimension. People lacked a spiritual ear with which to hear Jesus' counter-cultural message. For one thing, Jesus didn't act like people thought a religious person should act. He was often accused of being irreligious. He was called a drunk and a glutton. He interacted with tax collectors and prostitutes—among the worst social outcasts of the time.

The local religious leaders, the Pharisees, complained that Jesus didn't keep their religious ceremonies or hold to their beliefs. More than that, they felt he was slighting, even attacking, them. The Pharisees thought: He keeps knocking our religion. He's accusing us of giving up the true faith so we can keep our own traditions. Imagine that? The gall of this *upstart*. Does he think he personifies true religion? Yes, Jesus did think so. He claimed to be the originator, the embodiment, the perfect example and the High Priest of the way, the truth and the life. If you didn't have him at your center, he insisted, then you had a useless religion.

Christ the center

Jesus gave us the answer to the question: What

is Christianity? Christianity is Christ living his life in Christians through the Holy Spirit. Jesus is not merely living religion in us. He is not primarily living doctrine in us. He is not living ceremonies and rituals in us. Jesus is living *himself* in us. When he does, that means we have his new life in us. We are his. What, then, is Christianity for us? It is Christ. Who is Christ for us today? He is the center of our lives; he *is our* life.

No scripture better summarizes what we are as Christians, and what Christianity is, than Paul's statement to the Galatian church. Paul wrote: "I have been crucified with Christ and I no longer live, but Christ lives in me. The life I live in the body, I live by faith in the Son of God, who loved me and gave himself for me" (Galatians 2:20). If Christ as our center is embedded in our hearts by the Holy Spirit, we are Christians indeed. Christianity will not be an empty religion. It will bear witness to and be an example of Jesus Christ to the world.

How can Christ become the center of our lives? It can come about only through God's revelation to us, and his rescue of us. We must first be drawn by God to understand that we must be rescued. Humanity without God leads only to death. This hearing—this understanding—comes by revelation of the Holy Spirit.

At one point, Peter recognized something about who Jesus was—the Son of God. Peter didn't figure it out on his own. Jesus told him, "This was not revealed to you by flesh and blood, but by my Father in heaven" (Matthew 16:17). The Holy Spirit must give us a hearing ear so we can recognize who Christ is—and our need for rescue. The rescue is our transformation through a renewed mind that frees us from conformity to the evil in the world. However, we must respond positively to God's revelatory call and rescue.

Jesus explained it by a farming example. God is a sower scattering the seeds of understanding in human minds. Some seeds never germinate because they fall on hardened minds enmeshed in the world. Such people don't understand what they're hearing. Other seeds fall on shallow minds. The seeds of understanding germinate and grow to a point, then die. Such people catch a momentary glimmer of the truth, but the light is overpowered by the glitter of material things. The worries of life, the desire to make it in the world and to live a life of worldly pleasure—with no place for God—choke out the seeds that bring the revelation of God.

But in some people the seeds of truth grow into magnificent plants. They "hear the word, accept it, and produce a crop," said Jesus (Mark 4:20). Such Christians understand the revelatory call of rescue from God and continue to respond to it. Today, God is calling each of us to a relationship with him that rescues us from the clutches of our society and its values—and saves us to eternal life. The question is: Are you answering God's revelation and rescuing call?

What's in a name?

The word *Christian*, which describes those who follow Jesus Christ, was first used by pagan outsiders, probably as a term of ridicule and abuse. Luke tells us, "The disciples were called Christians first at Antioch" (Acts 11:26). Pagans in Antioch probably coined the word as a term of derision to mock people who believed in Jesus as the Messiah. (Antioch, in the province of Syria, was the site of major Christian evangelizing work among Gentiles in the A.D. 40s.)

The word *Christian* appears only twice more in the New Testament (Acts 26:28; 1 Peter 4:16). Once, it's on the lips of a Jewish king who tells the apostle Paul it won't be as easy as he thinks to convince him to be a Christian. In the second instance, the apostle Peter used the word *Christian* in the context of accusations made by the enemies of the church. (The word *Christianity* does not appear in the New Testament.)

Only a few references to Christ and Christians occur in secular literature of the time. The Latin historian Suetonius spoke of an action taken by emperor Claudius (A.D. 41-54): "Since the Jews constantly made disturbances at the instigation of Chrestus, he expelled them from Rome" (*Claudius*

25.4). *Christ* would have been a generally meaningless name to the Latin-speaking Romans. It's easy to see why Suetonius confused it with the common name *Chrestos,* which meant "good" or "kind."

The Roman historian Tacitus wrote that the emperor Nero (A.D. 54-68) had "inflicted the most exquisite tortures on a class hated for their abominations, called Christians by the populace" (*Annals* xv.44). However, the church in those earliest decades called itself by terms other than Christian. Some of them are described below.

Names for disciples

The church referred to itself as the group that followed "the Way" (Acts 19:9). This showed that Christianity was more than an abstract philosophy. It was a description of the way to fellowship with God through Jesus Christ in the Spirit.

Christians also called themselves "the believers" (Acts 4:32) and "God's elect" (1 Peter 1:1). The first title explained that the disciples believed in Jesus Christ as Savior. The second pointed to the special place Christians had within God's plan as the heirs of his promises.

The church often referred to its members collectively as "the disciples" – a word that means "people who learn" (Acts 6:2). The early Christians were carrying on Jesus' teachings and following his example. They were a living community that embodied the teachings of their Master. The disciples also called themselves "brothers and sisters" (Acts 9:30; 17:14). The name stressed the intimate, familial relationship of believers to one another.

Another designation for the followers of Jesus was "friends." Jesus had called his disciples his friends (John 15:14-15). John used this designation for believers in one of his letters (3 John 14).

"Saints" was the apostle Paul's favorite name for Christians (Romans 1:7; 8:27). The name is also used 13 times in the book of Revelation. The word did not emphasize any special holiness achieved by individual obedience, but rather the individual's special calling to salvation. The perfect righteousness of Jesus Christ was credited to people who were called out by God and separated for his purpose. Such people were holy, or saints, in God's sight.

Christians also called themselves "the congregation," from the Greek *ekklesia.* We use the word *church* rather than *congregation,* but they mean the same thing (2 Corinthians 1:1). They define the presence of God's people in the world at large or in a particular place.

"Christian" wins out

The word *Christian* seems to have had no special significance for the earliest church. If used, the word was but one of a number of self-designations. (The apostolic church apparently did not have a single official name for itself.) Eventually, however, the word *Christian* became the common way to designate the collective church. By the beginning of the second century, the word was used by both outsiders and insiders to refer to the followers of Jesus.

Today, the term *Christian* has lost some of its meaning because it is so loosely used. It seems everything is Christian. We have Christian churches, schools, political parties, cultural associations, kings and even geographical areas such as the Christian West. Because of that, it would be well for us to reflect on what we mean when we call ourselves Christians. A Christian is one who belongs to Jesus Christ, one who is transformed by him, and one in whom Jesus Christ dwells.

Paul Kroll

The Goal of the Christian Life

What is the goal of the Christian life, and how do we help one another get there? One old catechism says that our chief purpose in life is to glorify and enjoy God forever. This is true. We were created for God's glory and to proclaim his praises (1 Corinthians 10:31; Ephesians 1:11-12; 1 Peter 2:9). We exist to worship God, and in order to be genuine, this worship must come from the heart. It must be an expression of our real feelings. We adore God above everything else, and we submit to his every command.

How do we help people get to this point? We are unable to achieve such a task. It is God who changes people's hearts; it is God who converts the soul, who leads people to repentance, who touches people with love and grace. We can describe God's amazing love and his astonishing grace and we can set an example of adoration and dedication to our Savior, but after all is said and done, it is God who changes each person's heart.

Yet another way to describe our goal in life is to become more like Christ—and here I think we can briefly sketch some practical ways in which we can help one another submit to God's work in us as we grow toward that goal.

It is God's plan for each of us that we "be conformed to the likeness of his Son" (Romans 8:29). Even in this life, we "are being transformed into his likeness with ever-increasing glory" (2 Corinthians 3:18). Paul labored with the Galatians "until Christ is formed in you" (Galatians 4:19). He told the Ephesians that our goal is "attaining to the whole measure of the fullness of Christ" (Ephesians 4:13).

In Christ, we have a new identity and a new purpose for living. The new self is "to be like God in true righteousness and holiness" (Ephesians 4:22-24). What a concept! We are to be like God not just in the resurrection, but even, to the extent possible, in this life. We are becoming like Jesus, who showed us what God is like when living in the flesh. We are not just hoping to be like him in the next life—we are to be like him in this life.

We do not need to look like Jesus physically. We do not try to match his carpentry skills, his language skills, or his knowledge of agriculture. Rather, we are to be like him "in true righteousness and holiness." In our behavior and in our devotion to God, we are to be like Jesus Christ.

Be transformed!

How is the transformation accomplished in our lives? Paul exhorts, "Be transformed by the renewing of your mind" (Romans 12:2). Our new self "is being renewed in knowledge in the image of its Creator" (Colossians 3:10). Both heart and mind are involved. Behavior is, too. These three work together in those who are being transformed by Christ.

The mind alone is not enough. If only the mind is involved, we may be like demons who know truths about God but do not obey him. Simply knowing the truth is not enough. We must not only hear, but we must also *do* (Matthew 7:24). Behavior alone is not enough. If we go through the motions without really believing in God, we are play-actors. Even if we believe in God and do the right actions, if our heart is far from God, our worship is in vain. If we sing God's praises without feeling any affection for him, we are hypocrites.

In short, we need right beliefs, right actions, and right emotions. If the heart is right and our beliefs are right, then right behavior will be the result. We *want* right behavior, but we need to remember that it is the result of other things, and not the ultimate goal. Now, as I asked in the introduction, how do we help one another grow toward our Christian goal? How do we help one another become transformed to become more like Christ in righteousness and holiness?

Several steps

I see three or four steps in the process. First, there is conversion. We can preach the gospel, but God is the one who must change the hearts and produce a response. We should present the gospel message as clearly as we can, in as many ways as we can, with biblical terms and with modern terms, but we do not claim credit for the effectiveness of God's message. We just want to be faithful stewards, delivering the truth that God so loved the world that he sent his Son to rescue us from our sin.

Second, there is nurture. Jesus commanded his disciples to make more disciples, to make more students, to teach them the things he commanded. Paul instructed Timothy, Titus, and others to teach the truths of the Christian faith. Doctrine is important, and this is an area that Scripture says we should work on. Every church leader should strive for accuracy in doctrine, as defined by Scripture. However, we cannot make every doctrinal conclusion a test of true Christianity. We need to distinguish essential doctrines from nonessential ones.

Third, in addition to doctrinal nurture, there is also nurture of the heart. This is why Christian growth should occur in *community* with other Christians. Social experiences, the things we do *together*, help us grow emotionally. These may be positive emotions such as love and forgiveness, or the negative emotions that result from the sin that inevitably comes with interpersonal relationships. These painful experiences can help us grow as we learn to work through them with God's loving support and help.

Social and emotional nurture cannot be done by reading a book—it is done locally, through small groups and other relationships, guided and modeled by pastoral leadership. The pastor helps people grow not by doing everything for them (even if that were possible), but by teaching and equipping members to do it themselves, for one another. The best quality of pastoral care is found in small groups or small churches. Members who choose to be in a small group are choosing to get themselves more intimately involved in the pastoral care of the church. Small groups help people grow.

Behavioral changes

When members are growing in doctrinal understanding, coming to *know* God more, and in emotional maturity, coming to *love* God more, they will be growing in other ways, too. Their behavior will be changing. They will be treating one another with more love, patience, joy, peace, humility and forgiveness. They will be avoiding sexual immorality, greed, and dishonesty. The more we know and love God, the more we live like him. The heart change causes the change in behavior. The heart change comes from the Holy Spirit, and gives him room to work in our lives.

These behavior changes are rooted in a changed heart, but the process is often slow. Pastors have a responsibility to encourage behavioral changes so that Christians new and old, strong and weak, will be encouraged to live the new life God is creating in them. God is working in us, but he does not do it all for us. He changes our hearts and gives us what it takes to respond to him in righteousness. He wants us, in faith, to use our freedom in a good way.

We welcome repentant and struggling sinners, but not unrepentant, uncaring ones. Our model is Jesus Christ, who welcomed white-collar criminals and prostitutes, but did not welcome people who thought they had no need for repentance. As we strive to imitate our Savior and Teacher, Jesus Christ, we need to look especially at his relationship with the Father, and his relationship with the people around him. His relationship with the Father was characterized by prayer and by his thorough knowledge of and reliance on Scripture. Prayer and study have for centuries formed the core of Christian spiritual growth. They are important! Why? Not as another "duty" or a way of earning God's love. Rather, they are the way of being with God so that we can hear his voice in our lives and be reminded of our true condition: We are redeemed from sin, we belong to him, our salvation is secure in him, he loves us infinitely, he is our ever-present Helper and he will never leave nor forsake us.

Jesus was committed to people—he loved the lost, and he criticized people who thought they were religiously superior to others (a feeling that often stems from a works-oriented approach to worship). He was committed to a close relationship among believers—his disciples related not just individually to him as students to their teacher, but also to one another. Jesus formed them into a group, a body, that would in time give itself mutual support, a community that would reach out to others and invite them in.

Joseph Tkach

The Purpose of Blessings

People often ask why God allows trials. When we are in a trial, we want to know why. Why has this pain come upon us? Why me? We may even stay awake at night thinking about it, praying about it.

But have we ever considered why God allows blessings? We usually don't lie awake at night wondering why God has allowed such a thing to happen to us. We act like it's normal for God to give us a good life. We accept these blessings, sometimes give thanks, and enjoy them without a lot of further thought.

But we do not deserve blessings, so when they come, we ought to ask, Why? God doesn't owe us anything. He has not promised us health and wealth. Yet every one of us has blessings, and we need to ask, Lord, why has this happened to me?

What is normal?

The parable of the fig tree in Luke 13 gives us an illustration about blessings. Verse 1 gives the context of the parable: "There were some present at that time who told Jesus about the Galileans whose blood Pilate had mixed with their sacrifices." The people apparently assumed the victims were more sinful than other people. So Jesus answered in verse 2: "Do you think that these Galileans were worse sinners than all the other Galileans because they suffered this way? I tell you, no! But unless you repent, you too will all perish."

The common assumption was that people got what they deserved, that pain and suffering are a result of sin. But the cause is not always the sin of the people who are suffering. Sin hurts *innocent* people—that is one reason that God hates it so much—so people who suffer are often suffering because of someone else's sin.

The people of Jerusalem used an example of Galileans who suffered. Jesus uses an example of Judeans who suffered: "Or those eighteen who died when the tower in Siloam fell on them—do you think they were more guilty than all the others living in Jerusalem? I tell you, no! But unless you repent, you too will all perish" (verses 4-5). In this fallen world, disasters are normal, and our response to them should be repentance. That is the context of the parable of the fig tree.

A tree with a purpose

Then Jesus told the parable:

> A man had a fig tree, planted in his vineyard, and he went to look for fruit on it, but did not find any. So he said to the man who took care of the vineyard, "For three years now I've been coming to look for fruit on this fig tree and haven't found any. Cut it down! Why should it use up the soil?" "Sir,"

the man replied, "leave it alone for one more year, and I'll dig around it and fertilize it. If it bears fruit next year, fine! If not, then cut it down." (verses 6-9)

The owner could have used the space for grapevines, but he wanted figs, so he planted a fig tree. But the tree wasn't doing what it was supposed to do. The owner made a business decision: Get rid of it. It's taking up space.

Jesus was not giving us agricultural advice. The parable is not really about trees—it is about people. When Jesus first gave the parable, he was talking about the Jewish people. But the same principle applies to Christians today. God wants people to bear fruit—good results. He wants them to love him, but most people are just taking up space, doing nothing in particular. But God did not create us to do nothing—he created us to do good works (Ephesians 2:10). Good works are not for our own benefit, just as fruit does not benefit the tree that produced it—good works are to help others.

God doesn't want us doing nothing. He made us for more than being selfish. We are to love our neighbors. That means doing something. It means producing fruit. It means making a difference in other peoples' lives. We can't fill every need of every person. But each of us is able to help some people in some ways. Are we a blessing to other people?

Blessings for the tree

Jesus also offers forgiveness. The parable doesn't end with the removal of the fig tree. It has a different twist, and that's what we need to focus on. The gardener asks for patience and mercy. "Wait," he says. "Let me give the tree some special attention. Let me dig around it and put in some manure to fertilize the tree. If it still doesn't produce any fruit, then we'll cut it down."

The gardener is saying, in effect, "Let me give this tree lots of blessings, and if it doesn't start producing fruit after it has been blessed, then we'll get rid of it." So, if we have blessings in our lives, perhaps we should consider them as fertilizer given to us so that we will bear some fruit and do some good and not just take up space.

We have all had times in our lives when we have been unfruitful. God is patient and merciful. He gives us blessings anyway, with the hope that we will begin to bear fruit again. We deserve punishment, but we get grace and sometimes blessings, and the purpose is that we bear fruit. Blessings afford us an opportunity to be a blessing to others.

Can't judge by appearances

If people saw the tree being fertilized, they might assume that the tree was especially good to deserve such treatment. But the truth would be the opposite. In this case, the tree with blessings is the bad tree. Likewise, a person who is being richly blessed may not be particularly righteous. Maybe the person is, but maybe not — the blessings may have been given because the person was unfruitful. He or she is being fertilized in the hope that those blessings will help the person become a blessing to other people.

This parable challenges some common assumptions. People don't always get what they deserve. People who have trials may have been fruitful Christians. It may be that they are simply being pruned for a while to help them produce more fruit in the future. On the other hand, when we are blessed with abundance, we would like to think that we are being rewarded for good behavior. Perhaps, but it's not necessarily so.

Even worse, when we have blessings, it is easy to look down on people who have trials. But the well-fertilized tree is not necessarily better than the vines that have been pruned. We cannot judge by appearances.

Blessings are for sharing

It is easy for people to receive blessings and enjoy them for themselves. Ironically, though, blessings can distract us from God and into ourselves. But blessings are given to us so that we might produce more fruit, and if we don't, there is a word of warning here. Blessings are a sign of God's grace — his goodness to us even though we don't deserve it — not a reward for good works.

We need to use them in the way that God wants.

Grace is given to us so that we will bear fruit for God and for other people, so that we might help others and become a blessing to others. Grace enables us to become a conduit of God's love and grace and blessing to others. Just as he has loved us, we should also love others. Just as he has been forgiving toward us, we should be forgiving toward others. Just as he has been generous with us, we should be generous with others.

The good things God gives us should be used to serve others. Let us think about how we might use our physical blessings for God's glory. We all have spiritual blessings, too, and we need to think about how God may want us to bear fruit with those, to use them for the common good (1 Corinthians 12:7). Blessings are wonderful, and as God's people, we can learn how to share them with others, just as God shares his good gifts with us.

Joseph Tkach

Trials and Faith

Some Christians think that they have a guaranteed a way to escape trials. They point to biblical promises that God will intervene for those who have faith in his Son.

However, God not only promises to help us in our trials—he also promises us trials! Christ did not come to bring us a trouble-free life. Instead, he warned us that we would have strife within our families because of him (Matthew 10:34-36), that we would have trials (John 16:33) and that we would be persecuted (John 15:20). We enter the kingdom through many trials (Acts 14:22), and every Christian will suffer persecution (2 Timothy 3:12). We should not think it unusual when trials afflict us (1 Peter 4:12). Jesus suffered when he was in the flesh; that should remind us that we will also suffer.

Nevertheless, Scripture also says that if we ask for anything in Jesus' name, then he will do it for us (John 14:12-14). So some Christians conclude that we can ask for a trouble-free life, and if we have enough faith, then Jesus will make sure that we have no troubles. Can we claim John 14:12-14 as a promise for whatever we want? No—in a passage like this there are unstated qualifications, limitations that are explained elsewhere in Scripture. Consider this fact: Some Christians earnestly prayed that a certain person would be president. Others prayed in Jesus' name for someone else. Christians in each group prayed in faith, but Jesus did not answer all their requests in the same way.

The unstated qualification is that God answers only according to his will (1 John 5:14). God will not respond to prayers that go contrary to what he wants to do. He often has reasons we cannot see. We do not know his will perfectly, and it is possible for us to believe something that is not true. Our faith is no guarantee that the answers we seek will happen, since our faith may be mistaken. I have yet to hear of a literal mountain moving into the sea.

In various competitions and wars, some Christians ask God to give them victory; people on the other side ask the same, and God cannot give both of them what they want. We may ask God for a million dollars—many Christians have—but not receive, no matter how many things we buy "on faith," confident that God will supply. We can have full confidence in Jesus Christ—confidence that he saves us—without having faith that he is a genie performing all our requests made in his name just because we use the right words and believe.

Faith and healing

Many Christians have firmly believed that God would heal a loved one. They prayed in faith. Some believed that they had confirmation from other believers or from other miracles. So they were surprised, even dumbfounded, when the loved one died. What they had believed with such certainty turned out not to be true. Their faith could not heal the person—only God could heal, and he chose not to, despite their prayers, their faith, God's love and God's promises.

When such disappointments happen, a new trial sets in. If faith in the healing turned out to be a mistake, what about faith in Christ? Was it also a mistake? That is one of the dangers of the "word of faith" teaching—it links faith in our Savior to faith in specific predictions. Did Jesus promise to heal every disease? He did not heal Epaphroditus, as least not as fast as people wanted him to (Philippians 2:27). Even in his earthly ministry, Jesus did not heal everyone (John 5:3-9).

Didn't Jesus suffer for us? Doesn't that mean

that we need not suffer? Some say so, but we should test this line of thinking with another fact: Jesus died for us. Does this mean that we should never die? We already have eternal life (John 5:24; 11:26). But every Christian dies. There is something wrong with the line of thinking. We do not yet experience everything Jesus accomplished for us.

There will come a time when we will be raised imperishable. There will come a time when we never experience pain. There will come a time when we receive the full benefits of Jesus' redemption. But that time is not yet. In this age, we share in Jesus' sufferings (1 Peter 2:20-21). Jesus promised persecution, not freedom from pain and sorrow. When Paul was beaten, stoned, and imprisoned, he felt pain. Paul had great faith, but also many sufferings (2 Corinthians 1:5; Philippians 3:10; 4:12). Although Jesus atoned for all sin, Christians still suffer despite their faith—and sometimes *because* of their faith.

We suffer from persecution, and we suffer the incidental pains of living in a world in which sin is still common. Sin hurts innocent people, and sometimes we are the innocent people who are hurt. Sometimes it results in early death, sometimes a slow and pain-filled death. We may suffer physical damage from a burning, a beating, a car accident or asbestos fibers. Our health may suffer from exposure to cold, from smoke in a house fire or chemicals in our food. We may be hurt by wild animals, large or small, or even microorganisms. God has not guaranteed to protect his people from all possible problems.

Is it always God's will to heal people who have faith in Christ? The biblical evidence is that he sometimes does, and sometimes does not. Stephen was killed, James was killed. Eventually all the first Christians died of something. Yet, how many times did God save them out of danger before they eventually died? Perhaps many times.

Have you ever wondered about preachers who claim to heal all infirmities, yet they themselves wear eyeglasses? There is no reason why biblical promises would apply to one kind of ailment but not the other. The scriptures sometimes cited in support of a universal promise of healing do not make any exceptions for eyesight, age, accidents or anything else. Both Scripture and experience tell us that these verses were not intended as universal guarantees.

Yes, some have been healed, sometimes dramatically. These are examples of special favor, grace and mercy. We should not create universal promises out of these examples of exceptional grace. We especially should not imply that people who aren't healed do not have faith. Sometimes their faith is demonstrated through their suffering—they remain cheerfully confident that God will do what is best for them. Whether they live or whether they die, whether they have prosperity or poverty, whether they are sick or in heath, they trust in God. There is nothing wrong with their faith. What is wrong is a teaching that implies that they are somehow not doing enough.

Purpose of trials

Since God promises us trials, and he promises to help us in and through our trials, what are they for? Why does God allow any evil? We do not fully know, but we know that God does allow evil, and Jesus himself was willing to endure it, and he is still enduring it patiently. The Scriptures tell us about a few benefits of trials:

- "Suffering produces perseverance; perseverance, character; and character, hope" (Romans 5:3-4).
- "No discipline seems pleasant at the time, but painful. Later on, however, it produces a harvest of righteousness and peace for those who have been trained by it" (Hebrews 12:11).
- "You may have had to suffer grief in all kinds of trials. These have come so that your faith—of greater worth than gold, which perishes even though refined by fire—may be proved genuine and may result in praise, glory and honor when Jesus Christ is revealed" (1 Peter 1:6-7).

We learn things from suffering that we cannot learn from studying. Suffering shapes our character in a way that words cannot fully describe. Even Jesus learned from his sufferings (Hebrews 5:8), and we are also called to take up a cross and suffer with him. "If we are children, then we are heirs—heirs of God and co-heirs with Christ, if indeed we share in his sufferings in order that we may also share in his glory" (Romans 8:17).

Trials are not pleasant, but we are comforted by the fact that God is at work in our lives, and he is able to retrieve good from all things. He has the knowledge and the compassion to work in our lives for his glorious purpose. We do not always understand what specific lessons we are supposed to learn from a particular trial, but the overall lesson is always to trust in God. Often, a physical trial is also a trial of faith. In trials, we must trust God despite our physical circumstances, and by trusting God, we are growing in our faith relationship with him. This is of infinite importance, since in Christ we are everything we can be, and without him we are nothing.

An untried faith can be weak. Anyone can persevere when things are good. A tried faith is stronger, and the bond between us and God grows stronger. God wants a personal relationship with his children, a relationship characterized by faith, trust and love. This bond of faith can be strengthened by our difficulties. Trials teach us to rely on God for our every need. Whether our trial is health, or money, or relationships, or a problem in the church, we are to look to Christ.

Joseph Tkach

Life in Christ: Living Like a Christian

Christians are saved by God's gift, not by works (Ephesians 2:8-9). Good behavior cannot earn us salvation. But Christianity does have behavioral expectations. It involves changes in the way we live. God created us for relationships, and so he has certain desires for the way we interact with other people.

We are to live for Christ, not for ourselves (2 Corinthians 5:15). One of the last things Jesus told his disciples was to teach people "to obey everything I have commanded you" (Matthew 28:20). Jesus gave commands, and as his disciples, we also teach commands and obedience. These commands are not a means of salvation, and are not a standard of condemnation, but they are instructions from the Son of God. People are to obey him not out of fear of punishment, but simply because their Savior says so. We trust that his instructions are for our own good.

Perfect obedience is not the goal of the Christian life – the goal of the Christian life is to love God. God is transforming us into the image of Christ. By God's grace and power, we are becoming more like Christ. His commands involve not just outward behavior, but also the thoughts and motives of our hearts. These thoughts and motives of our hearts need the transforming power of the Holy Spirit – we cannot change them just by willpower.

Christ lives in us, and he leads us by the Holy Spirit toward obedience. Part of faith is trusting God to do his work in us. The greatest command — love for God — is also the greatest motive for obedience. We obey him because we love him. It is God who works in us, both to will and to behave according to his good purpose (Philippians 2:13). What should we do when we fall short? Repent and ask forgiveness, in full confidence that forgiveness has already been given to us.

A basic list

What does the Christian life look like? There are hundreds of commands in the New Testament. We are not lacking in guidance for how a faith-based life works itself out in the real world. There are commands for how the rich should treat the poor, commands for how husbands should treat their wives, commands for how we should work together as a church.

1 Thessalonians 5:12-22 contains a basic list:
- Respect those…over you in the Lord….
- Live in peace with each other….
- Warn those who are idle,
- encourage the timid,
- help the weak,
- be patient with everyone….
- always try to be kind….
- Be joyful always;
- pray continually;
- give thanks in all circumstances…
- Do not put out the Spirit's fire;
- do not treat prophecies with contempt.
- Test everything.
- Hold on to the good.
- Avoid every kind of evil.

Paul knew that Christians need some basic exhortations or reminders about the Christian life. Paul did not threaten to kick anyone out of the church if they failed to measure up — he simply gave commands that instructed them in the paths of faithfulness.

Live by the Spirit

Paul had high standards. Even though we are forgiven in advance for our sins, the New Testament gives us plenty of commands. We can see that in Paul's letter to the Galatians. Christians are not under the law, Paul says, but neither are they lawless. Paul warns the Galatians about people who would try to prevent them "from obeying the truth" (Galatians 5:7).

Christians are called to be free — "but do not use your freedom to indulge the sinful nature; rather, serve one another in love" (Galatians 5:13). Freedom comes with obligations, or else one person's "freedom" would infringe on another's. "The entire law is summed up in a single command," Paul says in verse 14: "Love your neighbor as yourself." This summarizes our responsibility toward one another. The opposite approach, fighting for self-advantage, is self-destructive (verse 15).

"So I say, live by the Spirit, and you will not gratify the desires of the sinful nature" (verse 16). The Spirit will lead us to love, not to self-centeredness. Selfish thoughts come from the flesh, but God's Spirit produces better thoughts. "The sinful nature desires what is contrary to the Spirit, and the Spirit what is contrary to the sinful nature. They are in conflict with each other…" (verse 17). Because of this conflict between Spirit and flesh, life does not always go smoothly. "…you do not do what you want" (same verse). We sometimes sin, even though we don't want to.

What is the solution to the sins that so easily beset us? Bring back the law? No! "If you are led by the Spirit, you are not under law" (verse 18). Our approach to life is different. We look to the Spirit, and the Spirit will develop in us the desire and the strength to walk according to the commands of Christ.

Looking to Jesus

We look to Jesus first, and we see his commands as a way to express loyalty to him, not as rules that have to be kept "or else we'll be punished." We have not come to Mt. Sinai, where punishment is prominent. Rather, we have come to the heavenly Jerusalem, where joy and salvation are prominent, where the blood of Jesus speaks forgiveness (Hebrews 12:18-24). It is a different approach to worship, a different outlook on salvation. The commands of Christ are commands, but they are not like the old covenant laws that brought punishments. The Spirit is leading us to become more like Jesus Christ.

"The only thing that counts is faith expressing itself through love" (Galatians 5:6). In Galatians 5, Paul lists a variety of sins: "sexual immorality, impurity and debauchery; idolatry and witchcraft; hatred, discord, jealousy, fits of rage, selfish ambition, dissensions, factions and envy; drunkenness, orgies, and the like" (verse 19-21). Some of these are behaviors, some are attitudes, but all of them are self-centered. Paul warns us: "Those who live like this will not inherit the kingdom of God" (verse 21). This is not God's way of life; this is not the way we want to be; this is not the way we want the church to be; this is not the way we want eternity to be.

Forgiveness is available for each of these (1 Corinthians 6:9-11). The church should be a place where grace and forgiveness is expressed and extended, not a place where sin is given permission to abound unchecked. The church preaches against such sins, as well as preaching forgiveness for those same sins.

"The fruit of the Spirit is love, joy, peace, patience, kindness, goodness, faithfulness, gentleness and self-control" (Galatians 5:22-23). This is the product of a heart devoted to God. "Those who belong to Christ Jesus have crucified the sinful nature with its passions and desires" (verse 24). With the Holy Spirit living and working in us, we grow in the desire and the habit of rejecting the works of the flesh. We bear the fruit of God's work in us.

Paul's message is clear: We are not under the law — but we are not lawless. We are under the authority of Christ, under the guidance of the Holy Spirit. Our lives are based on faith, motivated by love, characterized by joy and peace and growth. "Since we live by the Spirit, let us keep in step with the Spirit" (verse 25).

Michael Morrison

Jesus Helps Us in Everyday Trials

From birth to death, Jesus had a difficult life. He had moments of joy, and hours of pain — and we are no better than he is, so we cannot expect a trouble-free life. In this world, Jesus said, we will have trials. He warned his disciples about the cost of following him: They would have to take up the cross each day, willing to suffer and die, if need be, for their faith in Jesus Christ (Luke 9:23).

Whether or not we believe in Jesus Christ, we will have troubles. But when we believe in him, we can be confident that he understands our troubles. He knows what we are going through. That does not make our troubles go away, but it helps us when we know that not even God in the flesh was exempt from trouble. Jesus learned from the things he suffered (Hebrews 5:8) and because of that, he is "able to help those who are being tempted" (Hebrews 2:18).

When we struggle with the downside of being human, we take comfort in knowing that our Savior struggled with it, too. We have a Savior who knows what it's like. In Jesus, we can see that God himself is willing to suffer. That means that even if we can't understand our trials, we know that they are not a complete waste of time. Paul tells us that we will not only share in Jesus' resurrection life, we also share in his life of suffering (Philippians 3:10-11). We have difficulties in this life, but many joys as well. The two go together.

Rejoicing and trials

Peter wrote, "In this you greatly rejoice, though now for a little while you may have had to suffer grief in all kinds of trials" (1 Peter 1:6). Most non-Christians and even some Christians continue to be surprised and puzzled by this combination of trials and rejoicing. How is it possible to be joyful when we suffer? We are not rejoicing that we have a trial (there is no particular virtue in suffering itself), but we rejoice despite our trials. How can that be?

Let's notice what Peter wrote: "In this you greatly rejoice." What is the "this" that gives us great joy? In context, it is salvation, the fact that we can be confident that God will give us an eternal inheritance. We have a wonderful future guaranteed for us. This has been demonstrated to us by the resurrection of Jesus from the dead, and God's power is shielding us until we receive the promised glory (verses 3-5). The same power that raised Jesus will also raise us to glorious immortality!

Peter speaks of joy again in verse 8. He acknowledges that we do not yet see our Savior. We do not yet have our promised inheritance. We are suffering grief in all kinds of trials. Even so, we can rejoice. Why? Because "you are receiving the goal of your faith, the salvation of your souls" (verse 9). We rejoice in the salvation we are already receiving through faith.

Faith involves our minds, our hearts and our wills. It means that we understand and accept certain things about God. It means that we respond emotionally to these things, such as with love because we understand he loves us, and with joy because we understand that he is giving us so much, and with trust because we understand and believe his promises for our eternal salvation. When our understanding and our emotions are in agreement, then our wills are also. The decisions we make throughout each day are pleasing to God because he has brought us to the point that we want to do his will.

But we do not yet have the promised inheritance. We have not yet reached the time when there is no more crying and no more death.

We all experience both crying and death. Our pains and sorrows are caused by our enemy — sin. We rejoice because we know that Jesus has conquered our enemy, and he promises that we share in his victory!

We suffer because of our own mistakes and sins. We also suffer because the people around us are captives of sin, and sin hurts not only the sinner but innocent bystanders, too. *We* are often the innocent bystanders who suffer from the fallout of the sins of others. Satan, the enemy of God, tries to encourage the sinful nature in every person, thereby bringing even more pain and destruction to all, including persecution on the saints.

God not only promises to help us in our trials, he also promises us trials! Christ did not come to bring us a trouble-free life. Instead, he warned us that we would have fighting within our families because of him (Matthew 10:34-36), that we would have trials (John 16:33) and that we would be persecuted (John 15:20). We enter the kingdom through many trials (Acts 14:22), and every Christian will suffer persecution (2 Timothy 3:12). We should not think it unusual when trials afflict us (1 Peter 4:12).

Jesus said, "If you want to follow me, take up your cross. Be willing to suffer, even to lose your life, if you want to follow me." The Christian life involves suffering; we should not be surprised when it happens. Jesus said that a servant is not greater than the master. If Jesus, our Lord and teacher, became a human to suffer and die to serve us, if suffering was part of his training (Hebrews 2:10; 5:8), it should be no surprise that it is also part of ours. In these trials, we can rejoice because we know that Christ has promised us something far better.

Not worth comparing

Despite the suffering we sometimes experience, we rejoice in salvation. How can we rejoice? Paul gives an oft-quoted explanation: "Our present sufferings are not worth comparing with the glory that will be revealed in us" (Romans 8:18). Paul explains that we will receive a great inheritance — we are "co-heirs with Christ" (verse 17). We will share in his inheritance of glory. Today, we share in his suffering, but the day will come when we will share in his glory. The present suffering is part of God's plan for us. It is part of what prepares us to enter the glory of Christ. "We share in [Christ's] sufferings in order that we may also share in his glory" (verse 17).

Our Lord was a man of sorrow, yet he was also full of joy (Isaiah 53:3; Luke 10:21). When he suffered, he did so with the assurance that deliverance and glory would eventually follow (Hebrews 2:12). Jesus told his disciples to rejoice in their salvation. The glory ahead is so great that we can rejoice with Jesus and all believers despite our present-day difficulties. The joy of salvation and the hope of glory are so much greater than our present pains, that there is no comparison. It's infinitely more than a million-to-one ratio!

May God grant us the eyes and ears of faith to believe in and stand on his great and precious promises! We are his beloved children, and he is with us, even in our darkest moments. He never abandons us. He will see us through to the end, through every trial, every pain and every sin. He is always beside us and he never stops loving us, even when we are too weak to know it. Praise God for his eternal love!

Joy in the gospel

We have been promised great rewards, and that gives us great reason to rejoice — no matter what the circumstances we happen to be in now. Paul wrote, "In all our troubles my joy knows no bounds" (2 Corinthians 7:4). Our joy is increased all the more by the salvation of others. Paul put it this way: "What is our hope, our joy, or the crown in which we will glory in the presence of our Lord Jesus when he comes? Is it not you? Indeed, *you* are our glory and joy" (1 Thessalonians 2:19-20). Just as there is joy in heaven whenever a sinner repents, there is also joy on earth, in all who see life from God's eternal perspective.

The people of God find great joy in the spread of the gospel. To the church at Philippi, Paul wrote:

"The important thing is that in every way…Christ is preached. And because of this I rejoice. Yes, and I will continue to rejoice" (Philippians 1:18). Paul rejoiced to learn of people who believed the message and would be in God's family when our Lord and Savior comes. The apostle John had a similar joy: "It gave me great joy to have some brothers come and tell about your faithfulness to the truth and how you continue to walk in the truth. I have no greater joy than to hear that my children are walking in the truth" (3 John 3-4).

As the children of God, we share this joy with all believers, with the angels in heaven, and with God himself — joy in the preaching of the gospel, joy in hearing that people come to faith in Christ and joy in people who continue to walk in faith. Such joy in the redemption and salvation of people, such fruit of the Holy Spirit at work in us, shapes our passions, values and goals.

The use of our time, the habits of our thoughts, the health of our emotions and the quality of our words and actions toward one another are positively influenced by this life-cleansing joy in the love, kindness and power of God. Our private worship time, our worship with the church, our volunteer work, our giving of time both to the church and to people in need, our participation in small groups for prayer, study of the Word and worship — all these spring from the joy of God in us, joy produced by his gracious work in our lives and in the lives of others.

Our financial support for the work of the church is also a reflection of our joy in the things God values. Our donations to the church show the importance we place on the treasures of the kingdom of God as compared to the things of this world. Through the church we reach out as the body of Christ with the gospel message, and we give the gospel credibility as we give ourselves to God's transforming work in us. God desires that we each serve him in a personal way and that we serve him and one another as a body, the body of Christ.

"You are all members of one another," Paul wrote. We are not called to be in relationship with God without one another. We are called into the fellowship of the people of God, into the household of God. In Christ, we have communion with God and, through Christ, with one another. Jesus' command is that we love one another, and as his body, the church, we proclaim the gospel in the world and teach his ways. Together, we can have an even greater impact than we can as individuals, even though our individual impact is also essential to the health of the whole body. The gospel is a great source of joy for us all — joy in receiving the message and in giving it to others!

Joseph Tkach

Five facts about trials

- We have difficulties whether or not we believe in Jesus.
- Jesus promised that his followers would have trials.
- Jesus also promised that eternal joy would be vastly more than our temporary trials.
- There is joy in heaven and on earth whenever anyone turns to God.
- Faith in the future gives us reason to rejoice despite our troubles.

A Balanced Approach to Bible Prophecy

Many Christians need an overview of prophecy, to put prophecy into perspective. That is because many Christians overemphasize prophecy and make claims about prophecy that cannot be substantiated. For some, prophecy is the most important doctrine. That is what occupies most of their Bible study, and that is the subject they want to hear about the most. Armageddon fiction sells well. Many Christians would do well to notice the real purpose of prophecy.

> Bible prophecy reveals God and his will and purpose for humanity. In Bible prophecy, God declares that human sinfulness is forgiven through repentance and faith in the saving work of Jesus Christ. Prophecy proclaims God as Sovereign Creator and Judge of all, it assures humanity of his love, mercy, and faithfulness, and it motivates the believer to live a godly life in Jesus Christ.

The above paragraph has three sentences. The first one says that prophecy is part of God's revelation to us, and it tells us something about who he is, what he is like, what he wants and what he is doing. The second sentence says that Bible prophecy announces salvation through Jesus Christ. It does not say that *all* prophecy is concerned with forgiveness and faith in Christ. Nor does it say that prophecy is the only place that God reveals these things about salvation. We could say that prophecy is one of the many ways in which God reveals forgiveness through Christ.

Since God's plan centers on Jesus Christ, and prophecy is part of God's revelation of his will, it is inevitable that prophecy relates, either directly or indirectly, to what he is doing in and through Jesus Christ. (We are not trying to pinpoint every prophecy here — we are giving an overview.) The most important thing about prophecy is not about nations, and not about the future — it is about repentance, faith, salvation, and life right now.

If we took a survey in most denominations, I doubt that many people would say that prophecy is about forgiveness and faith. They think it is focused on other things. But prophecy is about salvation through Christ, as well as a number of other things. When millions are looking to Bible prophecy to discern the end of the world, when millions always associate prophecy with events still future, it is helpful to remind people that one purpose of prophecy is to reveal that human sinfulness can be forgiven through the saving work of Jesus Christ.

Forgiveness

Human *sinfulness* can be forgiven. I am referring to the fundamental condition of humanity, not just the individual results of our sinfulness. It is true that individual sins are forgiven, but it is even more important that our flawed nature, which is the root of the problem, is also forgiven. We will never have the time nor the wisdom to repent of every sin. Forgiveness does not depend on our ability to itemize them all. Rather, what Christ makes possible for us is that all of them, and our sinful nature at its core, can all be forgiven in one fell swoop.

Next, we note that our sinfulness is forgiven through faith and repentance. We have assurance that our sins are forgiven, on the basis of what Christ has done. The coming of Jesus to rescue us from our sinfulness was prophesied in the Old Testament; this is something that prophecy is about. Faith and repentance are two sides of the same coin.

People can experience forgiveness simply

through faith in Christ, without having any precise beliefs about how Christ is able to forgive us. No particular theory about Christ's atoning death is required. No special beliefs about his role as mediator are required for salvation. However, the New Testament teaches that our salvation is made possible through the death of Christ on the cross, and that he is our High Priest interceding for us. When we believe that what Jesus did is effective for our salvation, then we experience forgiveness. We acknowledge and worship him as Savior and Lord. We realize that he accepts us in his love and grace and we accept his wonderful gift of salvation.

Prophecy is concerned with our salvation. We find evidence for that in Luke 24. There, the resurrected Jesus is explaining things to two disciples on the road to Emmaus:

> Jesus said to them, "How foolish you are, and how slow of heart to believe all that the prophets have spoken! Did not the Christ have to suffer these things and then enter his glory?"… Beginning with Moses and all the Prophets, he explained to them what was said in all the Scriptures concerning himself. (Luke 24:25-27)

Jesus did not say that the Scriptures spoke only of him, or that every single prophecy was about him. He didn't have time to cover the entire Old Testament. Some prophecies were about him, and some were about him only indirectly. Jesus explained the prophecies that were most directly about him. The disciples believed some of what the prophets had written, but they were slow of heart to believe it all. They were missing part of the story, and Jesus filled them in and explained it to them. Even though some prophecies were about Edom, Moab, Assyria, or Egypt, and some about Israel, other prophecies were about the suffering and death of the Messiah, and his resurrection to glory. Jesus explained these to his disciples.

Jesus began with the books of Moses. They have some messianic prophecies in them, but most of the Pentateuch is about Jesus in a different way — in terms of typology, in the rituals of sacrifice and priesthood that prefigured the work of the Messiah. Jesus explained these concepts, too.

Verse 44 tells us more:

> He said to them, "This is what I told you while I was still with you: Everything must be fulfilled that is written about me in the Law of Moses, the Prophets and the Psalms."

Again, he did not say that every single detail was about him. What he said is that the parts that were about him had to be fulfilled. We could add that not everything had to be fulfilled in his first coming. Some prophecies seem to point to the future, to his return, but like he said, they must be fulfilled. Not just prophecy pointed to him — the Law also pointed to him, and the Psalms pointed to him and the work he would do for our salvation.

> Then he opened their minds so they could understand the Scriptures. He told them, "This is what is written: The Christ will suffer and rise from the dead on the third day, and repentance and forgiveness of sins will be preached in his name to all nations, beginning at Jerusalem. You are witnesses of these things." (verses 45-48)

Here Jesus explains more prophecies concerning himself. Prophecy was pointing not only to the Messiah's suffering, death, and resurrection — prophecy also pointed to the message of repentance and forgiveness, a message that would be preached to all nations.

Prophecy touches on many things, but the main thing it is about, the most important thing it reveals, is that we can be forgiven through the death of the Messiah. Jesus highlighted this purpose of prophecy on the road to Emmaus. If we are interested in prophecy, we should be sure not to miss this. If we don't get this part of the message, it won't do us any good to get anything else.

It is interesting to read Revelation 19:10 with that in mind: "The testimony of Jesus is the spirit of prophecy." The message about Jesus is the spirit of prophecy. That is what prophecy is all about. The essence of prophecy is Jesus Christ.

Three more purposes

Our third sentence adds several more details: "Prophecy proclaims God as Sovereign Creator and Judge of all, assures humanity of his love, mercy, and faithfulness, and motivates the believer to live a godly life in Jesus Christ." Here are three more purposes of prophecy. First, God is Sovereign Judge of all. Second, God is loving, merciful and faithful. Third, prophecy motivates us to live right. Let's look at these three.

Bible prophecy tells us that God is sovereign, that he has authority and power over all things. Isaiah 46:9-11 supports this point:

> Remember the former things, those of long ago; I am God, and there is no other; I am God, and there is none like me. I make known the end from the beginning, from ancient times, [I make known] what is still to come. I say: My purpose will stand, and I will do all that I please. From the east I summon a bird of prey; from a far-off land, a man to fulfill my purpose. What I have said, that will I bring about; what I have planned, that will I do.

God is saying that he can tell us how everything ends up, even when it is only starting. Only God can make the end known even when he is in the beginning. Even in ancient times, he was able to make predictions about what would happen in the future.

Some people say that God can do this because he sees the future. It's true that God knows the future, but that isn't Isaiah's point here. What Isaiah is bringing out is not so much that God sees or knows in advance, but that God will intervene in history to make sure that it happens. He will bring it about, even though he may call upon someone from the east, in this case, to do the work.

God makes his plan known in advance, and that revelation is what we call prophecy — something said in advance about what is going to happen. So prophecy is part of God's revelation of his will and purpose. Then, because it is God's will, his plan, his desire, he makes sure that it happens. He will do everything he wants to do, because he has the power to do that. He is sovereign over all nations.

Daniel 4:17 tells us the same thing. Just after Daniel announces that King Nebuchadnezzar will be insane for seven years, he gives this reason:

> The decision is announced by messengers, the holy ones declare the verdict, so that the living may know that the Most High is sovereign over all kingdoms on earth and gives them to anyone he wishes and sets over them the lowliest of people.

This prophecy was given and carried out so that we would know that God is sovereign over all nations. He has the power to set someone up as ruler, even the most unlikely of people. God can give it to whomever he wants, because he is sovereign. That is one message conveyed to us by Bible prophecy. It shows that he has all power.

Prophecy tells us that God is Judge. We can see that in many of the Old Testament prophecies, particular prophecies of punishment. God is bringing unpleasant consequences because the people have done bad things. God is acting as a judge, with the power to reward and the power to punish, and the power to make sure that it is done.

> Enoch, the seventh from Adam, prophesied about these men: "See, the Lord is coming with thousands upon thousands of his holy ones to judge everyone, and to convict all the ungodly of all the ungodly acts they have done in the ungodly way, and of all the harsh words ungodly sinners have spoken against him." (Jude 14-15)

Here the New Testament is quoting a prophecy that is not in the Old Testament. This prophecy is in the apocryphal book of 1 Enoch, and it has become part of the inspired record as to what prophecy reveals. It reveals that the Lord is coming and that he is a judge of every nation.

Love, mercy, faithfulness

Bible prophecy reveals something about what God plans and what he does, and it is therefore inevitable that it reveals to us something about his character. His purposes and plans will inevitably reveal that he is loving, merciful, and faithful. I think here of Jeremiah 26:13 — "Reform your ways and your actions and obey the Lord your God. Then the Lord will relent and not bring the disaster he has pronounced against you." If the people change, then God will change. He is not anxious to punish; he is willing to wipe the slate clean. He does not keep grudges – he is merciful and willing to forgive.

As an example of his faithfulness, we can look at the prophecy in Leviticus 26:44. The passage is a warning to Israel that if they broke the covenant, they would be conquered and taken into captivity. But then this assurance is added: "Yet in spite of this, when they are in the land of their enemies, I will not reject them or abhor them so as to destroy them completely." This prophecy is highlighting God's faithfulness, mercy, and love, even without using those specific words.

Hosea 11 is another example of God's faithful love. After describing how unfaithful Israel has been, verses 8-9 say, "My heart is changed within me; all my compassion is aroused. I will not carry out my fierce anger, nor will I turn and devastate Ephraim. For I am God, and not a man—the Holy One among you. I will not come in wrath." This prophecy is showing God's persistent love for his people.

New Testament prophecies also assure us that God is loving, merciful and faithful. He will resurrect us and reward us. We will live with him and enjoy his love forever. Bible prophecy assures us that God intends to do this, and previous fulfillments of prophecy assure us that he has the power to carry it out, to do exactly as he has purposed to do.

Motivates godly life

Last, we say that Bible prophecy motivates believers to live a godly life in Jesus Christ. How does it do this? For one, it gives us a motive to turn to God, because we are assured that he wants the best for us, and we will receive good forever if we accept what he gives, and we will ultimately receive bad if we don't.

This is shown in 2 Peter 3. We can start in verses 10-12:

> The day of the Lord will come like a thief. The heavens will disappear with a roar; the elements will be destroyed by fire, and the earth and everything done in it will be laid bare. Since everything will be destroyed in this way, what kind of people ought you to be? You ought to live holy and godly lives as you look forward to the day of God and speed its coming.

We are to look forward to the day of the Lord, rather than fearing it, and we are to live godly lives. Presumably something good will happen to us if we do, and something less desirable will happen to us if we don't. Prophecy encourages us to live godly lives, because it reveals to us that God will reward those who faithfully seek him. Verses 12-15:

> That day will bring about the destruction of the heavens by fire, and the elements will melt in the heat. But in keeping with his promise we are looking forward to a new heaven and a new earth, where righteousness dwells. So then, dear friends, since you are looking forward to this, make every effort to be found spotless, blameless and at peace with him. Bear in mind that our Lord's patience means salvation, just as our dear brother Paul also wrote you with the wisdom that God gave him.

Bible prophecy encourages us to make every effort, to have right behavior and right thoughts, to live godly lives and be at peace with God. The only way to do this is through Jesus Christ. In this passage, prophecy is telling us that God is patient, faithful and merciful.

Jesus' ongoing role is essential. Peace with God is possible only because Jesus Christ sits at the right hand of the Father, interceding for us as our High Priest. The Law of Moses foreshadowed and prophesied this aspect of Jesus' saving work; it is through him that we are strengthened to live godly lives, to make every effort, and to be cleansed of the spots we incur. Through faith in him as our High Priest, we can be confident that our sins have been forgiven and we are assured of salvation and eternal life. Prophecy assures us of God's mercy and the way that we can be saved through Jesus Christ.

Prophecy is not the only thing that motivates us to live godly lives. Our future reward or punishment is not the only reason to live right. We can find motivations for good behavior in the past, the present, and the future. In the past, because God has been good to us, and in gratitude for what he has already done, we are willing to do what he says. Our present motivation for living right is our love for God; the Holy Spirit in us causes us to want to please him in what we do. The future helps motivate our behavior, too—God warns us about punishment presumably because he wants that warning to motivate us to change our behavior. He promises rewards, too, knowing that they also help motivate us. We want to receive the rewards he will give.

Behavior has always been a reason for prophecy. Prophecy is not just foretelling, it is also forth-telling: setting forth God's instructions. That is the reason many prophecies were conditional — God warned of punishment, and he hoped for repentance so that the punishment would not have to come. Prophecies were not given as trivia about the future — they had a purpose for the present. Zechariah summarized the message of the prophets as a call to change: "The earlier prophets proclaimed: This is what the Lord Almighty says, Turn from your evil ways…. Return to me, and I will return to you" (Zechariah 1:3-4). Prophecy tells us that God is a merciful judge, and because of what Jesus Christ does for us, we can be saved if we trust him.

Some prophecies were longer-range, and did not depend on whether people did either good or bad. Not all prophecies were designed for that purpose. Prophecies come in such a wide variety that it is difficult to say, except in a general sense, what all prophecies are for. Some are for this, some are for that, and there are some we aren't sure what they are for.

When we try to make a statement about something as diverse as prophecy, we will make a general statement, because that is accurate: Bible prophecy is one of the ways God tells us what he is doing, and the overall message of prophecy therefore tells us about the most important thing that God is doing: leading us to salvation through Jesus Christ. Prophecy warns us of judgment to come, assures us of mercy, and therefore encourages us to repent and get with the program of what God is doing.

Michael Morrison

How to Interpret Prophecy

There are many difficulties involved in interpreting prophecy, but if we take the Bible seriously, we need to study prophecy, because prophecy is a large part of the literature God has inspired to be written and preserved in the Christian canon. Since prophecy encourages us to know God and do his will, it is important for us to study it, even if it is difficult.

Prophecy has a spiritual message, and readers need the help of the Holy Spirit to be able to understand it. But even people who have the Holy Spirit can make errors, and people with the Holy Spirit may disagree with each other. All sorts of erroneous interpretations have been taught by people claiming to have God's Spirit and claiming to have the inspired interpretation. Therefore, as a practical matter, we cannot convince people of our interpretation if we are using special insight they don't have access to. If we did that, we would be asking them to have faith in us.

We need to base our understanding, our arguments, and our teaching on what the scriptures say and on what people can see for themselves, in the translations that are commonly available. We have to use an understandable method of interpretation, one that makes sense historically, linguistically and theologically. We need to examine the words, the grammar, the paragraph flow, the type of literature we are dealing with, and the overall message of the Bible.

Prophecy was not inspired to satisfy our curiosity about the future – it has always had a theological purpose. It tells us something about what God is doing with humanity, and it is given to help motivate people to do something in the present. Prophecy is not an end in itself — it supports a more important goal. God's primary purpose in dealing with humanity is to reconcile us to him, to give us salvation through Christ – and prophecy serves that larger purpose. It tells us something about what God is doing, and it may also tell us something about what we should be doing. Prophecy should lead us toward God, so that we know him, have faith in him, and seek him through Jesus Christ.

Poetic language

We need to understand the type of literature we are dealing with, because this is where many of the difficulties arise. Prophecy is not written in the same way as history is. Prophecy is often poetic, and ancient poetry, like modern poetry, uses words in a metaphorical or symbolic sense more often than history does. Psalm 23 is a familiar example of poetic metaphors, with pastoral imagery. The Lord is my shepherd; he leads me beside still waters; my cup runs over. These are metaphors drawn from different aspects of life.

Psalm 18 is a good illustration. The subtitle says that it is about "when the Lord delivered David from the hand of all his enemies and from the hand of Saul." Saul tried to kill David, but David kept escaping.

The psalm begins with some common metaphors:

> The Lord is my rock, my fortress and my deliverer; my God is my rock, in whom I take refuge. He is my shield and the horn of my salvation, my stronghold. I call to the Lord, who is worthy of praise, and I am saved from my enemies. (verses 1-3)

David uses a variety of images to describe God as a place of safety – a defensive and passive role. He adds more images when he writes:

> The cords of death entangled me; the torrents of destruction overwhelmed me. The cords of the grave coiled around me; the snares of death confronted me. In my distress I called to the Lord; I cried to my God for help. From his temple he heard my voice; my cry came before him, into his ears. (verses 4-6)

From images of the underworld, David now turns to images of heaven, and he puts the matter in cosmic terminology:

> The earth trembled and quaked, and the foundations of the mountains shook; they trembled because he was angry. Smoke rose from his nostrils; consuming fire came from his mouth, burning coals blazed out of it. He parted the heavens and came down; dark clouds were under his feet. He mounted the cherubim and flew; he soared on the wings of the wind. He made darkness his covering, his canopy around him — the dark rain clouds of the sky. (verses 7-11)

David is using some of the same language that Canaanite myths use. He is speaking of earthquakes and thunderstorms. Is this the way that God rescued David from Saul? That is not in the history – David is speaking in imaginative, poetic terms.

We see more as we go on:

> Out of the brightness of his presence clouds advanced, with hailstones and bolts of lightning. The Lord thundered from heaven; the voice of the Most High resounded. He shot his arrows and scattered the enemies, great bolts of lightning and routed them. (verses 12-14)

This is primarily thunderstorm imagery. But then David adds something that was surely not involved in his escapes from Saul:

> The valleys of the sea were exposed and the foundations of the earth laid bare at your rebuke, O Lord, at the blast of breath from your nostrils. He reached down from on high and took hold of me; he drew me out of deep waters. He rescued me from my powerful enemy, from my foes, who were too strong for me. They confronted me in the day of my disaster, but the Lord was my support. He brought me out into a spacious place; he rescued me because he delighted in me. (verses 15-18)

In this psalm, we can see how poetic language can be applied to a historical event. It would be a mistake for us to take this literally – and we must be equally cautious about taking the language of prophecy literally, because it is also poetry. Some dramatic figures of speech may be involved. Poetic language about the valleys of the sea should not be taken literally, mountains may not be meant literally, and heavenly signs may not be meant literally.

Hosea 12:10 says some of the prophecies were given as parables, that is, in figurative language: "I spoke to the prophets, gave them many visions and told parables through them."

Literally?

One school of interpretation stresses the literal interpretation of prophecies. Prophecies are sometimes meant literally, but to begin with an advance assumption about prophecy runs contrary to the biblical evidence. We can't assume in advance that it is literal; nor can we assume in advance that it isn't. The literal approach has produced a lot of failed prophecies, and a lot of disappointment. Other schools of interpretation have their problems, too, all of which emphasizes our need to be cautious in our approach.

Amos' prophecy of blessings illustrates some problems of literal interpretation:

> The days are coming…when the reaper will be overtaken by the plowman and the planter by the one treading grapes. New wine will drip from the mountains and flow from all the hills. (Amos 9:13)

Will the reaper really be overtaken by the plowman? Why wouldn't the plowman stop and help the reaper? How can the grape-treader, who works in a wine press, overtake the planter, who works in a field? If streams of wine flow from the hills (other verses might make us wonder whether there will be any hills), why would anyone need a grape-treader? This is not meant literally. But how much of it is figurative? Will there be plowmen and grape-treaders at all? The verse cannot answer that question.

When we read that "mountains and hills will burst into song, and all the trees of the field will clap their hands" (Isaiah 55:12), we interpret it symbolically, because a literal fulfillment isn't possible. When we read that "the lion will eat straw like the ox" (Isaiah 11:7), we find something equally impossible without a miracle. Maybe it isn't meant literally, either.

When we read that everyone will sit under a vine and fig tree (Micah 4:4), we need not insist that everyone will have a vine and fig tree. We need to look at the picture before we look at the details. The details are artistic license used to support the picture of peace and prosperity, which is the context of verses 3-4. The details are like those in a photo of happy people. The photo can be representative of happiness, but we don't expect every detail to be representative. Sitting at home may illustrate peace and abundance, but those details are not required for peace and abundance.

As another example, Isaiah 40:3-4 says that the mountains will be brought low and uneven ground will be made level. Literally, this would mean that there will be no hills. However, Luke 3:4-6 implies that this prophecy was fulfilled by John the Baptist. Luke understood it figuratively, in a very non-literal way. He was not talking about mountains and roads at all.

Due to the way New Testament writers present Messianic prophecies, some readers may think there has been a "literal" fulfillment. But a comparison of Old Testament context and New Testament fulfillment sometimes shows a major shift in meaning. Sometimes the original verse in the Old Testament wasn't a prophecy at all – it was just given greater meaning in the life and ministry of Christ.

Joel 2:28-29 predicted God's Spirit on "all flesh" and dreams and visions, but Peter said that this was fulfilled on the day of Pentecost, when there was no mention of dreams and visions (Acts 2:16-17). Nevertheless, Peter said that Pentecost was a fulfillment of the prophecy. He did not press the details very far, and neither should we. Their understanding of fulfillment is different from the concept many people today have.

Let's look at an example from the book of Revelation: Does Christ hold a sword in his mouth (Revelation 19:15), or does it metaphorically mean words of war? Similarly in the Old Testament, when we read that people will "beat swords into plowshares," do we restrict the meaning to swords and plows, or do we update it technologically to include all instruments of warfare and productivity? In this case, the specific item (a sword) seems to refer to a general subject (violence); the same may be true with other details of prophecy. Each word may stand for something else.

What about people? Malachi 4:5-6 predicted an Elijah. But it wasn't literally Elijah; Jesus said that John the Baptist fulfilled that role. When Elijah comes again, will it be a resurrected Elijah, or someone in his role? What about the prophecies of a future David? In many cases, "David" may be a reference to his descendant and successor, Christ. If Christ fulfills the prediction, it isn't necessary that David himself will also. When we read that Christ will sit on the throne of David, should we expect the same physical throne, or is it a figure of speech depicting rulership of Israel? Will we all sit on the one throne of God (Revelation 3:21) while the apostles sit on other thrones (Matthew 19:28)?

Humility needed

We should interpret the Bible by asking, What did the writer mean? He may have intended a figurative meaning. However, to understand the figure of speech or the metaphor, we must first understand what the words mean literally. But we cannot reject all other possibilities in advance. Unfortunately, there is no simple formula to tell us which words are literal and which are symbolic, and even if we know the word is symbolic, there is no formula to tell us what the symbol means. That is why Bible prophecy is interpreted in many different ways.

Although we'd like to have an answer for every Bible question, we should say "We don't know" more often. "Some of us think this way, and some of us think that way. I understand how you got your view, and I might happen to disagree with it, but I cannot prove that either view is the only way of looking at it." This is the approach we need on several issues.

Because of the ambiguities that are involved in prophecy (probably by God's design), differences of opinion will exist, even among converted Christians. On such matters, we should not be dogmatic, and none of us should insist that the church teach our particular view. On many debatable issues, the church need not teach any view; it is not essential to Christian discipleship or to our commission. There are sections of the Bible we do not understand (even Paul didn't know everything), and we need to admit it. We cannot be dogmatic about many specific interpretations — and we cannot categorically reject everyone else's.

A brief word about dates, perhaps one of the most often misused aspects of prophecy: Bible prophecies are often purposely ambiguous about chronology. That isn't so we will study harder and make lots of guesses – it is because the chronology is relatively unimportant. The more important thing is our spiritual response, and that is more important even if we did know the chronology.

Prophecy is given not so much that we will know the future, but that we will know that God controls the future. It is far more important for us to know God, than it is for us to know the future. Any revelation of the future is given primarily so that we will do something now to be on the side of the One who wins in the end, the one who declares the end from ancient times, the one who will be sure to bring it all to pass just as he has purposed.

Michael Morrison

God's Wrath

The Bible tells us that "God is love" (1 John 4:8). He chooses to do good, to help human beings. But the Bible also speaks of God's wrath, his anger. How can a being of pure love also have anger?

There is no contradiction between love and anger. Actually, we should *expect* that love (a desire to do good) would also include anger or opposition against anything that hurts. God is consistent in his love, so he is opposed to anything that works against his love. Anything that opposes God's love is sin. God is against sin – he wants to counteract it, eventually eliminate it. Because God loves humanity, he dislikes sin. However, "dislikes" is too mild. God has strong feelings against sin. He *hates* sin, because it is an enemy of his love. This is what the Bible means by the wrath of God.

God loves human beings, even sinners (that's the only kind of human there is). Even when we were sinners, God sent his Son to die for us, to save us from our sins (Romans 5:8). We conclude that God loves the people, but hates (is implacably opposed to) the sin that hurts them. If God were not against everything that is against his creation and against a right relationship with him, God would not be loving. God would not be *for* us if he were not against whatever was against us.

The Bible occasionally says that God is angry at people. This is a figure of speech. God's desire is not that he wants to inflict pain on the people, but that he wants them to change their ways and to *escape* the pain that sin causes. His anger lasts only as long as they insist on sinning. This shows that God is not angry at the people for who they are, but only because of what they are doing. He is not angry at *them* – he is angry at their behavior. God wants a good outcome for the people, not a bad one. He did not create them for destruction, but for redemption and salvation (John 3:17). In contrast, God's anger at sin is permanent. God will never change his mind about the evil of evil and come to say, well, it really wasn't so bad, it really wasn't evil, but partially good or purely good.

God's wrath comes about because God's holiness and love have been violated by human sinfulness. Human beings who live their lives apart from God are antagonistic toward his way. People living in such estrangement are acting as enemies of God. Since humanity assaults everything good and pure that God is and stands for, God must oppose the way of sin. This holy and loving opposition to sinfulness in every form is called "God's wrath."

God is sinless – he is perfect holy Being by nature. If he did not oppose sinfulness in humanity, he would not be good. If he was not wrathful and warring against sin, if he did not care, God would then, in effect, be saying that sinfulness is not evil and can be tolerated. That would be a lie, because sinfulness is evil. But God cannot lie and be untrue to his essential Being, which is holy and loving. If God were to tolerate sin in not having a sustained hostility to it, it would mean that he accepted sinfulness as legitimate and that he finds human suffering caused by evil to be acceptable.

But God is supremely righteous – and he is pure love. Thus, his nature and Being cannot tolerate sinfulness and anything that violates who and what he is and who he created us to be. Therefore, it is impossible for a just God not to have "wrath" toward sin. Paul explains God's wrath as a just judgment that flows out of sinfulness against a holy God (Romans 1:18-26).

End of the enmity

However, God has already taken the actions

necessary in order to end the enmity between humanity and himself. These actions flow out of his love, which is the essence of his being (1 John 4:8). In love, God allows his creatures to choose for or against him. He even allows them to hate him, although he opposes such a choice because it hurts the people he loves. In effect, he says "no" to their "no." In saying "no" to our "no," he reinforces his "yes" to us in Jesus Christ. God has supremely expressed this love by sending his Son, Jesus Christ, to pay the penalty of sin and to end sinfulness (1 John 4:9-10) and reconcile us back to himself.

God has, at great cost to himself, taken all the necessary steps to have our sins be forgiven and blotted out. Jesus died for us, in our place. The fact that his death was necessary for our forgiveness shows the seriousness of our sin and guilt, and shows the results that sin would otherwise have for us. God hates the sin that causes death.

When we accept God's forgiveness in Jesus Christ, we admit that we have been sinful creatures in opposition to God. That's what it means to "accept" Christ as our Savior. We accept that we were sinful and in need of a Savior. We accept that we were alienated and in need of reconciliation. We acknowledge that through Christ and his redemptive work we have been given reconciliation, transformation and eternal life in God as a *free gift*. We repent of our "no" to God and thank him for his "yes" to us in Jesus Christ. Ephesians 2:1-10 describes the human journey from being the objects of God's wrath to receiving salvation by his grace.

God's purpose from the beginning was to express his love toward humans by forgiving the world's sin through the work of Jesus (Ephesians 1:3-8). This is instructive about humanity's situation in relationship to God. Whatever "wrath" God had, he also planned to resolve, even before the world was created (Revelation 13:8). He initiated from the foundations of the world a real reconciliation through Christ (Ephesians 2:15-18; Colossians 1:19-23). This reconciliation comes about not through human desires or efforts, but through the Person of and saving work of Christ on our behalf. That saving work was carried out as "loving wrath" *against* sinfulness and *for* us as persons. People who are "in Christ" are no longer objects of wrath, but live in peace with God.

In Christ, human beings are saved from wrath through his redemptive work and the indwelling Holy Spirit, who transforms us. God has reconciled us to himself (2 Corinthians 5:18); he harbors no desire to punish us. We respond and receive his forgiveness and new life in right relationship to him by turning to God and turning away from everything that is an idol in human life (1 John 2:15-17). Salvation is God's rescue program in Christ – "who rescues us from the coming wrath" (1 Thessalonians 1:9-10).

To repeat, human beings have become, in our very natures, enemies of God, and this animosity and distrust of God causes a necessary and spontaneous countermeasure from a holy and loving God – his wrath. But from the beginning, God has purposed out of his love to end the human-caused wrath by the saving work of Christ. It is through God's love that we are reconciled to him in his own saving work in the death and life of his Son (Romans 5:9-10; John 3:16).

In effect, even before it started, God planned to eliminate his own wrath against humanity. It is a hypothetical construct, since the solution was provided before the problem arose. God's wrath is not like human anger. Human language does not have a word for this sort of temporary-and-already-resolved opposition against humans who are opposed to God. They *deserve* punishment, but God's desire is not to punish but to rescue them from the pain that their sin causes.

The word *wrath* can help us understand how strongly God hates sin, but our understanding of the word must always include the facts that

1. God's anger is targeted toward sin, not the people in themselves,
2. God has already acted to end whatever wrath he had toward humans, and
3. his anger against sin will never end, because sin hurts the people he loves.

We thank God that God's wrath disappears when sin is conquered and destroyed. We have assurance in the promise of his peace toward us because he has once and for all dealt with sin in Christ. God has reconciled us to himself in the saving work of his Son, thus ending his wrath. God's wrath, then, is not against his love. Rather, his wrath serves his love. His wrath is a means to bring about his loving purposes for all.

While human wrath rarely if ever accomplishes loving purposes to even a small degree, we cannot project upon God our human understanding and experience of human wrath. Doing so is to commit idolatry, to think of God as if God were a human creature. The wrath of human beings does not work the righteousness of God, says James 1:20. God's wrath will not last forever, but his steadfast love will.

Key verses

Here are some key Scripture passages that demonstrate this relationship between God's love and his wrath unlike what we experience between fallen human beings.

- James 1:20: "Human anger does not produce the righteousness that God desires."
- Hosea 11:9; 14:4: "I will not carry out my fierce anger, nor will I devastate Ephraim again. For I am God, and not a man—the Holy One among you. I will not come against their cities.... I will heal their waywardness and love them freely, for my anger has turned away from them."
- Micah 7:18: "Who is a God like you, who pardons sin and forgives the transgression of the remnant of his inheritance? You do not stay angry forever but delight to show mercy."
- Nehemiah 9:17: "But you are a forgiving God, gracious and compassionate, slow to anger and abounding in love."
- Isaiah 54:8: "'In a surge of anger I hid my face from you for a moment, but with everlasting kindness I will have compassion on you,' says the Lord your Redeemer."
- Lamentations 3:31-33, 39: "No one is cast off by the Lord forever. Though he brings grief, he will show compassion, so great is his unfailing love. For he does not willingly bring affliction or grief to anyone…. Why should the living complain when punished for their sins?"
- Ezekiel 18:23: "Do I take any pleasure in the death of the wicked? declares the Sovereign Lord. Rather, am I not pleased when they turn from their ways and live?"
- Joel 2:13: "Rend your heart and not your garments. Return to the Lord your God, for he is gracious and compassionate, slow to anger and abounding in love, and he relents from sending calamity."
- Jonah 4:2: "He prayed to the Lord, 'Isn't this what I said, Lord, when I was still at home? That is what I tried to forestall by fleeing to Tarshish. I knew that you are a gracious and compassionate God, slow to anger and abounding in love, a God who relents from sending calamity.'"
- 2 Peter 3:9: "The Lord is not slow in keeping his promise, as some understand slowness. Instead he is patient with you, not wanting anyone to perish, but everyone to come to repentance."
- 1 John 4:18: "There is no fear in love. But perfect love drives out fear, because fear has to do with punishment. The one who fears [punishment] is not made perfect in love."

God's wrath against sin and his elimination of wrath against humans are simultaneously presupposed in his sending his Son, Jesus Christ, to win the final victory over this enemy of God. If God did not war against all forms of sinfulness – if he had no "wrath" against it – he would have seen no need to send his Son in human form as Jesus (John 1:1, 14) to destroy this enemy of his very Being and his purpose for humanity, to live eternally in right relationship with him. God's holiness is committed to making us holy. His righteousness aims to make things right, make all things new. His judgments, his revelation of what leads to life and what leads to death, are to *avoid* condemnation, the consequences of refusing to submit to his judgments fulfilled in Jesus Christ.

When we read that God so loved the world that he sent his Son – and that whoever believes in him will not perish (John 3:16) – we are to understand from this very act that God is "wrathful" against sin. But in his war against sinfulness, God does not condemn sinful humans, but saves them from sin for reconciliation and eternal life. God's "wrath" is not intended to "condemn the world," but to condemn and destroy the power of sin in all its forms so that humans may have an eternal relationship of love with him.

The Coming of the Lord

What do you think would be the biggest event that could occur on the world scene? Another world war? The discovery of a cure for some dread disease? World peace, once and for all? Contact with some extraterrestrial intelligence?

For millions of Christians, the answer to this question is simple: The biggest event that could ever occur is the second coming of Jesus Christ.

The Bible's message

The story of the Bible centers on the coming of Jesus Christ as Savior and King. As described in Genesis 3, the first human sinned and fractured their relationship with God. But God foretold the coming of a Redeemer who would repair that spiritual break. To the serpent who tempted Adam and Eve to sin, God said, "I will put enmity between you and the woman, and between your offspring and hers; he will crush your head, and you will strike his heel" (Genesis 3:15).

This is the Bible's earliest prophecy of a Savior who would smash the power that sin and death hold over humans ("he will crush your head"). How? By the sacrificial death of the Savior ("you will strike his heel"). Jesus accomplished this at his first coming. John the Baptist recognized him as "the Lamb of God, who takes away the sin of the world!" (John 1:29).

The Bible reveals the central importance of God becoming flesh at the first coming of Jesus Christ. The Bible also reveals that Jesus is coming now, in the lives of believers. The Bible also states that he will come again, visibly and in power. Jesus Christ comes in three ways:

Jesus has already come

We humans need God's redemption — his rescue — because we have all sinned, bringing death to everyone. Jesus redeemed us by dying in our place. Paul wrote:

God was pleased to have all his fullness dwell in him [Jesus Christ], and through him to reconcile to himself all things, whether things on earth or things in heaven, by making peace through his blood, shed on the cross. (Colossians 1:19-20)

Jesus healed the breach that occurred in the Garden of Eden. Through his sacrifice, the human family is reconciled to God.

Old Testament prophecy pointed to the kingdom of God. The New Testament opens with Jesus "proclaiming the good news of God. 'The time has come…. The kingdom of God is near,'" he said (Mark 1:14-15). Jesus, the King of the kingdom, was walking with humans! Jesus offered "for all time one sacrifice for sins" (Hebrews 10:12). We should never underestimate the importance of Jesus' incarnation, life and work 2,000 years ago.

Jesus came. Also —

Jesus is coming now

There is good news for those who believe in Christ: "You were dead in your transgressions and sins, in which you used to live when you followed the ways of this world…. But because of his great love for us, God, who is rich in mercy, made us alive with Christ even when we were dead in transgressions" (Ephesians 2:1-2, 4-5).

God has raised us with Christ, spiritually, now! Through his grace, "God raised us up with Christ and seated us with him in the heavenly realms in Christ Jesus, in order that in the coming ages he might show the incomparable riches of his grace, expressed in his kindness to us in Christ Jesus" (verses 6-7). This passage describes our present condition as followers of Jesus Christ.

People asked Jesus when the kingdom of God would come. He replied: "The kingdom of God does not come with your careful observation, nor will people say 'Here it is,' or 'There it is,' because the kingdom of God is within you" (Luke 17:20-21). Jesus Christ brought the kingdom in his person. Jesus lives within Christians (Galatians 2:20). As he now lives in us, he extends the influence of the kingdom of God. Jesus' coming to live in us also anticipates the ultimate revelation of the kingdom on earth at Jesus' second coming.

Why does Jesus live in us now? "It is by grace you have been saved, through faith — and this not from yourselves, it is the gift of God — not by works, so that no one can boast. For we are God's workmanship, created in Christ Jesus to do good works, which God prepared in advance for us to do" (Ephesians 2:8-10). God has saved us by grace, through no effort of our own. Although works cannot earn us salvation, Jesus lives in us so that we may now do good works and thereby glorify God.

Jesus came. He is coming. And —

Jesus will come again

After Jesus' resurrection, as his disciples watched him ascend to heaven, two angels asked: "Why do you stand here looking into the sky? This same Jesus, who has been taken from you into heaven, will come back in the same way you have seen him go into heaven" (Acts 1:11). Jesus will return.

At his first coming, Jesus left some messianic predictions unfulfilled. This was one reason many Jews rejected him. They thought the Messiah would be a national hero who would free them from Roman domination. But the Messiah was to come, first, to die for all humanity. Only later would he return as a conquering king, and then not just to exalt Israel, but to claim all earth's kingdoms as his own. "The kingdom of the world has become the kingdom of our Lord and of his Christ, and he will reign for ever and ever" (Revelation 11:15).

"I am going…to prepare a place for you," Jesus told his disciples. "And if I go and prepare a place for you, I will come back and take you to be with me that you also may be where I am" (John 14:23). Later, the apostle Paul told the church how "the Lord himself will come down from heaven, with a loud command, with the voice of the archangel and with the trumpet call of God" (1 Thessalonians 4:16). At Christ's return, he will raise to immortality the righteous dead and change to immortality the faithful who are still alive, and they will all meet him in the air (verses 16-17; 1 Corinthians 15:51-54).

But when?

Throughout the centuries, speculation about the second coming has caused uncounted arguments — and untold disappointment when various predictions failed. Overemphasizing the *when* of Jesus' return can divert our minds from the central focus of the gospel — Jesus' saving work for all humans, accomplished in his life, death, resurrection and continuing work as our heavenly High Priest. We can become so engrossed in prophetic speculation that we fail to fulfill the rightful role of Christians as witnesses to the world, exemplifying the loving, merciful, Christ-like way of life and sharing the good news of salvation.

When anyone's interest in the Scriptural announcements of the Last Things and the second advent degenerates into a subtle drawing up of precisely worked-out future events, then he has strayed a long way from the content and spirit of Jesus' prophetic utterances.[1]

Our focus

If knowing when Christ will return is not possible[2] (and therefore, by comparison to what the Bible does tell us, unimportant), then where should we focus our energies as Christians? Our focus should be on being ready for Jesus' second coming whenever it occurs! "You also must be ready," Jesus said, "because the Son of Man will

---

[1] Norval Geldenhuys, *Luke*, The New International Commentary on the New Testament (Grand Rapids, MI: Eerdmans, 1952), page 544.

[2] See Norman L. Shoaf, "No One Knows When Christ Will Return," in *40 Days of Discipleship, volume 1*, pages 157-160. Or: https://www.gci.org/articles/no-one-knows-when-christ-will-return-2/

come at an hour when you do not expect him" (Matthew 24:44). "He who stands firm to the end will be saved" (Matthew 10:22). The whole Bible revolves around Jesus Christ. As Christians, our lives should revolve around him, too.

Jesus came. He is coming through the indwelling of the Holy Spirit now. Jesus Christ will come again in glory to "transform our lowly bodies so that they will be like his glorious body" (Philippians 3:21). Then, "the creation itself will be liberated from its bondage to decay and brought into the glorious freedom of the children of God" (Romans 8:21).

I am coming soon, says our Savior. As Christians, disciples of Jesus Christ, we all can reply in unison: "Amen. Come, Lord Jesus" (Revelation 22:20).

Norman L. Shoaf

Here He Comes, Ready or Not

Don't you wish that Jesus would return? That all the wretchedness and wickedness that we see around us would end, and that God would usher in a time when "the earth will be full of the knowledge of the Lord as the waters cover the sea" (Isaiah 11:9)?

The New Testament authors lived in expectation of the Second Coming that would deliver them "from the present evil age" (Galatians 1:4). They exhorted Christians to prepare themselves spiritually and to be morally alert, knowing that "the day of the Lord will come like a thief in the night" (1 Thessalonians 5:2), unexpectedly, without warning beforehand.

Jesus answers the disciples

When Jesus lived, just like today, people were anxious to know when the end would come, so they could "get ready" for it. Jesus' reply implied that they should stop speculating and always be ready, without being prompted by prior indicators. Look at the accounts in Matthew 24 and Luke 21, where Jesus explains to the disciples that the temple would be destroyed (this happened in A.D. 70). What was Jesus saying? Was he telling us to look for the signs of the times?

"Tell us…what will be the sign of your coming and of the end of the age?" the disciples asked Jesus (Matthew 24:3). Believers have had the same question ever since. How will we know when our Master will return? We feel a need to know. But Jesus points us to a different need — the need to be ready regardless of history's times and seasons.

The answer Jesus gave conjures up (in the biblically literate mind) images of the figurative, frightening four horsemen of the Apocalypse (see Revelation 6:1-8) that have ignited the imagination of prophetic and fantasy writers for centuries. False religion, war, famine, deadly disease — sounds like our age right here and now? Yes, and it was meant to sound that way. It was meant to sound like every age.

Some have said that what Jesus meant is that when we see an *intensifying* of war, famine, and these other things, it means the end is near. Stimulated by this idea of things getting really bad before Christ returns, fundamentalists have tried, in their zeal for truth, to flesh out what they view as end-time references in prophetic scriptures, especially in the book of Revelation.

But what was Jesus saying? He does not discuss the idea of intensification. He seems, rather, to be discussing the constant condition of humanity. There have been – and always will be until he comes again – many deceivers who come in Christ's name, as well as "wars and rumors of wars…famines and earthquakes in various places" (Matthew 24:5-7). Has there been, since Christ came, a generation spared these things? These prophetic words of our Lord find fulfillment in every age of history.

Yet today, as in the past, people look at world events. Some, even some leading Christian opinion makers, claim prophecy is unfolding and the end is near. All of us *want* the end to be near, and we desire our Savior's return. However, Jesus said, in guiding our response to what some call the signs of the times: "See to it that you are not alarmed. Such things must happen, but the end is still to come" (verse 6).

Don't be afraid – be ready

Regrettably, sensational end-time scenario preaching in public campaigns or through television, radio and magazines is often used in the cause of evangelism to frighten people into believing in Jesus Christ. "Shape up or burn up" is an option given. If you don't give your life to Jesus, you will be a victim in the violence to come. We forget how Jesus himself evangelized – how he brought good news. He evangelized above all through kindness and mercy – look at the examples in the Gospels and see for yourself.

Paul explains: "Do you show contempt for the riches of his kindness, tolerance and patience, not realizing that God's kindness leads you toward repentance?" (Romans 2:4). It is God's goodness (expressed to others through us) that brings people to Jesus. We can be sobered by the concept of divine judgment, but we should not evangelize through threats.

Jesus pointed to the need to make sure we are spiritually ready for his return whenever it will be. That was his emphasis. That is more important than trying to establish something beyond the scope of human knowledge – "no one knows about that day or hour, not even the angels in heaven, nor the Son, but only the Father" (verse 36). Being better informed than the angels instead of being better prepared for his coming is where some people focus. Jesus concentrated on our being prepared.

In reinforcing this point to his disciples, Jesus used various illustrations and analogies. For example, "as it was in the days of Noah, so it will be at the coming of the Son of Man" (verse 37). At the time of Noah there were no signs of imminent disaster. No discussion of wars and rumors of wars and famine and disease. No threatening clouds on the horizon, just sudden rain. Relatively peaceful prosperity and moral depravity appeared to have gone hand-in-hand. They "knew nothing about what would happen until the flood came and took them all away. That is how it will be at the coming of the Son of Man" (Matthew 24:39).

What should we learn from the reference to Noah? To look at the weather patterns and watch for signs that might inform us of a date that the angels are ignorant of? No, it rather reminds us to "be careful, or your hearts will be weighed down with dissipation, drunkenness and the anxieties of life, and that day will close on you unexpectedly like a trap" (Luke 21:34).

Jesus also presented the parable of the 10 virgins to hammer this idea home. I understand this better after having lived in Africa for several years. Once I was to perform a wedding at noon, and even by 3 p.m. the bride had not arrived – she had delayed her coming! Some of the attendants fell asleep while waiting. At one point I noticed the bridegroom himself beginning to nod off.

What was the message of Jesus' story? Lest you fall asleep, have your lamps filled with oil so that your light can shine. Be led by the Holy Spirit. Be generous, welcome the stranger, visit the sick, be Jesus in your community (Matthew 25:31-46). If we do so, that is like giving people food in due season, when they need it. "It will be good for that servant whose master finds him doing so when he returns" (Matthew 24:46).

We know that Christ lives in us (Galatians 2:20), that his kingdom has begun in us and in his church, that there is a gospel work to be done now wherever we live, and that "in this hope we are saved" (Romans 8:24) – in the hope of the return of our Lord.

"The Lord is not slow in keeping his promise" (2 Peter 3:9). "So then, dear friends, since you are looking forward to this, make every effort to be found spotless, blameless and at peace with him" (2 Peter 3:14).

James R. Henderson

About the Authors

Gary W. Deddo received his PhD from the University of Aberdeen. He worked for many years as an editor for InterVarsity Press; he now works at Grace Communion International and is president of Grace Communion Seminary. He has written several books and e-books.

Neil Earle is a retired pastor for Grace Communion International. He teaches church history courses at Grace Communion Seminary.

J. Michael Feazell served for many years as Vice-President of Grace Communion International, as Executive Editor of *Christian Odyssey* magazine, and host of the *You're Included* video series. He earned his Doctor of Ministry degree from Azusa Pacific Seminary and has written *Liberation of the Worldwide Church of God*.

John Halford was a pastor, writer, and editor of *Christian Odyssey* magazine for Grace Communion International. He died in 2014.

James Henderson is the National Director of GCI churches in the United Kingdom.

Paul Kroll worked for Grace Communion International for many years, writing hundreds of articles for our magazines. He is now retired. He is the author of *Exploring the Word of God: The Book of Acts,* available in print or as a series of seven e-books.

Don Mears was a pastor for Grace Communion International.

Michael D. Morrison received his PhD from Fuller Theological Seminary in 2006. After working for Grace Communion International in various writing and editorial capacities, he is an instructor and Dean of Faculty at Grace Communion Seminary. He is also an associate pastor of Grace Life in Glendora, California. He has written several books and e-books, and is the editor of this volume.

Rick Shallenberger is a district pastor for Grace Communion International.

Norman L. Shoaf wrote and edited for Grace Communion International for many years.

Joseph Tkach is president of Grace Communion International and presenter of the video series *Speaking of Life*. He received a Doctor of Ministry degree from Azusa Pacific Seminary. He has written *Transformed by Truth* and numerous articles and e-books.

Some articles are a corporate product.

About the Publisher

Grace Communion International is a Christian denomination with about 50,000 members, worshiping in about 900 congregations in almost 100 nations and territories. We began in 1934 and our main office is in North Carolina. In the United States, we are members of the National Association of Evangelicals and similar organizations in other nations. We welcome you to visit our website at www.gci.org.

If you want to know more about the gospel of Jesus Christ, we offer help. First, we offer weekly worship services in hundreds of congregations worldwide. Perhaps you'd like to visit us. A typical worship service includes songs of praise, a message based on the Bible, and opportunity to meet people who have found Jesus Christ to be the answer to their spiritual quest. We try to be friendly, but without putting you on the spot. Come and see why we believe the gospel is the best news there could be!

To find a congregation, phone us or visit our website. If we do not have a congregation near you, we encourage you to find another Christian church that teaches the gospel of grace.

We also offer personal counsel. If you have questions about the Bible, salvation or Christian living, we are happy to talk. If you want to discuss faith, baptism or other matters, a pastor near you can discuss these on the phone or set up an appointment for a longer discussion. We are convinced that Jesus offers what people need most, and we are happy to share the good news of what he has done for all humanity. We like to help people find new life in Christ, and to grow in that life.

Our work is funded by members of the church who donate part of their income to support the gospel. Jesus told his disciples to share the good news, and that is what we strive to do in our literature, in our worship services, and in our day-to-day lives.

If this book has helped you and you want to pay some expenses, all donations are gratefully welcomed, and in several nations, are tax-deductible. To make a donation online, go to www.gci.org/donate. Thank you for letting us share what we value most — Jesus Christ. The good news is too good to keep it to ourselves.

See our website for hundreds of articles, locations of our churches, addresses in various nations, audio and video messages, and much more.

www.gci.org
Grace Communion International
3120 Whitehall Park Dr.
Charlotte, NC 28273
800-423-4444

You're Included...

We talk with leading Trinitarian theologians about the good news that God loves you, wants you, and includes you in Jesus Christ. Most programs are about 28 minutes long. Our guests have included:

Douglas A. Campbell, Duke Divinity School
Elmer Colyer, Dubuque Theological Seminary
Cathy Deddo, Trinity Study Center
Gordon Fee, Regent College
Trevor Hart, University of St. Andrews
George Hunsinger, Princeton Seminary
C. Baxter Kruger, Perichoresis
Paul Louis Metzger, Multnomah University
Paul Molnar, St. John's University
Cherith Fee Nordling, Northern Seminary
Andrew Root, Luther Seminary
Alan Torrance, University of St. Andrews
Robert T. Walker, Edinburgh University
N.T. Wright, University of St. Andrews
William P. Young, author of *The Shack*

Programs are available free for viewing and downloading at www.youreincluded.org.

Grace Communion Seminary

Ministry based on the life and love of the Father, Son, and Spirit.

Grace Communion Seminary serves the needs of people engaged in Christian service who want to grow deeper in relationship with our Triune God and to be able to more effectively serve in the church.

Why study at Grace Communion Seminary?

- Worship: to love God with all your mind.
- Service: to help others apply truth to life.
- Practical: a balanced range of useful topics for ministry.
- Trinitarian theology: a survey of theology with the merits of a Trinitarian perspective. We begin with the question, "Who is God?" Then, "Who are we in relationship to God?" In this context, "How then do we serve?"
- Part-time study: designed to help people who are already serving in local congregations. There is no need to leave your current ministry. Full-time students are also welcome.
- Flexibility: your choice of master's level continuing education courses or pursuit of a degree: Master of Pastoral Studies or Master of Theological Studies.
- Affordable, accredited study: Everything can be done online.

For more information, go to www.gcs.edu. Grace Communion Seminary is accredited by the Distance Education Accrediting Commission, www.deac.org. The Accrediting Commission is listed by the U.S. Department of Education as a nationally recognized accrediting agency.

Ambassador College of Christian Ministry

Want to better understand God's Word? Want to know the Triune God more deeply? Want to share more joyously in the life of the Father, Son and Spirit? Want to be better equipped to serve others?

Among the many resources that Grace Communion International offers are the training and learning opportunities provided by ACCM. This quality, well-structured Christian Ministry curriculum has the advantage of being very practical and flexible. Students may study at their own pace, without having to leave home to undertake full-time study.

This denominationally recognized program is available for both credit and audit study. At minimum cost, this online Diploma program will help students gain important insights and training in effective ministry service. Students will also enjoy a rich resource for personal study that will enhance their understanding and relationship with the Triune God.

Diploma of Christian Ministry classes provide an excellent introductory course for new and lay pastors. Pastor General Dr. Joseph Tkach said, "We believe we have achieved the goal of designing Christian ministry training that is practical, accessible, interesting, and doctrinally and theologically mature and sound. This program provides an ideal foundation for effective Christian ministry."

For more information, go to www.ambascol.org

Printed in Poland
by Amazon Fulfillment
Poland Sp. z o.o., Wrocław